AF506014

About CROP

CROP, the Comparative Research Programme on Poverty, is a
response from the academic community to the problem of poverty.
The programme was initiated in 1992, and the CROP Secretariat was
officially opened in June 1993 by the director-general of UNESCO,
Dr Federico Mayor.

In recent years, poverty alleviation, poverty reduction or even
the eradication and abolition of poverty has moved up the international agenda, and the CROP network is providing research-based
information to policy-makers and others responsible for poverty
reduction. Researchers from more than one hundred countries have
joined the CROP network, with more than half coming from so-
called developing countries and countries in transition.

The major aim of CROP is to produce sound and reliable knowledge that can serve as a basis for poverty reduction. This is done by
bringing together researchers for workshops, coordinating research
projects and publications, and offering educational courses for the
international community of policy-makers.

CROP is multi-disciplinary and works as an independent non-
profit organization.

For more information you may contact:

CROP Secretariat, Nygårdsgaten 5
N-5020 Bergen, Norway
tel: +47-5558-9739   fax: +47-5558-9745
e-mail: <crop@uib.no>
CROP on the Internet: <http://www.crop.org>

CROP is a programme under the International Social Science
Council (which has also helped finance this publication).

CROP International Studies in Poverty Research
published by Zed Books in association with CROP

ALREADY AVAILABLE

The International Glossary on Poverty, David Gordon and Paul
    Spicker (eds), CROP International Studies in Poverty Research,
    1999, 162 pp.

*Poverty Reduction: What Role for the State in Today's Globalized
    Economy?*, Francis Wilson, Nazneen Kanji and Einar Braathen
    (eds), 2001, 372 pp.

The Poverty of Rights: Human Rights and the Eradication of Poverty,
    Willem van Genugten and Camilo Perez-Bustillo (eds), 2001,
    209 pp.

Best Practices in Poverty Reduction: An Analytical Framework, Else
    Øyen et al (eds), 2002, 144 pp.

Law and Poverty: The Legal System and Poverty Reduction, Lucy
    Williams, Asbjørn Kjønstad and Peter Robson (eds), 2003,
    303 pp.

Elite Perceptions of Poverty and Inequality, Elisa P. Reis and Mick
    Moore (eds), 2005, 288 pp.

Indigenous Peoples and Poverty: An International Perspective,
    Robyn Eversole, John-Andrew McNeish and Alberto D. Cim-
    adamore (eds), 2005, 320 pp.

International Poverty Law: An Emerging Discourse, Lucy Williams
    (ed), 2006, 256 pp.

IN PREPARATION

*Poverty and Social Deprivation in the Mediterranean: Trends,
    Policies and Welfare Prospects in the New Millennium*, Maria
    Petmesidou and Christos Papatheodorou (eds), 2006, 416 pp

LUCY WILLIAMS | editor

International poverty law

An emerging discourse

CROP
International Studies
in Poverty Research

International Social
Science Council

Zed Books
LONDON | NEW YORK

International poverty law: an emerging discourse was first published by Zed Books Ltd, 7 Cynthia Street, London N1 9JF, UK and Room 400, 175 Fifth Avenue, New York, NY 10010, USA in 2006

www.zedbooks.co.uk

CROP International Studies in Poverty Research

Cover designed by Andrew Corbett
Set in Arnhem and Futura Bold by Ewan Smith, London
Index: <ed.emery@britishlibrary.net>
Printed and bound in Malta by Gutenberg Press Ltd

Distributed in the USA exclusively by Palgrave Macmillan, a division of St Martin's Press, LLC, 175 Fifth Avenue, New York, NY 10010.

A catalogue record for this book is available from the British Library.
US CIP data are available from the Library of Congress.

ISBN 1 84277 684 3 hb
ISBN 1 84277 685 1 pb

ISBN 978 1 84277 684 1 hb
ISBN 978 1 84277 685 8 pb

Contents

1 | Towards an emerging international poverty law

LUCY WILLIAMS

Legal rules significantly affect the distribution of income, assets and power. While often perceived as natural (both in the sense of arising without human intervention and reflecting a natural order), legal rules are chosen – frequently to benefit the interests of parties and/or nations in power. Specifically, the background rules of property (now including intellectual property), family, contract, legal capacity and tort law partially create and perpetuate wealth imbalances within and between nations. Thus whether one is considering current economic structures within nation-states, those earlier imposed by colonizers on colonized states, or those dominating the increasingly globalized economy, legal rules are deeply implicated in maintaining and strengthening status quo power and wealth inequalities, resulting in substantial poverty worldwide.

The Comparative Research on Poverty Programme (CROP) seeks to understand and expose the legal structures that perpetuate poverty and to develop new strategic models for reducing poverty, locally and globally. CROP works with poverty advocates worldwide, seeking to re-envision legal discourse and practices in the hope that transformative lawyering can become an even more effective tool for redressing poverty. Through CROP's Law and Poverty workshops, anti-poverty advocates explore trans-national and cross-cultural poverty issues within the context of the increasing integration of the world economy, with an eye towards understanding how the different cultures and sub-cultures within which we work either perpetuate poverty and/or offer sites in which to fight against it.

The chapters in this book are revisions of papers originally presented at the CROP Law and Poverty Workshop IV, which met at Onati, Spain, in May 2001. As a whole, the collection is intended as a contribution to the emerging discourse of international poverty law (IPL). IPL is committed to global poverty reduction and to trans-national, multi-disciplinary legal research and dialogue dedicated to that goal. We seek to incorporate IPL into the legal mainstream. Expansion of the boundaries and concerns of the legal discourse regarding poverty reduction is essential for at least two reasons, one related to nation-state borders and the other to disciplinary borders:

1) Advocates for economic redistribution and poverty reduction customarily operate and conceive their advocacy within a nation-state context. Anti-poverty legal policies are not generally formulated within a transnational perspective (with the exception of some work within the economic development literature). It is by now clear, however, given the steady integration of the world economy, that poverty cannot (if it ever could) be understood, let alone contested, solely within national borders. Acknowledging this in no way negates the critical importance of local grassroots mobilization. Local anti-poverty empowerment initiatives cannot, however, be viewed in isolation from cross-border poverty reduction strategies. Thus, while anti-poverty advocates must work to establish or increase public education, nutrition programmes and effective public health systems within their respective nation-state contexts, we must also understand and position our work within the global economy by immersing ourselves in and challenging the structures of international finance, production and trade which perpetuate poverty on a world scale.

2) While establishing its identity and discursive unity, IPL must critically appreciate and draw upon a wide range of legal discourses. Indeed, most disciplines within law, for example property, trade and finance, labour, contract, tort, taxation, intellectual property, immigration and international law, have implications for poverty, and the legal rules that constitute and perpetuate poverty are intimately shaped by law and policies deriving from those other disciplines. Yet advocates and scholars in those legal fields often ignore the centrality of poverty to their respective disciplines, and virtually all have failed to appreciate how their fields intersect to support systems that perpetuate poverty and a grotesque maldistribution of resources on a global scale. As it develops, IPL must identify the connecting threads in legal thought and practice that reinforce poverty. At the same time, IPL must assimilate mainstream legal learning across disciplines in order to develop more sophisticated legal analyses for addressing poverty.

This introduction seeks to provide an intellectual framework within which readers can position and understand the book's chapters. My major purpose is to set out the theoretical and practical threads that draw the chapters together and to provide a possible springboard for future work, criticism and methodological development within IPL.

International poverty law: theory and methodology

Individually and in dialogue, the chapter authors seek to advance the theoretical range and sophistication of IPL and, thereby, its usefulness in developing legal strategies to reduce poverty. They work within and approach issues of poverty from numerous, distinct geographical, disciplinary and methodological contexts and perspectives. Many of the authors, although by no means all, rely heavily on human rights discourse and United Nations (UN), International Labour Organization (ILO) and World Trade Organization (WTO) initiatives as their primary legal sources. The tension between the particularity of local knowledge and problems, on the one hand, and the ambition to find global, common legal ground, on the other, generates a series of rich insights. These, in turn, problematize the human rights discourse.

The first two chapters provide a framework within which to position the theoretical development of IPL. St Clair explores the virtues of addressing poverty reduction through a human rights discourse. She carefully considers two major objections to this methodology, namely that human rights discourse is empty rhetoric because of weak or non-existent legal enforceability, and that human rights discourse is pervasively informed by libertarian perspectives. St Clair acknowledges that the ambiguous notion of liberty in the *UN's Human Development Report 2000* (HDR 2000) appears to endorse dichotomies between negative and positive rights, and between first- and second-generation rights,[1] and she criticizes the rights model as one that may 'import many market values incompatible with the practical fight for poverty reduction'. She attempts to recast rights rhetoric by invoking Amartya Sen's capabilities approach and rights-goals theory. Although ultimately she embraces the human rights approach as one tool for reducing poverty, she exposes many of its flaws and cautions that a rights model must be supplemented by other moral and political approaches, including theorizing some human rights as 'global public goods'.

Fortman also draws on HDR 2000, although he recognizes that rights are only 'abstract acknowledgements of claims'. He differentiates between rights, entitlements (a 'legitimate command' over a particular good or service) and claims (the 'concrete act of acquirement'), incorporating Sen's entitlement-failure theory. He rejects the distinction between moral rights (rights without remedies) and legal rights, noting that all rights 'require performing behaviour on the part of those who hold them'. He emphasizes that rights enforcement can be achieved through the informal mechanisms of 'living law', as well as through formal legal processes. Thus, even if human rights are difficult to enforce, human rights discourse provides political instruments and can establish a normative statement of a moral code that might support social change.

Building on the theoretical framework set forth in these first two chapters, the next five chapters explore specific international human rights

International poverty law

initiatives that address a particular aspect of poverty. The authors grapple with many of the questions raised by St Clair and Fortman within distinct local and methodological contexts, seeking to expand IPL's capacity to address discrete aspects of poverty.

Prieto-Acosta explores the relatively new field of international intellectual property (IP) law as applied to biological products and processes and the ways in which this international law is undermining food security. Initially focusing on the Agreement on Trade Related Aspects of Intellectual Property Rights (TRIPs) and US intellectual property law, she documents the legal advantages enjoyed by developed nations which have a more advanced biotechnological sector and IP legal structure. She questions whether, by allowing biotechnology companies in these countries to patent food crops, seeds and genetic material that have been 'natural' for generations in lesser developed countries (LDCs), a new form of 'privatization' is occurring, i.e. ownership by private companies of previously publicly held genetic material. The result of this 'biopiracy' is that farmers in the LDCs are increasingly dependent on the biotechnology companies, by, for example, farmers being required to 'buy back' previously indigenous seeds. Prieto-Acosta articulates specific counter-measures that might address this issue, particularly focusing on the Convention on Biological Diversity.

Like Prieto-Acosta, Aoued takes on issues of hunger and malnutrition, albeit from a quite different perspective. Aoued situates his discussion within the international human rights discourse of right to food (RTF), discussing the framing of RTF in UN development documents that focus on adequacy and sustainability. He highlights the appointment of a UN Special Rapporteur on the Right to Food as indicative of the growing normative body of law supporting this concept, and discusses the pros and cons of the three 'axes of intervention' provided for the Special Rapporteur to further the RTF. While critically questioning the ability of international public law to serve as the site for IPL development, he advocates ongoing international dialogue and exploration of this field as a forum for poverty reduction.

Olivier and Van Rensburg articulate the discussion of poverty reduction within the circumstances of the new South Africa, addressing the linkages between international human rights undertakings and the developing interpretation of the 1996 South African constitution, which entrenched socio-economic rights in the constitution with no first-generation/second-generation distinction. Noting the constitutional mandate that the judiciary must consider international human rights law in interpreting the social rights contained in the constitution, the authors explore the ways in which the Constitutional Court has relied on language or interpretations of international human rights initiatives in their decisions, primarily focusing on *The Government of the Republic of South Africa and Others* v. *Grootboom and Others*. This chapter presents an alternative vision of constitutional law, one in which social and economic rights are justiciable, and one in which the principles of human dignity and solidarity (within South Africa, *ubuntu*) are central not only in structuring a social security system, but also in preventing social exclusion.

Saini draws connections between poverty, illiteracy and child labour in India. He focuses on poverty as a lack of opportunity and argues that one of the most basic opportunities in addressing poverty is the availability of primary education. He documents the extent and causes of child labour and lack of school attendance in India. Recognizing the inertia of the Indian government in addressing these issues, he evaluates the impact of international human rights initiatives connected to child labour. While persuasively demonstrating the importance of international (primarily ILO and UN) poverty directives in pressuring states to articulate specific human rights for children, he also questions the fundamental effectiveness of such measures. Saini then moves into the trade agreement negotiation arena, taking on the complex and highly controversial issue of incorporating or attaching 'social clauses' to WTO trade agreements. Recognizing the multiple and often disingenuous motives of developed nations' actors in trade initiatives, he assesses the national impact of international pressure generated by these discussions and ultimately advocates the use of social clauses to the extent that they reduce child labour and encourage primary education.

Voiculescu pushes our thinking beyond national or even international governmental regulation, agreements or initiatives to consider how poverty reduction advocates must engage with transnational corporations (TNCs) and incorporate them into the anti-poverty discourse. She explores the possibilities of bridging gaps between economic growth and human development, or 'privatized' human rights, through corporate codes of conduct encouraged by UN instruments, ILO conventions and OECD guidelines. She suggests reasons why TNCs might support such codes (not the least of which is to maintain their self-regulatory status), and views voluntary codes of conduct as particularly useful in areas that would prompt public outrage (such as child labour). She cautions, however, that anti-poverty advocates utilizing voluntary codes must carefully develop and incorporate democratic checks and balances into their strategies.

The book concludes with Amitsis's chapter, which provides an overview of human rights documents and connects IPL to this textual framework. He looks at a number of the human rights instruments discussed earlier (including the Universal Declaration of Human Rights, the International Covenant on Economic, Social and Cultural Rights, UN Action Programmes implementing the Vienna Declaration of Human Rights and the Copenhagen Declaration on Social Development), analysing each in terms of the specific principles and concepts that comprise the legal discourse of poverty reduction. He positions each initiative within the varying conceptions of poverty (subsistence, basic needs, relative deprivation) and recommends specific steps to ensure the indivisibility and direct applicability of international human rights norms.

New directions for international poverty law

Together, these chapters advance promising legal arguments for the fight against poverty, yet they also provide certain cautionary perspectives for and reveal difficulties awaiting IPL as an emerging legal discipline. In these remaining comments, I build on the authors' work in order to highlight strengths and weaknesses of IPL as currently framed.

First, IPL must look beyond monetary indicators (financial income and assets) to embrace more inclusive strategies for poverty reduction. Historically, anti-poverty advocates have viewed state-based *income* transfers as the primary instrument of poverty reduction. Of course, transfers are an important and, in certain countries, a highly successful tool for combating poverty. Their implementation reflects a significant political achievement which should not be abandoned; indeed, progressives everywhere should fight to expand direct redistribution of monetary wealth and income.

Several of the authors show, however, how class (and the reader should add gender and ethnicity) deeply affects one's options and opportunities in ways that go well beyond monetary concerns. Saini discusses poverty not just as a lack of resources, but of opportunity, specifically in the context of an opportunity for primary education. Invoking Sen's capabilities approach, St Clair sees poverty reduction as a process of expanding people's ability to make meaningful choices about their life paths. Aoued argues that anti-poverty advocates must move beyond a fixation on basic needs (understood in terms of economic indicators) to an approach in which the fulfilment of subsistence needs is a precursor to the enjoyment of broader rights and self-realizing experiences. Thus, anti-poverty strategies that are based on the insight that poverty means more than lack of income and which incorporate the multiple ways in which poverty impacts on and restricts people's lives might result in structural changes that would allow impoverished people to become and experience themselves as full, productive and self-determining members of society.

This formulation provides a possible framework within which IPL might challenge the traditional dichotomy between first- (civil-political) and second-generation (socio-economic) rights. Several authors argue the necessity of addressing this dichotomy. Olivier and Van Rensburg, for example, base their discussion on the new South African constitutional dispensation, which entrenches both first- and second-generation rights. St Clair challenges the mainstream assumption that first-generation rights are enforceable because they are merely negative prohibitions on government, whereas 'positive', second-generation rights lack the quality of enforceability because of the difficulties of locating duty-bearers or articulating justiciable standards by which to judge them. The conventional wisdom distinguishing first- and second-generation rights conveniently assumes that there is no connection between the two; in other words, that people who are socially and economically deprived should be able to meaningfully enjoy or exercise civil and political rights. In the multi-dimensional view, however, one of the defining features of poverty is the inability of poor people to enjoy 'first-generation' rights unless they are guaranteed 'second-generation' rights. In other words, arguing that many economically deprived individuals cannot actively participate in civil and political rights, i.e. framing poverty as the inability of some poor to actualize 'first-generation' rights when they are not provided with 'second-generation' rights, connects the two in a way that might provide a theoretical structure within which to upend the notion that only first-generation rights are enforceable.

While I see important benefits that might result from this intellectual path, however, I also caution against embracing it without a critical perspective. In exploring the implications of poverty beyond an economic perspective, many policy-makers have equated poverty with the concept of 'social exclusion'.[2] Like all other legal terms, 'social exclusion' does not have a fixed meaning among, or indeed within, cultures, but rather is indeterminate – different legal structures utilize the term to validate highly different social, political and legal regimes and initiatives. IPL must struggle with the complex ways in which the definitions of 'social exclusion', which view poverty as more than lack of income, can be deeply problematic.

For example, current poverty policy in the US, as developed largely by neo-liberals, discusses 'social exclusion' as if it entails isolation, lack of community networks, failure to invest in community endeavours, and inability to maintain social interaction. As a result, the discourse of 'social exclusion' within the US labels many highly functioning individuals as dysfunctional. Single mothers receiving social assistance benefits are viewed as outside mainstream economic structures, ignoring the fact that the majority regularly move in and out of low-wage labour and that many, whether moving in and out of wage work, have significant social and community networks that allow them to survive. Thus, in the US, 'social exclusion' implies individual fault – blames the poor for their condition – without acknowledging the structure of low-wage labour (which is not responsive to parenting needs and does not provide lone mothers with either adequate income or health insurance to sustain their families). Social exclusion incorporates autonomy in wage work as the primary value; in other words, the concept assumes a norm for social inclusion within the arena of 'first-generation' rights, while failing to address or incorporate the absence of 'second-generation' rights. As a result, the concept of social exclusion has been used to argue for reducing social assistance benefits as an incentive to modify the behaviour of those in poverty rather than addressing structural causes of poverty.

Second, explicitly or implicitly, most of the chapter authors ground their analysis and advocacy in the discourse of human rights. This methodological focus provides a platform for innovative work on poverty reduction that is quite encouraging, indeed rejuvenating for many, and, at the same time, highly problematical.

Human rights discourse provides an important idiom in which to formulate demands for poverty reduction, draw attention to unrealized or 'unacquired' rights, and mobilize opposition to economic imbalances (Prieto-Acosta, Amitsis, Fortman and Olivier/Van Rensburg). Human rights principles, while empty vessels in the abstract, can be defined to serve as the foundation of an articulable moral code (Amitsis). St Clair views human rights as emphasizing the 'justice aspect of poverty reduction' and rejects the 'objection that only rights matched with duties have any power at all'. Fortman rejects as false the dichotomy often drawn between morality (rights without remedies) and law (legally enforceable entitlements), arguing that, while often not enforceable through ordinary legal claims, human rights can provide general principles of justice that 'guide judicial decision-making'. He sees human rights concepts as potentially offering 'political instruments to mobilize dissent, protest, opposition and collective action aimed at social and economic reform'. Similarly, Voiculescu highlights the moral value and mobilization potential of voluntary codes of conduct for TNCs. Thus human rights discourse, as jurisprudence and as norms entrenched in international and multilateral legal sources, can provide an important rhetorical medium for advancing an anti-poverty political agenda within an IPL framework.

The authors note, however, at least two major difficulties with grounding IPL analysis and advocacy exclusively in human rights discourse. Initially, although useful as a tool for mobilization, the fact that human rights are not generally enforceable as ordinary legal entitlements is a serious limitation of the approach. While urging IPL to embrace a 'universally recognized human rights framework' for poverty reduction, several authors recognize the difficulty of building a network to address poverty without the option of legally enforceable entitlements; consequently, they argue for the development of effective enforcement mechanisms. This line of argument should be continued and deepened. Anti-poverty advocates must devise and promote imaginative solutions to the problem of enforcement. For example, several progressive legal thinkers have proposed that victims of human rights violations be granted a remedy akin to the mechanism of 'investor standing' to sue for breach of treaty obligations as provided under Chapter 11 of the North American Free Trade Agreement. IPL would do well to make exploration of this and similar proposals a research priority.

In addition, while as a historical matter human rights concepts and rhetoric have a progressive ring, human rights concepts have no inherent, self-defining content. Rather, as with general norms in all law fields, the precise legal meaning of human rights is indeterminate. Put another way, human rights concepts and principles are sites of political contestation. Both Fortman and St Clair note that human rights discourse is filled with cases in which the rights of different groups or interests clash. For example, rights of family privacy often conflict with a family member's right to well-being and physical safety; similarly, rights of cultural self-determination often conflict with rights of sub-group resistance, which may appeal to other fundamental rights (for example, gender equality). Human rights discourse itself – without reference to moral and political arguments external to rights discourse – provides no method or decision process to resolve such conflicts or precisely define the legal implications of a human rights principle. This doesn't mean that choices cannot be made or that balances cannot be struck. It means only that decisions in the presence of human rights conflicts must be made by appeal to arguments, considerations and sensibilities outside the discourse.

Third, it is common knowledge that legal rights on the books, whether or not enforceable by action, do not automatically translate into acquired rights on the ground. Therefore, IPL must go beyond the question of enforcement mechanisms and devise practical strategies to implement rights in people's lived experience.

Legal rights such as a 'right to food' or a 'right to housing' acquire meaning through legal interpretation in the context of political practice. Thus, Saini documents the 'bureaucratic inertia and indifference and façades of only symbolic legal measures'. Voiculescu discusses the difficulty of 'practical implementation, finding a way to internalize external values and standards into a corporation's organizational charter, influencing the ethos in which that corporation conducts its business'. Fortman describes rights as performative, that is 'they require performing behaviour on the part of those who hold them'. By way of example, Prieto-Acosta notes the lack of farmer representation in decisions about the use of seeds that they have contributed to seed banks. Thus IPL, recognizing that 'performing behaviour' operates within a context of economic and power imbalance, must focus on stakeholder voice and the ability of less powerful stakeholders to exercise or claim rights.

Several authors argue that, in our search for strategies to turn paper rights into acquired rights, poverty reduction advocates should consider informal as well as formal legal tools (see particularly Fortman). Olivier and Van Rensburg present *ubuntu* (social solidarity), a fundamental constitutional principle in the new South Africa, as one vehicle for accomplishing that goal, by focusing poverty-reduction efforts on building group solidarity and collective responsibility. Amitsis discusses recent EU anti-poverty initiatives conducted through the 'Open Method of Coordination', an innovative compromise between formal and informal legal processes, as a promising model capable of incorporating communal values and commitment. At the ideological level, several authors advocate that IPL should juxtapose the human rights appeal for solidarity and collective responsibility with the concept of individual autonomy, and thereby challenge dominant US legal and political thinking that underlies aspects of economic globalization in general, for example IMF Structural Austerity Programmes.

Fourth, an important message of this book is that advocates of the human rights approach for fighting poverty must begin to engage with the difficult issues of and controversies within the field of development economics. This book modestly begins that work. In general terms, Saini criticizes mainstream 'economic discourse, parading as scientific rationality', which 'may be oblivious to prevailing social and cultural infirmities, rent-seeking potential of certain actors in the economic system, restrictions on free flow of information, and the susceptibilities of the poor and powerless in the political power dynamics'. St Clair, while recognizing possible benefits that might emerge from 'well-balanced market structures', emphasizes that 'efficient and legitimate market structures must be informed by the social and cultural values of the societies in which they are embedded'. Voiculescu discusses how 'direct investment and undeniable economic growth accompanying the presence of TNCs are not necessarily linked to the reduction of poverty', but rather tend to 'bestow net benefits on advanced economies'.

More specifically, Prieto-Acosta describes the destruction of local markets based on IMF Structural Austerity Programmes that require the abolition of farm subsidies, and, thereby, food security, in LDCs while mandating tariff-free importation of heavily subsidized crops from developed countries. Aoued, Prieto-Acosta and Fortman all discuss the effects of moving from self-sustaining, production-based economies to export-led economies. They argue that this transition within a global economy dominated by the US negatively affects people's entitlement positions and seriously diminishes their socio-economic security. Prieto-Acosta criticizes developments within intellectual property law that threaten to carry out a privatization of genetic materials previously in the 'public' domain. It is important to note, however, that several chapters call for a more nuanced and less knee-jerk approach than progressives often take to the question of privatization. For example, Voiculescu articulates a form of 'privatization' of human rights through TNCs' voluntary codes of conduct. Saini, Voiculescu and Prieto-Acosta all explore ways of building protections into global markets through means other than government action, whether at national or supranational level.

In their focus on market reconstruction, poverty-reduction advocates must criticize and work to transform the gendered nature of much contemporary economics discourse. Market structures, as traditionally understood, do not acknowledge the contribution of 'non-wage' work (such as care-giving in the home) to economic production. In discussing questions of allocative efficiency, productivity and economic growth, mainstream lawyers and economists regularly ignore subsidies provided by unpaid labour in the household. As IPL expands its theoretical repertoire and begins to grapple with questions of development economics and market structure, it must conceptualize basic building blocks such as 'work', 'efficiency', and 'productivity' in new gender-sensitive ways.

Of course, there are many other connections to be drawn among the chapters – for example, both Amitsis, who discusses the use of UN documents, and St Clair, who applies Sen's capability-approach theory, develop a right to food, the central topic of both Aoued and Prieto-Acosta's chapters. Voiculescu suggests that child labour (Saini's central topic) may be amenable to voluntary codes of conduct. Fortman applies his theoretical analysis to Olivier/Van Rensburg's South African constitutional analysis. Amitsis's call for 'participatory minimum standards' schemes connects both to Saini's embracement of a trade agreement social clause addressing child labour and Olivier/Van Rensburg's discussion of the rejection of internationally articulated (in the General Comments to the ICESCR) minimum standards in the *Grootboom* case.

Conclusion

As a whole, the papers presented at Law and Poverty (LAP) IV open a new venue, that of the emerging legal field of IPL. But the discussion at LAP IV as contained in this book is only the beginning of a more developed sense of how law can be a tool to reduce poverty on a global level.

As noted, the primary focus at LAP IV on 'globalization' was to situate anti-poverty concerns in the rhetoric of international human rights. The human rights arena is an important addition to the tools of poverty advocates. But it is not sufficient, because it is both internally contradictory and unenforceable. In other words, it is ultimately an incomplete and limited strategy.

Thus IPL discourse must move beyond a human rights focus, not viewing human rights law in isolation, but rather connecting it to additional areas of law. For too long, anti-poverty advocates have operated within their isolated fields of immigration, environmental, low-wage labour, social welfare benefits (including both social security and social assistance), healthcare and family law without exploring the connections between their fields so as to provide a fuller picture of legal structures that perpetuate poverty. In addition to immersing itself in development economics, IPL must bring together the threads from these multiple areas of law in order to provide a multi-disciplinary approach to poverty reduction.

Perhaps most importantly, however, the legal human rights arena continues to assume and not challenge the validity of the background rules of property, torts, family and contract law, and to carve out often modest exceptions within the current legal framework. An isolated human rights analysis deflects attention away from, and therefore, unwittingly accepts as inevitable, the background legal structures that shape and steer economic life – both at the level of nation-state law and at the level of international economic law.

While advocacy for incremental change is an essential component of legal representation for the poor, ultimately poverty cannot be eradicated or even seriously challenged without changes in market-structuring rules (again, both national market-structuring rules and the rules that structure international economic activity). If IPL does not challenge the background legal rules of markets that bear significant responsibility for causing and/ or perpetuating gross inequality, it will ultimately fail to address poverty reduction.

IPL has the potential to serve as the basis for one of the most innovative and transformative legal discourses of the twenty-first century, grappling with pervasive global poverty. This book begins that process.

Notes

1 Traditional discussions of citizenship separate rights into two categories: first-generation rights (civil and political), which are considered negative rights, i.e. no person should be able to infringe on one's right to vote, right to free speech, right of association. These are assumed to have a known duty-bearer, an individual (or in some cases the state) who is interfering with another individual's right. Second-generation rights entail socio-economic rights, viewed as positive rights.

2 Olivier/Van Rensburg and Amitsis incorporate the language of social exclusion in their chapters, while importantly recognizing that poverty and social exclusion can be, but are not necessarily, related.

2 | How can human rights contribute to poverty reduction? A philosophical assessment of the *Human Development Report 2000*

ASUNCION LERA ST CLAIR

Looking back, the experience of exile, in spite of a lot of suffering, has been very fruitful. I have learnt a lot, I have learnt to read and write, I have learnt Spanish – before I could only speak with people from my own group – I have learnt that I have rights, that there are human rights, but maybe the most important of all, we have learnt to organize in order to claim our rights and in order to create a better life. *Peasant from La Quetzal, a returnee community in Guatemala*[1]

The vast majority of humanity just has the right to see, to hear, and to remain silent. *Eduardo Galeano (2000)*

In one of his last speeches as administrator of the United Nations Development Programme (UNDP), Gustave Speth claimed that poverty must be viewed as a denial of basic human rights. 'For the 1.3 billion people – one third of the population of the developing world – who live on less than a dollar a day, there can be no doubt that poverty is a brutal denial of human rights' (UNDP 1998: 27). According to Speth, a charity model is not sufficient to reduce poverty. The poor have a claim for fairness and equity, a claim for justice, and human rights is the best moral framework to emphasize the justice aspect of poverty reduction. Since 1998, the UNDP has worked to mainstream and integrate the principles of human rights with other core concepts on their agenda, mostly concerning human development.

But what can human rights do for poverty reduction? It may seem that the ethical language used by Speth in the 1998 Oslo symposium should be enough to answer this question: given that the discourse of human rights situates poverty concerns as a justice issue, such a view mandates that individuals and institutions work towards the reduction of poverty. Indeed, thinkers in the field of development ethics had been defending human rights approaches to development and poverty as a means to advocate and justify a better, more ethical development policy, which at the same time could have more political force and thus achieve positive practical results.[2] Certain rights were constructed to avoid threats to our humanity and to protect the dignity of otherwise marginalized humans. As the quote from the Guatemalan peasant at the beginning of the chapter shows, knowledge of human rights can be an important tool to help the poor build a valuable conception of themselves, but it is an important tool only if the poor are actually able to claim their rights. Unfortunately, as Galeano's quote states, that is not commonplace. Human rights discourse ends up too often benefiting those in power and bypassing the poor. The excluded, dispossessed and vulnerable, in short the poor, rarely can *claim or practise* their rights. Defining poverty as a denial of human rights seems a very promising path, but unless those rights are fully implemented and the poor are able to use them, such a path raises an important ethical problem. Human rights could end up being no more than empty rhetoric that raises the hopes of the poor without giving them the practical tools to better their lives.

The UNDP document that argues most forcefully for a human rights approach to development and poverty is the *Human Development Report 2000* (HDR 2000). HDR 2000 offers two main arguments to justify the shift in approach:

1) Human rights are double-edged tools that look at the law as well as at morality, and they represent already accepted international standards in both areas.
2) Human rights approaches add analytical force to the implementation of human development, since rights place claims on others (individuals or institutions) to fulfil their requirements. Rights entail duties, and duties bring with them responsibility, accountability and culpability.

Focusing on the philosophical underpinnings of HDR 2000, provided by Amartya Sen's rights-goals theory, this chapter analyses what the human rights conception of HDR 2000 can do for poverty reduction in practice. After describing HDR 2000's view of rights and Sen's conception of rights-goals, the chapter argues that human rights can be instruments to help reduce poverty if and only if we are able to develop models of rights that do not bring with them the values and assumptions of laissez-faire capitalism and the primacy of the market economy as it is currently conceived and legally constructed based on the *Homo economicus* assumption. But most importantly, the chapter argues that a unique framework of justice is not enough to accomplish the goals of poverty reduction. Human rights must be complemented by social virtues, such as solidarity, as well as by instrumental approaches, such as global public goods, that appeal to those in positions of power.

Two objections

Philosophers have contested the notion and construction of human rights for many generations. Disagreements regarding the justification of natural rights, the primacy of *the right* over *the good*, the differences between negative and positive rights, disagreements about the individualistic principles underlying human rights – the principle of personal autonomy, the principle of the inviolability of the person, and the principle of the dignity of the person – the interrelation between social and economic rights and liberty rights, how to resolve conflicts of rights, as well as many other issues, are the subject of an extensive amount of philosophical literature. If the goal of espousing human rights is to reduce poverty, two of these philosophical objections and their consequences are of paramount importance.

The first objection claims that human rights as an approach to poverty reduction is problematic because it can very easily become empty rhetoric. In the absence of a clear, moral and institutional division of labour to fulfil the duties that flow from human rights, such an approach raises the hopes of the most vulnerable without giving them real tools with which to exert their claims on others. Such a division of labour can only be achieved if the human rights views rest on a universally accepted underlying conception of liberty. Poverty reduction requires the successful implementation of social and economic, as well as civil and political, rights. Yet the latter kinds of rights are the only ones that allow for the identification of specific duty-bearers. Objectors claim that rights would only be accessible to everyone if *all* rights rested on some universally accepted concept of liberty. Although it is unnecessary to make artificial divisions between different conceptions of liberty, there is an important gap between the conception of liberty underlying civil and political rights and that underlying social and economic rights, with substantial consequences for the success of poverty reduction policies. The first category, liberty rights, takes a negative view of liberty as 'freedom from interference'. The most basic rights from this liberal point of view are rights to speech, thought, association, and to economic activities such as buying and selling, without interference from others, including the state. First-generation rights – civil and political – belong to this category. Second-generation rights, on the other hand, take a more positive view of freedom and claim that people must have rights to secure whatever is needed to undertake activities. Under such a view, basic rights include those rights to some means of life or rights to have certain needs met. Social, cultural and economic rights, whose conception of positive liberty differs from the negative one seen above, belong to this category.

The identification of the duty-bearers for the fulfilment of negative liberty rights is quite easy. Either obligations are universal, and everyone can fulfil them, or one can point to specific agents in each specific case. Rights to non-interference can be ascribed to both, universal as well as special agents. Such rights entail what philosopher Immanuel Kant called 'perfect duties', i.e. duties with an associated right. Yet the fulfilment of social and economic rights cannot be performed by everybody, nor can we point out specific actors. 'Nobody can feed all the hungry, so the obligation to feed the hungry cannot be universal, and most of those who are hungry have no special relationship in virtue of which others should feed them, so special obligations will not be enough to remedy poverty and hunger' (O'Neill 1986: 101–2). In her later work, O'Neill expresses the consequences of such gaps between rights and obligations in the following terms:

> Unfortunately much writing and rhetoric on rights heedlessly proclaims universal rights to goods and services, and in particular 'welfare rights', as well as to other social, economic, and cultural rights that are prominent in international Charters and Declarations, without showing what connects each presumed right-holder to some specific obligation bearer, which leaves the content of these supposed rights wholly obscure. This obscurity has been a scene and source of vast political and theoretical wrangling. Some advocates of universal economic, social and cultural rights go no further than to emphasize that they can be institutionalized, which is true. But the point of difference is that they *must* be institutionalized: if they are not there is no right. (O'Neill 1996: 132)

In short, this objection claims that social and economic rights cannot be implemented unless they are institutionalized, but since one cannot identify the duty-bearers of the designated rights, it is difficult, if not impossible, to justify the obligations necessary to respect and promote such second-generation rights.

The second and related objection claims that the argument that rights are an internationally recognized standard in law and in morality does not have many practical consequences for the poor. The most widely accepted understanding of human rights is the libertarian tradition, which underlies many contemporary understandings of democracy and market economy. Libertarian rights articulate civil and liberty rights in the negative sense – that is, liberty rights as protections against violations of individual freedoms – thus entailing restrained rather than pro-active actions on the part of duty-bearers. Libertarians fail to acknowledge, however, the conflict among individual freedoms – the ways in which one's 'freedom' infringes on another's 'freedom'. While certain liberty rights are essential in order to achieve the goals of poverty reduction, the narrow interpretation of liberty rights often articulated by libertarians leads to the neglect of social and economic rights. Although it was the Declaration of the Rights of the Man and Citizen of 1789 which made explicit that 'the mere will of the strong is not a final justification for actions which affect the vital interest of individuals, and that the mere fact of being human is enough title for claiming goods which are necessary for an autonomous and dignified life' (Nino 1991: 2), the focus of libertarian rights is reduced to the protection of the individual against the possible abuses of those in power which affect people's civil and political choices as well as their property. The idea that some goods are needed by all humans in order to have a dignified life is lost in the libertarian tradition. The problem, objectors claim, is not only that rights to non-interference do not offer any ethical grounds to help the poor, but that liberty and social and economic rights have incompatible assumptions. Libertarian rights assume the values of laissez-faire capitalism and the market to be above the needs of marginalized people.

The two notions of liberty spelled out above show that liberty rights are entangled with the basic principles of laissez-faire capitalism. If liberty rights include a defence of freedom of economic action, rights to a minimum of economic means are seemingly impossible within our current market structure. Viewed from that perspective, liberty and economic and social rights are incompatible. 'If there are unrestricted economic rights to run life on commercial lines and accumulate private property, there cannot be rights to food or welfare; if there are rights to food or welfare or health care or employment there cannot be unrestricted rights to engage in commercial activity' (O'Neill 1986: 107). Also, respect for human rights requires absolute respect for people's autonomy, which is easily undermined by power relations and by social stigmatization, two common characteristics in the lives of the poor. Yet autonomy, 'like freedom, requires social conditions for its realization that demand significant constraints on the scope of the market and private property rights ... Protection of autonomy may sometimes require prohibiting the commodification of some things' (Anderson 1993: 142). In short, autonomy requires that many rights are non-tradable.

Analysing the differences between human rights as understood in the United States and in China, David Hall and Roger Ames (1999) claim that liberal rights are constructed in abstraction from explicit economic assumptions and that the conception of the person that flows from liberal rights is directly linked to the *Homo economicus*. The model of the self or the conception of the person that flows from liberal rights is based on the idea of an autonomous will. The individual is entitled to rights prior to her entrance in society. She is a solitary individual motivated by the pursuit of her own life project and entitled to the non-interference of others, mostly the state, in her goals and property. 'If an individual is construed primarily in materialistic, economic terms, the proposed alternatives among which one is to decide are likely to be those which fulfill the sorts of desires the *homo economicus* is thought to possess' (ibid.: 115). Rights-based liberalism, these authors add, trumps the possibility of assessing alternative views of human life that could take into account a broader conception of human flourishing, one that may include concerns for educational and cultural opportunities, or even concerns for others. Yet, '[the] liberal argument for not constructing a society in which specific notions of the good are promoted is that this contravenes the very notions of freedom and autonomy upon which a society is based. In the mind of the liberal, such an effort smacks of a condescending and paternalistic state that quite conceivably could move toward totalitarian excess' (ibid.).

In short, the traditional understanding of first-generation rights could trump the achievement of second-generation rights and thus leave human rights approaches unable to provide solutions for poverty reduction. The *freedom* espoused by the market is 'the freedom to disconnect; to treat others as objects' (McNeill 2001). Yet poverty reduction requires social connection not only because this is very important for societies where most of the poor live, but also because institutions cannot guarantee full respect for principles of justice. Institutionalized principles of justice do not guarantee non-violation of those principles by certain individuals, such as corrupt government bureaucrats. The ethic of the market destroys many of the social virtues necessary to maintain and protect people's connectedness, particularly that of the most vulnerable. The moral virtues that promote social connectedness are also necessary because the changes and costs associated with poverty reduction require a minimum level of agreement and acknowledgement that certain elements of human life are 'good' for people and thus worth protecting and promoting.

This chapter does not argue against the possible benefits that may be offered by well-balanced market structures, but rather aims to emphasize that economics and its instruments ought to be at the service of people and societies. Market institutions cannot occupy all the spaces, for example defining values, culture or family relations. In order to promote everyone's human rights, the market must be based on values and not the other way around. As we shall see in a later section, the concept of justice may not be enough to accomplish the goals of human rights. Also, poverty reduction may need to conceive of certain goods as being outside the currently articulated sphere of the market. As I shall argue later, human rights may need to be complemented by what is now called the territory of *global public goods*, an approach also endorsed by the UNDP.[3]

In order to assess whether HDR 2000 responds to the objections presented above and their consequences, the next sections of this chapter offer a description of HDR 2000's conception of human rights, and its philosophical underpinnings, provided by Amartya Sen's capability approach and his associated rights-goals theory.

Human rights and human development

HDR 2000 sees human rights as important tools for strengthening and implementing one of the UNDP's core concepts, human development. Human development, the process of enlarging people's choices, is an idea based on Sen's capability approach, which in turn represents an alternative conception of development economics and poverty that expands the informational basis of development to include concerns for the quality of life, social justice, entitlements and rights. Rather than focusing on goods and consumption or preference satisfaction or happiness, Sen's approach emphasizes widening people's options to live productive and creative lives according to their needs and interests, or, as Sen often says, 'those lives that people have reason to value' (Sen 1999). Capability is, according to Sen, the most suitable moral category in which to conceptualize the problems raised by development and poverty.

Accordingly, human development offers an explicit and thorough analysis of the ends and means to development which challenges the traditional confusion (mostly of neo-classical economics) of economic growth and consumption as ends in themselves. Consumerism and the economic means to it are, in Sen's view, instruments to a further set of valuable goals. Growth is simply a necessary means to achieve human development, while poverty reduction is implicitly an end in itself. This value analysis of development aims to shift the discourse of development from a charity- to a justice-oriented perspective. Most importantly, Sen's conceptualization represents a new analysis for public policy, given that his approach directs attention not only to the poor as an end, but also to their supporting infrastructures or 'social arrangements' as means that are created by society. In other words, the idea of human development leads policy-makers to concentrate on the ways in which the infrastructures of society can be transformed so as to help promote and respect people's choices.

Human development has its own correspondent conception of poverty. Poverty means 'that opportunities and choices most basic to human development are denied – to lead a long, healthy, creative life and to enjoy a decent standard of living, freedom, and dignity, self-respect and the respect of others' (UNDP 1997). The definition of poverty presented in HDR 2000 goes a step farther and focuses more on the social and economic structures that support society. Poverty is then viewed as a 'failure of institutions, communities, and groups to respect the rights of individuals' (UNDP 1998). It is in this respect that the UNDP sees human rights as having an important role to play in human development and human poverty.

Capabilities and rights in HDR 2000

HDR 2000 conceptualizes human rights using the terminology of Sen's latest approach to development, i.e. development as freedom. It sees rights in terms of freedoms, because such strategy conceptually links rights with the notions of capabilities and entitlements at the core of human development. HDR 2000 explains the relations between both sets of terms by claiming that even though rights are very diverse, they all entail the entitlement of help and non-interference from others in defence or protection of one's substantial freedoms. Human rights are, the report claims, grounded in the importance of freedom for human lives, the core idea of capability.

Given that, as we have seen above, human development focuses on the social arrangements or infrastructures provided by society to enable people to live fulfilling lives, HDR 2000 sees rights approaches as offering tools to locate accountability for failures in the social system and responsibilities for present and future tasks. Among other issues, HDR 2000 claims, ' ... human rights analysis involves assessments of the extent to which institutions and social norms are or should be in place to provide security to the human development achievements within society'. If human development shifts the conceptualization of development and poverty from being an issue of charity to a matter of justice, HDR 2000 sees human rights approaches as adding analytical force to the implementation of human development, since rights place claims on others (individuals or institutions) to fulfil their requirements.

In the words of the director of the Human Development Report Office, 'integrating human rights into development opens up a whole new agenda – of strengthening the institutions, consensus on norms, legal standards, and political processes to strengthen mechanisms of enforcing entitlements' (Fukuda-Parr 1998). Thus, according to HDR 2000, an articulation of human rights as encompassing basic needs for self-actualization is an excellent tool with which to implement the goals of human development. Human rights discourse transforms the goals of human development into rights and entitlements, responsibilities and accountabilities, through the institutionalization of the claims to well-being made by human development. Furthermore, as human rights evolve as established moral standards, such an approach strengthens the language of capabilities and functionings at the core of human development and helps create a universal consensus in moral norms.

Yet the notion of liberty in HDR 2000 is ambiguous. HDR 2000 endorses both the positive and negative liberty interests that this chapter has explained above, but it does not clarify the differences between or the historical misunderstandings of the notions of liberty pointed out there. At times, the text reads as if capabilities and rights were coterminous. In other sections, the text states that rights are the tools with which to institutionalize capabilities. 'Investing in capabilities and securing rights in law are a powerful combination – to empower poor people in their fight to escape poverty' (UNDP 2000: 74). This implies that rights can only do the job when transformed into laws. Indeed, the report explicitly says, 'Accountability of the state needs to be defined in terms of implementation of policies' (ibid.: 77).

In another section the report states that 'Building capabilities in one generation is a means to securing social and economic rights in the next – and to eradicating poverty in the long term' (ibid.: 76). This latter statement assumes that there must be a prior acknowledgement of capabilities – presumably to create a worldwide moral consciousness that recognizes that certain capabilities are good for people – before they can be implemented as rights. Yet HDR 2000 recognizes that for the purposes of poverty reduction we need solutions now, rather than waiting until the next generation: 'For the many economic, social, and cultural rights most central to poverty eradication – right to food, education, health care, housing, work – claims to support, facilitation and promotion are particularly pressing and important ... the right to such necessities is an entitlement to the social arrangements needed to facilitate them' (ibid.: 72).

This chapter attempts to clarify these ambiguities by looking at Sen's rights-goals theory, which provides the philosophical underpinnings of HDR 2000.

Rights-goals or capability-rights

The ideas of 'rights' and 'freedom' developed by Sen that are at the core of HDR 2000 are very different from the standard conceptions of Western liberal tradition. Sen equates capabilities with rights because he develops a particular conception of human rights as 'rights-goals' that breaks with the traditional libertarian view of non-consequentionalist constraint rights. Libertarian rights, for example Nozick's property rights, are procedural rights that claim their justification in the means through which an individual achieves either a good or a service.[4] Their emphasis is on a narrow conception of 'entitlement', one that provides grounds only for negative liberty. For example, in regards to my right to food, others are obliged only not to take my cultivated land by force or to coerce me to give away my food involuntarily. But no one is obliged to make sure that I am not starving. Others may charitably help me obtain food or the means to get it, but I have no claim in that regard. Libertarian or procedural rights are justified merely because of a 'just' procedure, not based on their outcomes or consequences. 'For instance, the reason why people should have the right to food is not that by exercising this right they will achieve good outcomes such as freedom from hunger and the ability to live a healthy active life, etc. These outcomes may very well happen, but that is not the reason why people should have the right. They should have the right because in trying to acquire food they have followed a just procedure' (Osmani 2000: 275).

Thus, this understanding of rights entails only negative obligations on other parties, usually called constrained-focused obligations, and has nothing to do with a society's idea of what is good for people or with what may be required to fulfil people's potential.

Sen developed his conception of rights-goals precisely to avoid such limitations. He aims to include the concept of the good as well as the concept of the right, to recognize the value of first- and second-generation rights, and to point towards their interrelation. Libertarian rights can accomplish little for the concept of capability as the core idea of human development. Such a conception of rights is not compatible with the claim that certain capabilities are necessary for people's well-being. 'A basic right for Sen is a right to a minimum amount of basic capabilities or freedoms' (Crocker 1995: 186). This means that Sen links the concept of 'right' with the concept of the 'good'. According to Sen, rights can be justified because they provide 'good' consequences as well as because they may be the result of a 'just' process. Some rights, for example, are defined as 'basic', not because they are indispensable to the fulfilment of any other right but because they are 'a way of formulating the urgency of minimal levels of eminently valuable human functionings' (ibid.: 186). In other words, the right to food is basic because it allows people to function in a state of being well nourished, a good in itself for any human being.

The goodness of rights has as much importance as the goodness of the consequences of such rights. Sen points to the dangers of an excess emphasis on the importance of rights in the following terms:

If rights were to be seen as not only important but also as having priority over any accounting of consequences, then the rights would have to be accepted unconditionally. Indeed, in libertarian theory, this is exactly what happens to the delineated rights, which are seen as appropriate no matter what consequences they yield. These rights would, then, be appropriate parts of social arrangements irrespective of their consequences. (Sen 1999: 212)

On the other hand, Sen insists that one cannot evaluate any sense of rights without taking into consideration the possible negative consequences that may come from their enactment. Drawing on Indian moral philosophy, Sen uses the example of two warriors, Arjuna and Krishna, reflecting on a major imminent battle, to show that one cannot do one's duty irrespective of the consequences. Arjuna tells Krishna that although he does not doubt that this battle is part of a just war, and that theirs is a just cause, he also recognizes that engaging in the battle will entail killing many people who have done nothing wrong except agreeing to support one side or the other. He will have to do the killing himself and he will have to kill people for whom he has personal affection. Krishna dismisses Arjuna's qualms, pointing out that since this is a just battle, Arjuna's duty as a warrior is to fight regardless of the consequences. Arjuna's moral position is consequentialist; he incorporates an evaluation of the consequences of his action. Krishna's moral position, on the other hand, is deontological; she argues for the primacy of the concept of duty irrespective of the consequences.

Through this example, Sen attempts to reflect on a particular type of consequentialism that is compatible with the specific responsibilities a moral agent has because of her situation. When Arjuna assesses the moral reprehensibility of the battle, he does so from his own perspective. He is not free to evaluate consequences as he likes: 'Arjuna has the responsibility – indeed cannot escape the responsibility – to take note of the special badness of events as he must evaluate them, because he himself would have to do some of the killing, and victims would often be quite innocent persons for whom Arjuna has affection' (Sen 2000: 485). In other examples, Sen argues for the importance of considering the consequences that a rights approach may have on goods that are not attached to a particular individual but to all human beings. 'In the context of reproductive rights, the fact that they are taken to be significant does not entail that they are so overarchingly important that they must be fully protected even if they generate disasters and massive misery and hunger' (Sen 1999: 213). This view points towards the compatibility of rights with other global responsibilities.

Finally, Sen's conception of rights acknowledges the importance of legislation but argues that the moral side of human rights cannot be reduced to laws. This conception allows him to reject the objection that only rights matched with duties have any power at all. Human rights may or may not be legislated for, 'but in so far as they are valued, that valuation can include the importance that is attached to the relevant person's freedoms and also the responsibility that others have – irrespective of citizenship, nationality, and other denominations – to help this person attain these freedoms. If others can help, then there is a responsibility that goes with it' (Sen 2000: 494). Why can there not be unrealized rights, asks Sen, for whom the sphere of the moral is envisioned as broader than the sphere of the legal. To see moral rights as aspiring pre-legal rights misses the point of rights demands. In Sen's view, human rights can be invoked in cases where an appeal for legality may not be appropriate. For example, a wife's human right to participate in family decisions is important to fight for, but many would not want this to be legally enforceable.

In short, Sen argues for a conception of rights that respects a conse-quential responsibility (both individual and collective) compatible with deontology. This philosophical framework focuses on three necessary elements:

1) human rights refer to the freedom of right-holders to do and to achieve certain conditions;
2) human rights demand correlate obligations on others, both negative and positive, to help the right-holder fulfil such rights;
3) human rights may or may not be legislated for because their moral content ought to be broader than their legal sense.

Sen's view, then, seems to offer some arguments in opposition to the first objection posed above. There can be unrealized rights, even rights that are very hard to implement. This, however, does not make human rights a matter of empty rhetoric. Thus, according to Sen, the problem stated by O'Neill ' ... arises partly from her implicit attempt to see the use of rights in political or moral discourse through a close analogy with rights in a legal system, with its demand for specification of correlated duties' (ibid.: 497). If we see human rights as an expression of Sen's capability approach with the value of a moral code, in which rules may or may not be legislated, capability-rights seem to escape many of the traditional objec-tions to rights. From this perspective, the statements of HDR 2000 that emphasize legislation of rights are compatible with those that claim that recognition of capabilities in one generation may eventually lead to the legislation of rights later on. Yet we must keep in mind that the implication here is that *capability-rights* are something very different from traditional understandings of *human rights.*

While rights and capabilities are the same in the sense that both terms refer to our shared human nature, capabilities need to be seen as broader than rights; only in that way can one avoid the philosophical trap raised in the first objection. The language of capabilities and functionings refers to what people actually do or are, whereas rights refer too often to a nominal entitlement, which may have no real value in terms of implementation. As Nussbaum points out, women in many countries, for example, 'have a nominal right of political participation without having this right in the sense of capability: for example, they may be threatened with violence should they leave the home' (Nussbaum 2000: 98). In Nussbaum's view, it is actually more instructive to understand rights in terms of capabilities because capabilities refer to the ways people actually live – that is, the notion of capability tells us whether a right has actually been fulfilled. If we conceptualize the right to shelter as a right to a certain amount of resources, then that right may not lead the very poor to obtain better housing, given that they have become accustomed to very low standards of living. Analysing economic and material rights in terms of capabilities, however, Nussbaum argues, leads to justifying more clearly the need to spend more resources on the most vulnerable and disadvantaged or to creating programmes that would enable them in their transition to full capability. In short, by defining rights in terms of capabilities we can ensure that people in a particular country have certain rights, say the right to political participation, not just because that right is written down on paper: people have a right to political participation only if a country has 'effective measures that make people truly capable of political exercise' (ibid.: 98).

Yet the measures needed to make people truly capable of exercising their rights require a much more complex moral framework than that provided by a human rights approach. In fact, such a framework, as I shall argue below, is also necessary to accomplish the implementation of Sen's capabilities approach. I favour O'Neill's insistence that 'Rights to goods and services are easy to proclaim, but until there are effective institutions their proclamation may seem bitter mockery to those who need them. Liberty rights, however, are different because far more is determined even if institutions are missing or weak' (O'Neill 2000: 105). Also, even though Sen views development in terms of freedom and capabilities, and his conception of poverty entails an idea of the person that is very different from the *Homo economicus*, neither he nor HDR 2000 pays sufficient attention to the problem that a human rights approach may import many market values incompatible with the practical fight for poverty reduction. A hasty equation of pro-rights approaches with pro-poor policies ignores the fact that all these objections are practical obstacles to the implementation of rights.[5]

Poverty reduction requires more than an established discourse on rights. Unless the powerful are motivated by solidarity with the poor to implement rights and to ensure that the poor can in fact exercise their rights, a human rights approach to poverty reduction is rather weak. It may be attractive to those who want to promote a sense of moral obligation that has nothing to do with love, care, trust, friendship, sympathy or solidarity. But, as Rorty claims, we want moral progress to have its roots in the lived experiences of those at the lowest levels in society, rather than waiting patiently upon the condescension of the privileged. Fundamentalist beliefs on rights are popular because they make a strong rhetorical demand on those in a position to help the poor (Rorty 1998). But reality is rather different. If we want human rights to work for the poor, we must enquire, 'How can we make human rights work? How can we spread the human rights culture? How can human rights be complemented?' The focus ought to be on the implementation of human rights and the assurance that all people, particularly the poor and vulnerable, are able to exercise their rights. I argue, then, that poverty reduction requires that rights approaches be complemented by other moral and political frameworks, as well as by accounts of international cooperation that offer the rich a sense of security. An ethic of sympathy that promotes and creates feelings of solidarity with distant others, and the new literature on 'global public goods', which gives those in power reasons for promoting rights as a means to promote their own security, seem the best ways to complement human rights discourse.

Justice, virtues and global public goods

Gustave Speth's claim that human rights are the best possible justice framework for poverty reduction has widespread acceptance. Yet we have seen that human rights cannot fully respond to the demands of poverty reduction. This does not entail a rejection of human rights approaches to poverty reduction. On the contrary, I argue that rights are a very useful framework for justice, yet to use that approach as the sole conception of justice would be a mistake. A single justice approach (whether via human rights or any other) cannot provide all the needed strategies and answers to poverty reduction. We need to conceive the scope of our moral concerns globally as a mixture of principles of justice – human rights among others – certain virtues, and even some more instrumental frameworks.

First, it would be a mistake to endorse a 'one size fits all' account of justice. Alternative accounts of justice, for example the Kantian emphasis on obligations rather than rights, should not be abandoned. Second, a focus on rights – a justice framework – usually neglects other moral alternatives that are necessary just to implement rights. For example, an emphasis on rights neglects virtues such as generosity or beneficence in public affairs. An exclusive focus on rights precludes the possibility that some of these virtues could act as obligations. Particularly since human rights are by no means acknowledged, let alone legally entrenched, all over the world, such a coupling of justice and virtues is necessary in order to make progress towards poverty reduction. A 'virtue' approach is needed if we are truly to influence people's beliefs and attitudes, a prerequisite to expanding the boundaries of moral communities, which, in turn, is a necessary condition for the global implementation of second-generation rights. Thus, in the absence of certain virtues, it may be difficult, if not impossible, to implement social and economic rights in the near future (as urged by HDR 2000). And to make the poor *wait* is indeed unethical.

As O'Neill claims, it seems quite arbitrary to insist that living by principles of justice is all that is ethically required in our actions towards others. As we have seen in former sections, social cohesion and connectedness are necessary elements of all human beings, and even more so for the most vulnerable. Such connectedness cannot be promoted and respected under a human rights approach, even if all rights were institutionalized. Institutionalized principles of justice do not guarantee protection against certain abuses or violations (O'Neill 1996).[6] Institutions are supposed to take care of certain vulnerabilities; yet at the same time, we become vulnerable in other senses to other people's actions and to those same institutions whose goal is to protect us. For example, the actions of particular officials or bureaucrats give us support, but at the same time expose us to their possible inefficiency or corruption; international food aid, which supposedly improves the nutrition of the hungry, creates dependence on those who supply it. Justice, O'Neill claims, does not take into account the different ways in which human beings are connected, i.e. mutually vulnerable. Personal indifference and neglect are not an unjust act: 'Yet no vulnerable agent can coherently accept that indifference and neglect should be universalized, for if they were nobody could rely on others' help; joint projects would tend to fail; vulnerable characters would be undermined; capacities and capabilities that need assistance and nurturing would not emerge; personal relationships would wither; education and cultural life would decline' (ibid.: 194).

Third, effective poverty reduction requires taking into consideration the conflicts between our conception of global justice and the ethical content of other global institutions, such as the market. The objection raised at the beginning of the chapter – that liberty rights endorse an economic view of people and their relations – still stands. HDR 2000 does not question market values and how these may enhance the idea that pro-rights strategies are pro-poor. But, as currently formulated, many market values have an alienating and desocializing effect incompatible with the virtues necessary to implement social and economic rights for all. The market promotes and intensifies inequalities between the poor and the non-poor. In fact, critics of human development can attribute the same objection to the idea of human development itself. They may ask, 'How poverty-oriented is human development?' It is usually argued in the UNDP that the concept of human development places poverty at the forefront of any development strategy. Yet human development indices are still per capita measurements that do not include, e.g., an inequality index. If poverty has anything to do with inequality, then human development per se is not a poverty-oriented idea. There can be, for example, a polarization in human development, whereby some sectors of the population enjoy high human development but others (the poor) do not. Critics may also argue that the cause, or one of the causes, for such polarization is the still-pervasive emphasis in the human development paradigm on market principles. Rather than offer a critique of the market or of capitalism, it seems more practical for the purpose of implementing rights and reducing poverty in the short term to follow a strategy that does not take for granted the idea of an unregulated market – a strategy that a) makes explicit the values brought about by the market, b) looks for ways to overcome the failures and 'bad' outcomes of the market, and c) engages with the concept of global public goods beyond its original economic sense, as an important element of social life. I propose that one of the ways to achieve these goals is by endorsing the conceptualization of some human rights as global public goods.

Global public goods (GPGs), as opposed to private goods, have two main characteristics: a) they are goods marked by non-excludability and non-rivalry, i.e. their benefits are public and benefiting one person or group does not exclude benefiting others, and b) the benefits of these goods are global or almost global (Kaul et al. 1999). As the effects of globalization reach the remotest corners of the world, GPGs such as good health or the care of the environment are becoming more and more important in order to promote and protect people's well-being. The quality of the ozone layer or the effective control of highly contagious diseases such as Aids can have tremendous effects on all inhabitants of the planet, but these are issues that allegedly fall outside the scope of the market. Economists call them 'cross-border externalities'. 'A cross-border externality occurs when actions of one country have consequences for another, unmediated by classically competitive markets. Examples of negative externalities are: water use in countries that share rivers and water tables, atmospheric pollution, infectious disease control, financial contagion and the spillover effects of civil war' (Kanbur 2001).

Even from this narrow economic perspective, it is highly utopian to think that the discourse on human rights is going to take care of all these negative externalities. But it might be possible to do so by supplementing rights with GPGs. For example, investment in medical knowledge for diseases of the poor, such as malaria, has no market benefit given that the poor cannot afford to pay for its cost. In the absence of an implemented global justice framework, an appeal to the right to health of the poor is not very convincing, even if we assume that individuals in the position to help have a strong sense of social virtues and their obligations. Poor health 'creates situations in which the poor are further disempowered as their rights are eroded or neglected, compounded by their inability to respond because of their lack of economic and human resources' (Harcourt 2001: 4). Conceptualizing health as a GPG can correct such market failure. Health as a GPG would also require the transfer of affordable drugs to the poor, for example Aids drugs to sub-Saharan Africa. An appeal to the right to health may not be enough to mobilize support and cooperation, whereas health as a GPG may help in the realizing of that right (Kaul 2001).

There is a further conceptualization of GPGs that could help bring about the goals of poverty reduction as well as the de facto implementation of rights: GPGs seen from the perspective of justice and solidarity, as instruments to maximize and better social relations. Many GPGs are social, in that they refer to social relationships as well as to shared understandings of what is good for all people (Holmstrom 2000). Also, the design and elaboration of social goals help build a sense of solidarity as well as a sense of justice among the parties involved (Fisk 2000). Given that GPGs are the outcome of social planning and shared understandings, supplementing human rights approaches to poverty with GPGs could help overcome the negative effects of individualism without compromising people's freedom and autonomy. As a justice approach, GPGs are a compelling challenge to a free market that does not serve the well-being of all.

Conclusion

This chapter has argued that human rights are a necessary, but not sufficient, way to accomplish the goals of poverty reduction. Poverty reduction requires more than a single framework of justice; it requires the construction of social values and a sense of solidarity with the poor on the part of those who have power to promote and implement human rights. As endorsed by HDR 2000, the conceptualization of rights as rights-goals or capability-rights aims at using human rights as a tool with which to implement the goals of human development. HDR 2000 argues that human rights approaches transform these goals into entitlements and responsibilities. This discourse avoids some of the traditional philosophical objections to rights, but leaves unanswered criticism that rights approaches to poverty reduction could end up being empty rhetoric that provides false hopes to the poor and vulnerable. This chapter argues that human rights approaches do not have a unified conception of liberty. Some understandings of human rights – for example, those of libertarians – may argue for a conception of liberty that might in fact trump the realization of social and economic rights. Liberty rights emphasize the rights to economic activities such as buying and selling, as much as the rights to free speech or association. Such rights to non-interference in one's economic life do not offer any grounds to help the poor, nor do they build any sense of solidarity among people, particularly with the poor. Objectors even claim that libertarian rights place the values of laissez-faire capitalism and currently espoused market values above and before the needs of the poor. 'Market freedom', these objectors add, breaks or forgoes the connections people have with each other and destroys social virtues that are necessary to protect the vulnerable. This chapter proposes that we conceive the scope of our moral concerns as a mixture of principles of justice – rights being the best candidate, but not the only one – the endorsement and promotion of certain social virtues, and the supplementation of moral views with more instrumental approaches, such as global public goods.

Notes

1 Quoted in Stølen (2000), where the author claims that the indigenous refugees that have returned to Guatemala have gone from being exploited peasants to cooperative members.

2 For an overview of the field of development ethics see <www.development-ethics.org>.

3 See UNDP (1999).

4 Nozick (1974).

5 There are other possible incompatibilities that I do not discuss in this paper. For example, the right to practise one's culture may in fact keep people in poverty.

6 Notice that this is exactly Nussbaum's claim.

References

Anderson, E. (1993), *Value in Ethics and in Economics*, Cambridge, MA: Harvard University Press

Crocker, D. (1995) 'Functioning and capability: the foundations of Sen's and Nussbaum's development ethic,' in M. Nussbaum and J. Glover (eds),

Women, Culture and Development: A Study of Human Capabilities, Oxford: Clarendon Press.

Fisk, M. (2000) 'Surviving with dignity in a global economy: the battle for public goods', in A. Anton et al. (eds), *Not for Sale: In Defense of Public Goods*, Boulder, CO: Westview

Fukuda-Parr, S. (1998) *Human Development and Human Rights*, Report on the Oslo Symposium, 2–3 October

Galeano, E. (2000) *Upside Down: A Primer for the Looking Glass World*, trans. M. Fried, New York: Metropolitan Books

Hall, D. L. and R. T. Ames (1999) *The Democracy of the Dead: Dewey, Confucius, and the Hope for Democracy in China*, Chicago, IL: Open Court

Harcourt, W. (2001) 'Editorial note: freedom for the poor', *Partnership in Health and Development, Journal of Development* (special issue), 44: 1

Holmstrom, N. (2000) 'Rationality, solidarity, and public goods', in A. Anton et al. (eds), *Not for Sale: In Defense of Public Goods*, Boulder, CO: Westview

Kanbur, R. (2001) 'A note on cross-border externalities, international public goods and their importance for aid agencies', personal website

Kaul, I. (2001) 'Health as global public good', *Development*, 44 (1)

Kaul, I, I. Grunberg and M. A. Stern (eds) (1999) *Global Public Goods: International Cooperation in the 21st Century*, New York: Oxford University Press for the United Nations Development Programme

McNeill, D. (2001) 'Ethics and economics', Background paper for the annual meeting of the board of governors of the Inter-American Development Bank, Chile, March

Nino, C. (1991) *The Ethics of Human Rights*, Oxford: Oxford University Press

Nozick, R. (1974) *Anarchy, State, and Utopia*, Oxford: Blackwell

Nussbaum, M. (2000) *Women and Human Development: The Capabilities Approach*, Cambridge: Cambridge University Press

O'Neill, O. (1986) *Faces of Hunger: An Essay on Poverty, Justice and Development*, London: Allen & Unwin

— (1996) *Towards Justice and Virtue: A Constructive Account of Practical Reasoning*, Cambridge: Cambridge University Press

— (2000) *Bounds of Justice*, Cambridge: Cambridge University Press

Osmani, S. R. (2000) 'Human rights to food, health, and education', *Journal of Human Development*, 1 (2): 273–98

Rorty, R. (1998) *Truth and Progress*, Cambridge: Cambridge University Press

Sen, A. (1999) *Development as Freedom*, New York: Knopf

— (2000) 'Consequential evaluation and practical reason', *The Journal of Philosophy*, 97 (9): 477–502

Shue, H. (1996 [1980]) *Basic Rights: Subsistence, Affluence and US Foreign Policy*, Princeton, NJ: Princeton University Press

Stølen, K. (2000) 'Participatory communitarian development among returned refugees in Peten Guatemala', Mimeographed working paper, Oslo: Centre for Development and the Environment, University of Oslo

UNDP (United Nations Development Programme) (1997) *Human Development Report 1997*, New York: Oxford University Press

— (1998) *Human Development and Human Rights: Report of the Oslo Symposium*, Copenhagen: UNDP

— (1999) *Global Public Goods: International Cooperation in the 21th Century*, ed. I. Kaul et al., New York: Oxford University Press

— (2000) *Human Development Report 2000*, New York: Oxford University Press

3 | Poverty as a failure of entitlement: do rights-based approaches make sense?

BAS DE GAAY FORTMAN

The *Human Development Report 2000* of the United Nations Development Programme (UNDP) noted: 'People are turning more and more to the law – including international human rights law – to claim their rights.' But what has to be claimed is access to resources necessary to acquire what people need. Rights are abstract acknowledgements of such claims. In order to get one's claims *honoured*, the rights acknowledging them have to be *asserted*. But will that help? Whether 'rights-based approaches' can be conducive to poverty eradication is the principal issue addressed in this chapter.

Notably, the 'rights of the poor' were declared more than fifty years ago in the Universal Declaration of Human Rights of 1948 (UDHR). Article 25, for example, is quite explicit: 'Everyone has the right to a standard of living adequate for the health and well-being of himself and of his family, including food, clothing, housing and medical care and necessary social services, and the right to security in the event of unemployment, sickness, disability, widowhood, old age or other lack of livelihood in circumstances beyond his control ... '

Strong and compelling language, indeed, but what has it meant for the world's poor? The international community responsible for such 'rights language' appears to be unable to guarantee its enforcement. Indeed, the global endeavour to realize these human rights suffers from a huge *deficit* in implementation, which all too often is submerged in the general euphoria of human rights declarations, conferences, committee meetings and work-shops. Non-implementation is notably reflected in the language used with regard to poverty, for example 'poverty *alleviation*', 'poverty *reduction*' and 'pro-poor growth'. Taking human rights seriously, however, would seem to imply just one type of terminology: that of poverty *eradication*.

A fundamental weakness in human rights discourse concerns its relationship to felt social reality: the focus on *declared* rights, frequently at the beginning of long and enduring struggles for implementation, rather than *acquired* rights, i.e. formal legal protection of freedoms and titles that have already been granted societal recognition as sources of *entitlements*. This chapter examines the meaning of such a *declaratory* approach to rights with particular emphasis on the rights of the poor.

Human rights as *declared* rights

The tendency to abuse power is as old as human history. Therefore the use of power should always be tied to certain norms. Where such norms express legal protection of fundamental freedoms and basic entitlements of each and every human being, we speak of 'human rights'. Since here human dignity itself is at stake, claims based on these rights should normally trump other types of claim, both private and public.

The purpose of *rights*, as interests protected by law, is to put conflicts of interests in a normative setting and thus to prevent their manifestation as pure power struggles. But although rights are abstract acknowledgements of claims in the sense of a general commitment to offer legal protection for their realization, the world is full of denials of claims founded upon people's fundamental freedoms and basic entitlements. In fact, while the whole idea of rights is based upon the expectation that evident violations will lead to contentious action resulting in redress, *human* rights often remain without effective remedies. This is due to two crucial deficiencies: first, the often prevailing inadequacy of law as a check on power, and second, the lack of receptivity to these rights in many cultural and politico-economic contexts.

In terms of the role and rule of law, society is expected to function in such a way that rights are respected and claims based on entitlements connected to those rights are honoured. Dispute settlement is confined to cases in which there are conflicting claims protected by different rights (for example, between landlord and tenant). In the case of human rights, however, adequate embodiment in positive law is all too often lacking, resulting in little redress for violations in and from centres of power. Of course, there are notable differences in context here. In the Netherlands, for example, freedom of speech is protected by a historically *acquired* right, while in China freedom of speech is based on an internationally *declared* right that is structurally divorced from the national political centre.

The character of human rights as 'declaratory' rather than 'conclusive' is applicable to economic, social and cultural rights in particular and manifests itself especially in countries in the South. This is not just a matter of *socio-economic* context, i.e. no jobs, no access to land and hence extreme pressure on scarce productive resources, which breeds frustration and aggression rather than recognition of other people's freedoms and needs. There is also a *political* setting that finds its background in the history of colonialism and affects the distribution and control of power, both internationally and in local contexts. As a result, the fight for *social justice* in a modern economy and polity has a long way to go. Currently that struggle has not yielded impressive fruits internationally. Over the past two centuries, the gaps between the richest and the poorest countries have widened immensely, while in absolute terms, in the poorest region, sub-Saharan Africa, the number of people living on less than one US dollar a day increased considerably during the 1990s.[1] As a result of decisions taken in the name of economic progress, the world's poor often face increasing daily hardships.[2] In that dim light, the toughness of the struggle for social justice within so many developing countries is hardly surprising.

(Non)-implementation of economic, social and cultural rights

From a legal-philosophical perspective, human rights may be seen as connecting general principles of justice with the conception of human beings as individuals with subjective rights. Each distinct human right has a *core* that relates to human dignity. Behind that core is a general principle connected with *public justice* in the sense of a communal conviction of what is so crucial for the integrity of the public-political community that it should be enforced. Examples of such principles of justice reflected in the International Bill of Rights are liberty, equality, due process (with sub-principles such as habeas corpus and objectivity and impartiality in judicial decision-making), humanity (respect for human life), the integrity of the body, privacy, stability of possessions,[3] and participation.[4] The next step in terms of standard-setting is to elaborate these principles in domestic legal texts. The relative success of such attempts to further embody human rights in positive law depends first on the functionality of the country's legal systems, second on the country's judicial and political openness to the issue of legitimacy as a notion transcending pure formal legality, and third on country-specific cultural factors. Indeed, the spiritual roots of a human rights language can be found in different social and cultural contexts.[5] Hence, in accepting their responsibility for the implementation of human rights, states are well advised to look for religious and other types of moral support for efforts made within the environment of their specific jurisdiction, as well as in an international setting. This applies to the North as well as the South. Particularly problematic in the US setting, for example, is the principle of recognition of need – *social justice* – which lies behind Articles 22 to 25 of the Universal Declaration of Human Rights and the International Covenant on Economic, Social and Cultural Rights. The struggle for social justice appeals to people's sense of solidarity and collective responsibility. But in the context of a settlers' society like the US – a country that has such a dominant influence on global culture – it is individual autonomy rather than social justice which dominates legal and political thinking. ('Your well-being is not my concern. I made it, now you have to make it!') Of course, this type of politico-legal thinking is not confined to the US. Notably, the culture underlying economic globalization is generally based on possessive individualism rather than social justice.

Apparently, the international community still lacks the means to enforce the fundamental freedoms that have been declared as universal rights. With regard to basic entitlements for each and every human being, even a human rights *profile* has not yet been established. Yet the formulation of basic entitlements to education, healthcare, food, clothing, housing and employment as *rights* has raised expectations and 'rights-based approaches' further increase these. Thus, the world of human rights is a world of unfulfilled expectations. While, inevitably, human rights have to be incorporated in the systems of our time ('mainstreaming'), a serious concern today is that they have become a *system* of their own, involving inter-governmental and non-governmental centres, compliance and complaints procedures with commissions, committees and courts of law, training programmes and academic teaching courses, often quite far removed from real-life perspectives. The term 'secular religion' is used in this connection, particularly in an institutional sense.

Is it advisable, then, to capitulate and abandon that whole international venture for the protection of human dignity through rights? My answer is no, because in the global struggle to bind all use of power to essential standards, we have nothing that could better suit the requirements of protecting people's human dignity in a modern setting. Rhetoric, true, but a strong and morally compelling rhetoric. Rights do, indeed, fulfil the important function of providing legal protection to subjective claims based on recognized interests, and hence the incorporation of human rights in functioning legal systems must be seen as essential. Even where not yet incorporated, human rights discourse can still be seen as *normative statements of* a *moral* code.

My use of the word 'moral' here indicates that the grounding of these rights is in morality and does not imply that human rights should be considered as 'moral rights' as opposed to 'legal rights'. Political science circles in North America particularly seek to bifurcate moral and legal rights, with the term 'moral rights' standing for rights that cannot be enforced or, in other words, rights without remedies.[6] But remedies are never automatic; rights-holders always have to claim what they are due. So the term 'acquired rights' should not be misinterpreted to mean rights with automatic remedies. Rights are *performative*, i.e. they require action on the part of those who hold them. In the case of human rights the struggle is often to acquire the entitlements that are supposed to be protected by internationally declared law. In other words, of primary interest to people living in poor sanitary conditions is not the internationally declared right to health but their daily access to clean water. The latter rests upon a concrete entitlement. In many respects, then, that struggle for entitlements is still in its early stages; hence human rights often cannot offer immediately effective realization.

The word 'right', then, holds a *legal* significance – that what is confirmed in such terminology *ought to be* protected by law so as to guarantee enforcement. Like law itself, rights find their meaning in order and justice. As human rights are rooted in justice, their realization is not just a matter of enforcing positive law, but a moral issue as well.

Poverty as entitlement failure

The strategic model on which the global human rights venture is based consists of international standard-setting and monitoring coupled, principally, with local struggles for enforcement and implementation. In this endeavour, international agencies for development cooperation such as the UNDP have chosen to concentrate their efforts on 'enabling environments' in the sense of enhancing the right type of conditions under which people can exercise their human rights. Many people, however, live in environments that, far from being conducive to local implementation, must be regarded as hostile to any effort for the protection of basic human dignity. In such *disabling conditions*, human rights tend to function not so much as legal resources but as *political instruments* to mobilize dissent, protest, opposition and collective action aimed at social and economic reform.

Particularly in adverse conditions such as situations of extreme pressure on scarce resources, a political economy analysis, i.e., one implying a meta-juridical approach that looks beyond disciplinary boundaries, may be enlightening.[7] Crucial to the analysis is the interface of and interaction between economic, political and legal aspects of problems and policies.

Political economy of human rights, then, is a way of looking behind systemic violations and structural non-implementation. Remarkably, its contribution is not restricted to economic, social and cultural rights. Lack of implementation of civil and political rights, too, must be assessed in a politico-economic context. With regard to poverty these so-called first-generation rights should be seen as 'empowerment rights', indispensable in any struggle to transform declared socio-economic rights into a meaningful basis for actual entitlement. Conversely, in respect of the realization of civil and political rights, economic, social and cultural rights may be seen as 'sustainability rights'.

The core focus of political economy vis-à-vis human rights is acquirement: why and how do people succeed in acquiring what they need for sustainable livelihoods. The methodology I propose starts with Amartya Sen's notion of *entitlement failure*, as advanced in his *Poverty and Fam-*

ines.[8] Behind failing claims to essential goods and services are deficient entitlement positions, and behind entitlement failure are malfunctioning entitlement systems.

For example, in his analysis of several cases of famine in Bengal, Ethiopia and the Sahel countries, Sen found no instance in which the explanatory factor was a decline in the availability of food; indeed, during the great famine in the Sahel in the 1980s, the export of groundnuts to the world market continued while people were starving to death. Each case of famine analysed by Sen appears to have been caused by *entitlement failure.*

In this connection, Sen distinguishes between production-based and trade-based entitlement. Subsistence economies typically rest on the former: production for one's own needs. While labour productivity is low, socio-economic security may be relatively high. Specialization in production, division of labour and technologies based on economies of scale will increase productivity. But the transition from a production-based to a trade-based economy may negatively affect people's entitlement positions and thus diminish their socio-economic security. Activities to increase productivity imply change, and change produces conflict about rights and obligations. Entitlement analysis offers insight into such processes. Sen bases his entitlement analysis primarily on direct access to resources. Two factors determine the entitlements of a person living in a society whose economy features private ownership and exchange in the form of trade (exchange with others) and production (exchange with nature): the *endowment* of the person (what he or she owns) and what Sen calls *exchange entitlement mapping* – the specification of the alternative commodity 'bundles' the person can command for each endowment bundle.

Elsewhere, I have expanded this methodology into an *entitlement systems analysis.*[9] Briefly, a basic distinction first has to be made between rights, entitlements and claims. A right implies neither more nor less than an *abstract* acknowledgement of claims. Entitlement is concrete: actual legitimate command over a good or service in a specified use.[10] A claim is a concrete *act* of acquirement. For example, the owner of a house is generally presumed free to use it. This includes the presumption of an entitlement to live there. Hence owners may well claim actual occupancy of their premises. But it is quite possible that another person is already entitled to occupy that house, for example a tenant. If two distinct individuals claim occupancy at the same time, the judge in question will look behind the conflicting claims and weigh the relative strengths of the respective rights as well as the different interests of the parties. If, in light of the case's facts, there is no completely on-point precedent (as there usually is not), general legal principles may assist in finding developing law for this specific dispute. With regard to this type of case, for example, an old *regula iuris* says 'Nemo de domo sua extrahi debet' (people cannot be evicted from their own house); a modern principle is 'Sale can break no rent'. The latter means that a new owner cannot terminate the occupancy of the tenant without consent.

Just as the relationship between abstract rights and concrete entitlements[11] is not mechanical, neither is there an automatic link between entitlements and honoured claims (actual acquirement). Usually, in order to claim what one wants, certain activities must take place within processes of production, distribution and consumption of goods and services, for example land has to be worked, commodities have to be manufactured and sold, services have to be delivered, consumer goods have to be bought in shops, a door has to be opened with a key. Entitlements provide neither more nor less than access to such processes; actual acquirement also requires activities and action.

Now, suppose a person is homeless simply because he or she lacks an entitlement to occupy any premises. What is the effect of the housing right as defined in Article 25 of the UDHR and Article 11 of the International Covenant on Economic, Social and Cultural Rights (ICESCR) in terms of that individual's concrete entitlement? Unfortunately, this human right does not generally function as a direct source of concrete entitlements. If, however, a landless individual takes direct action to use land currently belonging to absentee owners, the right to food as recognized in international law may well play a part in processes of ex-post legalization. This is, in fact, the way in which the 'Sem tierra' movement of landless peasants in Brazil tends to operate. In terms of poor people's 'coping strategies', this may be termed *quiet encroachment.*

A consequence that might follow from the general housing right articulated in international human rights law is a judicial prohibition on depriving human beings access to their sole resort without offering an alternative. Thus, in public interest litigation, the Indian Supreme Court ruled that homeless beggars cannot be simply removed from street pavements where they sleep. Olivier and Van Rensburg's chapter in this book discusses in detail the South African Constitutional Court's judgment of far-reaching strategic importance in *The Government of the Republic of South Africa and Others* v. *Grootboom and Others,*[12] which obliged the state to act positively to ameliorate the plight of the hundreds of thousands of people living in deplorable conditions, albeit within the South African constitutional 'progressive realization' parameters. Naturally, in carrying out these duties the state must prioritize. But in doing so, those who should be put highest on the list are the individuals belonging to the most vulnerable and deprived groups in society. Although the overall housing programme implemented by the state since 1994 had resulted in a significant number of additional houses, it failed to cater to the needs of the group requesting remedial action in this particular case. The court issued a declaratory order requiring the state to implement measures aimed at relief for those desperate people who had not been properly cared for in the state programme applicable in the Cape Metropolitan area. Such measures would have to be taken before the programme that had led to their forced removal from the spot where they had at least benefited from roofs over their heads could be implemented. In short, while generally economic rights have been declared as rights without pre-existing entitlements, through concrete action entitlements pertaining to the human right in question can be asserted. Human rights, in other words, are *transformational*: they establish a normative framework for processes of social change.

As there can be rights without entitlements, the opposite may equally obtain. Thus, a peasant may have lawful access to a plot simply because a relevant authority, for example the chief of his tribe, granted access for as long as that person worked that piece of land. Indeed, institutional relations may also serve as entitlement (sub-)systems. Generally, the titles of people living and working in the informal sector of the economy are unprotected by state law, leading to *possession without ownership* and similar juridical actualities. Highly relevant in this connection is the relationship between citizens and their state. Besides state law protecting already existing entitlements, state power may also serve as a source of new entitlements. The state may also interfere negatively in people's entitlements, however, for example through expropriation. Hence, for the purpose of human rights implementation, government policies and actions, in the broadest sense of enforcing entitlements for 'private' actors or in the more traditional sense of positive state regulation, have to be closely monitored in their effects upon the entitlement positions of those living in daily hardship.

The universality of human rights as internationally accepted standards of legitimacy facilitates the mobilization of international support in struggles against their violation. For example, international pressure, through reporting or other procedures by the United Nations Special Rapporteur for Housing, may contribute to processes that will result in actual recognition of people's housing needs. Indeed, it is often (international) non-governmental organizations rather than states which work with and support those carrying out their responsibilities in UN compliance mechanisms.

The rights of the poor: some alternative approaches

Notably, the possibility of judicially enforcing human rights abuses tends to be underestimated, particularly with regard to economic, social and cultural rights. Although, as pointed out, a homeless individual cannot usually sue the state for provision of a house, forced evictions or cutting off essential services can be contested in courts of law. There is a legally enforceable difference, in other words, between a state of non-implementation and a concrete act of violation. Now, if human rights were no more than subjective rights, albeit of a special type, the human rights deficit mentioned earlier would have a paralysing effect on the whole effort to protect human dignity by law. In that case, the issue would be confined to *justiciability*. But the main point is that precisely in situations where the use of legal resources becomes problematic, the function of human rights as *standards of legitimacy* is activated, through confrontation of power abuses with norms based on the protection of human dignity. Government housing policies, for example, must be based on the right of everyone to live in a decent house and government budgets should reflect the priority given to people's housing needs.

Specifically designated human rights, then, must be seen not merely as subjective rights – to be enforced through claims based on entitlements connected with them – but also as general principles of justice. As such, they play a role in adjudication, not as a direct basis for judicial acceptance of certain claims, but as normative principles that guide judicial decision-making, much as the old *regulae iuris* performed that function.[13] Consider, for example, the damages suffered by small fishermen when, in the name of development, big trawlers are introduced into shallow waters, destroying the breeding grounds for the fish that form the basis of the local fishermen's livelihoods. Those who have suffered as a result may fail to achieve judicial recognition of claims based on a subjective 'right to development', but the right to development may well be invoked in order to determine responsibility for a tort.[14]

Thus far, the emphasis has been on law in a modern universalistic sense, i.e. enforcement of rules through regularized mechanisms. If, however, the realization of fundamental norms binding the use of power were purely dependent on formal legal processes, in many places deficits in the enforcement of crucial standards would be much worse. Fortunately, however, law can also work through *informal* mechanisms or, in another terminology, as *living law*.[15]

While 'law' manifests itself as regulation of power, living law has the nature of 'anti-power'. An illustration may be taken from the social history of slavery in Barbados. Beginning at the end of the eighteenth century, records of slave births and sales show that infants were no longer sold separately from their mothers and that the nuclear slave family became a common phenomenon, in that husbands and wives were not sold separately.[16]

While slaves were still regarded as chattels and certainly not recognized as legal subjects, motherhood became a 'customary right, evidenced by the noticeable self-enforcement of human rights by informal means'.[17]

Moreover, as noted previously, human rights function not only as legal resources but as *political instruments*: standards of legitimacy, applicable to any use of power, whether by state or non-state actors. The processes through which this is effected may have a formal as well as an informal character. Besides living law, in other words, *living politics* also confront power with human rights standards. To illustrate the meaning of living politics, it may be helpful to juxtapose two distinct situations: a parliament without a free press and a free press without a parliament. The former means *dead* politics; a free press without a parliament, on the other hand, can lead to *living* politics. Likewise, in the case of the fishermen summarized above, those in power might be aware of the submerged, but significant, potential resistance likely to be activated when the local population see their fishing grounds destroyed, and might discourage big trawlers from fishing in the shallow waters. Indeed, *living politics* are likely to become increasingly relevant with regard to non-state actors.[18]

Notably, globalization today also affects interpretations of legitimacy. For example, as a consequence of globalization, principles regarding the use of power become more and more *general* in the sense of being shared in the whole *ius gentium*. This opens the way to more *inductive* approaches to envisioning a human rights discourse. A deductive approach derives concrete rights from international treaties and other formal sources; an inductive approach starts from what people themselves see as the fundamental freedoms and entitlements that everyone should enjoy and hence ought to be protected by law. Such a growing focus on real-life contexts influences the processes of legitimization. In Bangladesh, for instance, private wash places appear to be a strong priority for rural women. Such essential entitlements can be identified only inductively.

In short, then, institutional decisions that affect the lives of people are being increasingly confronted with universal standards of legitimacy, including modern human rights. While the international structure for the protection of human rights has been designed with a particular emphasis on the state, today growing attention is being paid to human rights observance by non-state actors such as (transnational) corporations, discussed in Voiculescu's chapter in this book. As historically the applicability of rules of justice has never been confined to the state, such a development is not surprising.

Poverty as a failure of entitlement

Conclusion

The project of protecting a decent life for each and every human being by *declaring universal rights* is not simple. Declared *rights* are rights, and a rights-based organization of society demands functioning legal systems. A crucial point is that while one can have rights without entitlements (for example, a displaced person who still owns his house but lacks access to it), the opposite may equally obtain: entitlements without rights. The poor are generally people with some actual possessions but few legal titles. This is the core of Hernando de Soto's argument in *The Mystery of Capital: Why Capitalism Triumphs in the West and Fails Everywhere Else.*[19] According to de Soto's calculations, the average assets possessed by the poor amount to US$8,000 per person. He deplores the fact, however, that poor people's daily access to certain resources and their claims are not protected by established legal titles, i.e. it is practically impossible for them to borrow, invest or accumulate. The assets of the poor, for example a piece of land with a shack, cannot be used for further accumulation because there is no title registered and protected through the modern, universalist legal system.

Therefore, if rights-based approaches are to effectuate change within the rubric of international poverty law, they should remove such constraints and ensure that the entitlements reflected among poor people are equally protected under our legal regime. In other words, policy should be aimed at moving from living law to formally protected entitlement.

Declaring rights implies that much more is necessary than just protecting already acquired bundles of entitlements. Human rights law is *laborious law*. In many a politico-economic context, the transformation of these declared rights into acquired rights that actually guarantee fundamental freedoms and entitlements for everyone requires long and enduring struggles. For civil and political rights, the political order has to be confronted. For economic, social and cultural rights, the entitlement (sub-)systems that lie behind structural non-implementation have to be changed, requiring a confrontation with existing economic powers.

In sum, the rights approach as launched in the *Human Development Report 2000* provides an important methodology for envisioning innovative and integrative strategies to tackle poverty and other violations of basic human dignity. What is needed now is a systematic evaluation of its implications. This might be based on the following elements:

1. Poverty is 'a brutal denial of human rights'.[20] Hence, rights-based strategies confront the status quo. As such, they differ from development approaches based on a harmonious striving for progress (development

interpreted as a pure positive-sum game). The basic orientation is not material resources, but the constraints in poor people's daily struggles for sustainable livelihoods.

2. The focus of a rights approach is not poverty as a general phenomenon, for example, the number of people who have to survive on less than so much per day, but rather on the lives and daily hardships of the poor. The centre of attention is people's needs rather than the state's resources.

3. The poor are *people with rights*. Economic, social and cultural rights are meant to offer people protection in order that they might obtain their basic human needs. Hence the injustices that lie at the *roots* of denied needs have to be addressed. An entitlement (sub-)systems approach may serve to reveal the causes of concrete entitlement failure. In other words, the strategy must move from an individual case-by-case response to addressing the structures behind non-implementation of human rights. When poverty is seen not as a natural hazard, but as a denial of basic human dignity, a strong normative component emerges.

4. Rights can be approached from a 'deductive' perspective, for example distilling some eighteen specified civil, political, economic, social and cultural rights from the international treaties and covenants while going into the juridical intricacies of legal definition. Another approach is 'inductive': what are people's own perceptions of what they are due in terms of fundamental freedoms and basic entitlements? Rights-based approaches will have to combine the two methods in spelling out the implications of human rights at the grassroots level.

5. A core notion of implementing a rights approach is *accountability*, meaning that institutions and persons exercising power (actors, in other words) become duty-bearers. In concrete situations of non-implementation, the challenge is to identify duty-bearers while specifying their duties. At times, the duty bearer appears evident, for example when Zimbabwean president Robert Mugabe ordered bulldozers to level people's shacks and destroy their possessions, simply because he wanted 'eyesores' out of view during a state visit by Queen Elizabeth II in the 1980s (recently this has become 'standard practice' in Zimbabwe). Likewise, in the South African *Grootboom* case the duty-bearer was identifiable. But often this is not the case, because behind non-implementation lie complicated social, political and economic structures.

6. Human rights are not just *legal resources* but *political instruments*. The latter implies that the use of power can be seen as legitimate only if human rights standards are followed. *Legitimacy* is a core concept referring to institutions and principles, procedures and outcome. Hence,

rights-based approaches have to track not just inputs but *outcomes*, identifying and utilizing specific standards within a context that is not merely local but also international. Indeed, rights-based approaches will remain meaningless if not connected to responsibilities for global injustices as well.

Within this context, the human rights regime faces three major internal threats. First, human rights might be viewed simplistically, as if universality were just a matter of international law – and furthermore an already settled issue. Although perceived as clear in a legal sense, in political and cultural terms universality remains a major challenge, requiring continuous mobilization of support from every possible quarter in the struggle to protect the dignity of all. Indeed, the global human rights venture necessitates much more than just the involvement of international lawyers, however important their role may be. Second, human rights may be conceptualized as a pure *system*, far removed from the real-life experiences of people struggling for their daily livelihoods. I am referring here to legal instrumentalism: law as an instrument of social change. In fact, the concept of 'rights with remedies' is as simplistic as that of 'rights without remedies'. The real tasks we are facing today are no longer primarily in standard-setting, but in the tribulations of implementation. The third risk is in capitulation: the feeling that human rights law is of such a laborious nature that we should abandon the whole discourse.

Human rights law is not impossible law, as long as one refrains from positivist dogmatism, while being prepared to look creatively for new ways of using human rights as legal resources – human rights as not just subjective rights in the conventional sense but general principles of justice which play their part in adjudication in a way similar to the old rules of law (the '*regulae iuris*'). With regard to economic, social and cultural rights and collective rights, this opens new avenues for litigation. Related to this, human rights operate as general standards of legitimacy. As such, they may function in alternative approaches to poverty, such as living law ('quiet encroachment') and also as instruments in the politics of protecting human dignity.

Finally, the word *approach* is somewhat weak, making a 'human rights approach' sound like the latest fashion in launching ideas on development. If the poor have rights – and they do – then there is no new 'approach' conceivable that would deny or ignore these rights. Indeed, human rights is a *commitment*, following from a *conviction* (well expressed in Article 1 of the UDHR), and hence for actors adopting 'rights-based approaches' there will be no way back.

Notes

1 See, for example, UNDP (1999) *Human Development Report,* New York, and the World Bank (2000) *Global Economic Prospects and the Developing Countries*, Washington, DC.

2 See B. Klein Goldewijk and B. de Gaay Fortman (1999) 'Development-oriented approaches', *Where Needs Meet Rights. Economic, Social and Cultural Rights in a New Perspective*, Geneva: WCC Publications, pp. 19–35.

3 I.e. the principle behind Article 17 of the UDHR which declares the right to property.

4 I.e. the principle behind Article 21 of the UDHR on the right to partici-pate in government. Cf. the *regula iuris* 'Quod omnes tangit debet ab omnibus approbari', as formulated in the *Corpus Iuris Canonicis* (SEXTI DECRETAL., LIB. V, TIT. XII., DE REGULIS IURIS, Bonifacius VII, Regula XXIX).

5 Michael Ignatieff signals a political crisis, a cultural crisis and also a *spiritual* crisis in human rights. See M. Ignatieff (1999) *Whose Universal Values? The Crisis in Human Rights*, Amsterdam: Praemium Erasmianum Essay.

6 Joseph Wronka, for one, sees human rights as a process from 'rights as ideals' via 'rights as enactments' to 'rights as exercised'. See J. Wronka (1998) *Human Rights and Social Policy in the 21st Century*, Lanham, MD: University Press of America, pp. 28–30.

7 For a definition of political economy I refer to the *Review of Political Economy* in its mission statement: 'Political economy is best defined as an approach to economics which puts first priority on practical, and policy 'issues, and tailors theoretical and empirical work accordingly. The economy is regarded as being located in historical time, interacting with a political, social and natural environment. Within the system the agents change and interact in a manner which cannot be described adequately by the assump-tions of neoclassical theory.'

8 A. Sen (1981) *Poverty and Famines. An Essay on Entitlement and Depriva-tion*, Oxford: Clarendon Press.

9 See B. De Gaay Fortman (1999) 'Beyond income distribution. an entitle-ment systems approach to the acquirement problem', in J. Van der Linden et al. (eds), *The Economics of Income Distribution: Heterodox Approaches*, Brookfield (US)/Cheltenham (UK): Edward Elgar, pp. 29–75.

10 In the essay referred to above I define entitlement as the possibility of making legitimate claims, and hence a function of both power and law. The term 'command' used in the present text constitutes a quite appropriate modifi-cation suggested by Suzanne Verstegen in her paper *Understanding and Prevent-ing Poverty-related Conflict*, presented at the workshop 'Resources, Entitlement and Poverty-related Conflict', The Hague: Clingendael Institute, 5 March 2001, p. 14.

11 This distinction provides more clarity than that between abstract rights and concrete rights, as used in the *Human Development Report 2000* (based on Ronald Dworkin's work).

12 2000 (1) SA 46 (CC).

13 In this way collective rights, too, can play their part. Thus, as an enlightening principle the right to a healthy environment, for example, or the right to development, may well determine a court case.

14 The right to development is based on UN General Assembly Resolution 41/128 of 4 December 1986. It stipulates, among other things, the duty of states to adopt development policies that aim at 'free and meaningful participation in development' and 'the fair distribution of benefits' resulting from development. Through a certain period of regular practice, supported by *Opinio Iuris*, principles formulated by the General Assembly may acquire the status of general principles of law. Another example is Sovereignty over National Resources. See N. Schrijver (1997) *Sovereignty over National Resources. Balancing Rights and Duties*, Cambridge: University Press, pp. 371ff.

15 While the term 'living law' is used with different meanings I use it here in the sense of *informal* processes of setting, monitoring and enforcing norms pertaining to order and justice within a certain community.

16 See H. McD. Beckles (1989) *Natural Rebels. A Social History of Enslaved Women in Barbados*, New Brunswick, NJ: Rutgers University Press, *inter alia* pp. 105 and 107.

17 Obviously, slave owners feared that non-compliance would imply a considerable risk of slave revolts and hence jeopardize the whole social system.

18 One of the most striking developments in this respect is the incorporation of human rights clauses in the general principles of transnational corporations. Shell International, for one, not only adopted such a human rights clause in its own code of conduct but also deleted the phrase 'Shell is not involved in politics'. While, naturally, party politics is a different matter, the universal responsibility for the observance of human rights implies that no actor in business can stay out of politics. The whole discussion on corporate responsibility and human rights was sparked off particularly by Shell's traumatic experiences in Ogoniland. See Amos Adeoye Idowu (1999) 'Human rights, environmental degradation and oil multinational companies in Nigeria: the Ogoniland episode', *Netherlands Quarterly of Human Rights*, 17 (2): 161–84.

19 H. de Soto (1999) *The Mystery of Capital. Why Capitalism Triumphs in the West and Fails Everywhere Else*, London: Bantam Press.

20 UNDP (1998) *Integrating Human Rights with Sustainable Development*, New York.

4 | Biodiversity versus biotechnology: an economic and environmental struggle for life[1]

MARGARITA GABRIELA PRIETO-ACOSTA

Some of the world's poorest people are peasant farmers and indigenous people who live at subsistence level in developing countries[2] around the world. Of the 1.2 billion people living in absolute poverty, 75 per cent live in rural areas and over 50 per cent of them depend directly on agriculture for their livelihoods.[3] Increasingly, economic pressure is mounting on these people as national and international intellectual property laws make it possible for biotechnology companies to obtain proprietary rights over medicinal herbs, staple food crops and the genetic resources they contain. Many seeds have traditionally been freely available to farmers in developing countries for generations, but can now be privately owned by companies that intend to sell them to farmers at a profit. These companies, mainly from developed countries,[4] are obtaining patents on specific plant varieties or genes from crops traditionally farmed in developing countries, such as Basmati rice, millet, cassava, sweet potato, enola, nuña and yacón. Similarly, pharmaceutical companies are finding traditional remedies in developing countries, deriving new marketable drug products and patenting and commercializing them at a profit, often without offering any reward or benefit to the communities through which the plants and their beneficial properties originally became known. This phenomenon is known as 'biopiracy',[5] a term explained more fully below. It raises serious concerns about the impact that intellectual property rights may have on poverty in developing countries.

In today's global economy, food is increasingly a commodity traded through markets rather than being grown for a family's own consumption. In these circumstances, food security[6] depends on having adequate financial resources. For weaker nations, equitable trading conditions, free of unfair barriers, are fundamental to food security. The biggest threat to equity in trade is an imbalance of power, especially today since the interests of transnational corporations are supported by a regulatory regime that plays to their strengths.

Non-governmental organizations (NGOs) and developing countries have claimed in recent years that the regulations of the World Trade Organization (WTO), in particular the Agreement on Trade Related Aspects of

Intellectual Property Rights (TRIPs), discriminate against poorer countries through a combination of cultural, financial and technological barriers.[7] One result of this discrimination is seen in farming, which provides a livelihood for 75 per cent of the population in developing countries.[8]

The security previously provided by state involvement in the development and organization of agriculture has been removed under pressure for market reforms, and with it the foundations of everyday life for farmers in developing countries. Consequent to the liberalization of global markets, agricultural produce has become a commodity traded for the lowest global price, as determined by powerful traders and market forces. While the profit motive holds greatest influence in international trade and workers around the world take up the strain to compete on cost, the bold dreams and promises of the past, such as the declarations of human rights and international expressions of commitment to solve environmental and social problems, are in danger of being forgotten. Yet while harsh economic realities have to be faced, welfare economists agree that the benefits to society as a whole decrease as the gap between rich and poor increases. Social inequalities are rarely taken into account by the corporate powers that drive and control most of the economic system, motivated necessarily, but perhaps excessively, by share price and profit.

As the power of nation-state governments around the world diminishes in the face of market forces, so the social commitments that nations have endorsed seem to receive a lower priority. The principles addressed in the 1948 Universal Declaration of Human Rights (UDHR), however, are still worthy of consideration, even if only as a reminder of our humanity and of our basic duties towards other people. Another valuable, if neglected, undertaking is the 1976 International Covenant on Economic Social and Cultural Rights (ICESCR), created to give effect to the UDHR. Out of 148 parties, 142 have ratified as of November 2003.[9] One of the main objectives declared therein is the protection of a fundamental human right of all people to have sufficient food,[10] an aspirational standard against which all governments, especially the signatories, must measure their performance.

This chapter shows how respect for humanity has been devalued as a consequence of the drive for profit from plants. The result is a decrease in the living standards of those who work with and depend upon the crop plants provided by nature.

In particular, the chapter looks at the role of the global intellectual property rights (IPR) model built into the WTO/TRIPs regulations, and specifically how this model relates to biological entities and what effect it is having on poverty in developing countries.

In the first section I analyse the effect of IPR laws on poverty in developing countries, looking specifically at the TRIPs agreement, national legislation in developing countries, United States law relating to IPR and the US Patent and Trademark Office (PTO), and the practices of the World Intellectual Property Organization (WIPO).

In the second section, I review the international conflict over the implementation of the TRIPs agreement and the Convention on Biological Diversity (CBD), analysed under four headings: the CDB, TRIPs and plants, the discord between the two treaties, and plants as genetic resources.

In the third section I look at how, in order to prevent the exploitation of their resources, developing countries implementing the CBD currently face risks in two areas: biopiracy and food security.

In the fourth section, I look at what can be done to protect the poorest people in developing countries from 'biopiracy' under TRIPs, specifically under the headings of countering problems of patents and plant variety protection and the defence of human rights.

The impact of IPR laws on poverty in developing countries

The TRIPs agreement, national legislation in developing countries, United States law regarding IPR and the US Patent and Trademark Office, and the practices of the World Intellectual Property Organization (WIPO) all significantly affect poverty in developing countries. This section first describes the connection between each of the above and plant varieties and then analyses the cumulative impact on poverty.

Patents and plant variety protection under WTO/TRIPs and UPOV In 1994 the international community completed the GATT negotiations at the Uruguay Round, which resulted in the founding of the WTO and its regulations, including the TRIPs agreement, which aims to harmonize legislation on IPR issues across the globe. TRIPs has introduced two mechanisms by which the economic interests in biological material can be protected for monopolistic purposes. In Article 27.3 (b), TRIPs provides IPR protection over micro-organisms and related processes through patents. The same section requires IPR protection over plant varieties through either patents or another 'sui generis system', intended by developed countries, especially the US, to be based on plant breeders' rights, as represented internationally by the UPOV organization (Union pour la Protection des Obtentions Végétales, translated as International Union for the Protection of New Varieties of Plants).[11] Both routes are available through genetic engineering, although each imposes distinct requirements.

For a patent to be granted, the invention must be new, involve an inventive step, i.e. be innovative (non-obvious), be useful, i.e. capable of industrial application (an aid to practical human activity) and not simply a discovery (Article 27.1, TRIPs). A patent-holder has the right to stop others from making, using or selling the invention without permission. The duration of a patent is twenty years, after which the invention becomes public property (Article 27.1, TRIPs).

For a plant variety to be granted protection under the UPOV 1978 convention, it must meet conditions of distinctness, uniformity and stability. Under the UPOV 1991 convention, the condition of novelty was added. The period of protection for holders of plant breeders' rights (PBR) under UPOV depends on the lifespan and reproductive cycle of the plant. During this period any plant 'essentially derived'[12] from the protected variety is also subject to control by the holder of the rights over the source plant.

TRIPs makes fine distinctions for granting rights, however, not only on biological grounds (micro-organisms versus plants and animals) but also on the grounds of what input the breeder or inventor has contributed to the 'product' or 'process' (Article 27.1, TRIPs).

National legislation in developing countries Few developing countries have a patent system covering plants. Most also do not have advanced biotechnology or plant breeding industries that can compete with the US, Japan and Europe. There are, therefore, few competitors in the field of patents. Those developing countries that currently recognize patents on plants have based their acceptance criteria on those in TRIPs for inventions, requiring particular evidence in forms not usually available in non-industrialized societies (Article 27.1, TRIPs).[13]

United States laws on IPR and the US Patent and Trademark Office The following US IPR rules and regulations, as administered by the US Patent and Trademark Office (PTO), have a bearing on privatization of plant genetic resources.

- US patent law does not admit sale or use of a product or process outside of the US as evidence of prior art.[14] Thus products or processes already in existence, which may prove that the subject of a patent application is not novel, may be ignored and conditions of inventive step and novelty not be fully tested.
- Farmers' varieties or landraces[15] found outside the US are not accepted as prior art, unless they have been patented or described in a printed publication in any country, or been in public use or on sale in the US for at least one year before the patent application or before the new plant variety was created.

- Patent applicants do not need to certify the sources of original biological samples or knowledge, or provide evidence that these were legally obtained.
- In order to have a patent revoked where its validity is questioned by virtue of another product or process previously in use or commercialized abroad, a full legal challenge must be made. The cost of this makes it impossible for most growers or farmers of plants in developing countries to press a claim that a patent is unjustified owing to lack of novelty, constituting a significant barrier to justice for growers in developing countries.
- The PTO is not required, as part of its examining procedure of plant material used in inventions, to check for traditional uses outside of the US and is therefore unable to properly test patent applications.

Thus the rules of the US PTO put innovators in other countries at a disadvantage when trying to assert their rights to the plant genetic resources they have developed and rely upon, especially those in the informal sector, where traditional IPR protection is inappropriate. In addition, the technology and science involved in genetics are new and complex. They are likely to be best understood by industry scientists. It seems at least possible that patent examiners may have difficulty in judging the true merit of some biotechnological inventions for which patents are sought, particularly over issues of novelty and obviousness.

The practices of the World Intellectual Property Organization (WIPO) The features of the US IPR system mentioned above are reproduced globally through a system of 'international' patent applications. This system is operated by WIPO and implements the objectives of the Patent Cooperation Treaty (PCT),[16] which was negotiated under its auspices. WIPO describes the process as follows.[17]

The PCT makes it possible for a national or resident of a contracting state to seek patent protection for an invention, simultaneously in any number of states chosen from those contracted to it, by filing an 'international' patent application. The effect in each designated state is the same as if a national patent application had been filed with the national patent office of that state. Where a designated state is party to a 'community' patent treaty, such as the European Patent Convention, the applicant may (and for certain countries must) opt for the effect of a community (rather than a national) patent application.

The international application is then subjected to an international search, carried out by one of the major patent offices,[18] which results in an 'international search report' listing the citations of published documents that might affect the patentability of the invention claimed in the international application. The applicant may at that stage decide to withdraw his application, but if not, the application and international search report are published by the International Bureau and communicated to each designated office. The applicant must then commence the national procedure before each designated office, furnishing a translation (where necessary) of the application into the official language of that office and paying to it the required fees. The advantages of using this system are that the timescales are quite generous, search and examination work can be considerably reduced, and third parties are in a better position to formulate a well-founded opinion about the patentability of the claimed invention.

The demand for international patent protection through the system is growing, increasing from 2,625 international applications in 1979 to 67,007 in 1998.

Given the US's membership of WIPO and the fact that it is a signatory to the PCT, US nationals and residents have the right to make international applications for patent protection of their inventions through the PCT system, and the US PTO is one of a selected group of patent authorities empowered by the PCT to receive and handle such applications. US patent law (United States Code [USC] Title 35 – Patents) reflects the powers and responsibilities of the US PTO in this and other PCT-related roles (USC 35 Chapters 35, 36 and 37).[19]

WIPO is constantly working to make globally enforceable patents easier to obtain. As of 1 January 2004, new arrangements under the PCT make the process easier still. Rather than applicants designating individual countries in which to apply for protection, all available countries are designated for protection at a national and regional level. A new, enhanced search and examination system, providing an international search and opinion on compliance with main patentability criteria, will be available very early in the procedure. The duplication of work in the processing of PCT applications will be reduced and centralized. International preliminary examination reports will be available to third parties through a request to WIPO.

A much more significant project is under way at WIPO, however, designed to harmonise patent regulation and enable a single patent to be automatically valid in signatory countries. The NGO Genetic Resources Action International (GRAIN) has been monitoring its development and wrote the following:

> For three years, a new international patent treaty has been under negotiation at the World Intellectual Property Organisation (WIPO) in Geneva.

This Substantive Patent Law Treaty (SPLT) would remove most of the remaining national flexibility in patent systems and pave the way for a future world patent, granted directly by WIPO. This is an appealing prospect for transnational corporations and large powers like the US and the EU, who see patents as the primary means to control a globalised economy. But a world patent system is bad news for developing countries and their citizens, who would lose even the limited freedom left by the WTO's TRIPs Agreement to adjust patent systems to national development goals. However, it is not too late for the developing world to say 'no thanks' and stop the negotiating process.[20]

Bias in favour of industrialized countries Many demonstrations against the WTO have brought attention to the defects in world trade regulation (Seattle, Genoa and those in opposition to the proposed Free Trade Area of the Americas at the 3rd Summit of the Americas in Quebec). While liberalization of world markets may provide some benefits for all participating countries, developed and developing alike, the balance of advantage seems to be in favour of those nations whose companies have accumulations of capital and control of technology. This advantage has been reinforced by the extension of industrial IPR systems to include biological products and processes, brought about primarily in developed countries and globalized through the WTO/TRIPs regulations.

Although patents on machinery, copyrights on songs and software and certifications of geographical origin have been well established for many years in industrialized countries, the idea of IPR protection for biological products and processes is relatively new and lacks international support among many nations. Through TRIPs, the WTO and its corporate backers are attempting, seemingly by economic power or by stealth (i.e. aggressive trade powers disguised as free trade laws), to establish a system whereby the exclusive rights provided through IPR can be extended to the products upon which vast proportions of humanity depend for use or trade, particularly in developing countries.

Numerous NGO reports describe crops, spices, medicinal herbs and other useful plants in developing countries becoming partly or fully subject to IPR protection. For example, the US firm RiceTek obtained a patent under US legislation for what it claims is a type of Basmati rice. Subsequently this patent was the subject of NGO campaigns in support of the Indian government, which has legally challenged twenty claims to novelty and the use of the name basmati[21] in connection with this genetically modified (GM)[22] rice grown in the US. Such challenges face substantial financial and legal obstacles, however, with lawyers often requiring hundreds of thousands of dollars up front. This is problematic for governments of developing countries and can be even more difficult for individuals and companies with far fewer resources.

An IPR ambush seems to have been set for producers of organic material in some developing countries, whether they produce fruits, crops, herbs, extracts or medicines. The trap consists of four main elements:

- First, producers in developing countries do not have strong legal arrangements to regulate and control access to their plants or genetic resources, despite the requirement for such arrangements in the CBD.[23] In these countries almost anyone can collect samples for research without contract or payment.

- Second, few developing countries, as compared to developed countries, have advanced biotechnology or plant breeding sectors, so it is unlikely that products or processes suitable for exploitation will qualify for protection under patent and Plant Variety Protection (PVP) criteria. The advantage of developed countries in technology and efficiency in capitalizing on intellectual property means that they can privatize these genetic resources more easily than organizations in the country of origin.

- Third, having collected the samples, developed a protectable product or process and obtained national protection, either at home or in the country of origin, the corporate owners of IPRs can use international IPR laws to enforce them in other countries. The WTO and TRIPs require all member states to adopt compatible IPR systems, and, through WIPO, IPR owners can extend the protections of their own country's rights to other countries.

- Fourth, the relatively late introduction of IPR legislation on plant genetic resources (PGRs) in developing countries puts their own breeders and growers at a great disadvantage. At the time that the legislation comes into force, many PGRs, probably including some native to the country concerned, will already be subject to IPRs under other national regimes. The owners of these IPRs can use the new legislation to enforce those rights in the enacting country. So the late introduction of such legislation by developing countries mainly benefits the companies that already have a large number of IPRs.

How biotechnology patents can worsen poverty The case against the current system of granting intellectual property rights over plants has been growing, especially in the case of crops. Vast numbers of farmers are currently dependent upon staple food crops that are becoming subject to protection by patents or Plant Breeders Rights (PBRs). Permission to use these crops must be paid for through licence fees.

Plant breeders and biotechnologists have for a long time been looking for ways in which to enforce their monopoly rights. Genetic engineering has provided some useful means for protecting the monopolies, such as the 'terminator'[24] and 'traitor' genes, collectively known as Genetic Use Restriction Technologies (GURTs).[25] The 'terminator' gene switches off the reproductive capacity of the plant after one generation unless a special chemical is applied. The more sophisticated 'traitor' gene requires an input to activate certain traits, such as disease resistance. Both of these methods prevent unlicensed seed-saving from current crops – the primary survival method of 1.4 billion people, including 90 per cent of farmers in Africa[26] – and would, if implemented, force poor farmers to buy new seed or chemical inputs each year.

In October 2000, a merger created the biotechnology giant Syngenta,[27] which then held over half of the world's patents for GURTs. Dr Sue Mayer, director of GeneWatch UK, has said that GURTs technology 'could threaten the rights and livelihoods of millions of small farmers in developing coun-tries by making them dependent on Syngenta's chemicals and seed for their survival. Increasing dependence on the use of chemicals could also have very damaging effects on the environment.'[28] The Fifth Conference of the Parties (COP) to the Convention on Biological Diversity (CBD), held in Nai-robi in June 2000, also called for an investigation into the socio-economic impacts of traitor technology before any further development.

Opponents of gene research argue that these so-called inventions are merely discoveries, as no one can yet claim to have created a new gene. They also say that laboratory technology such as automated gene analysis is making these discoveries more obvious, i.e. that there is little creativity in a process where automation means that the revelation of certain informa-tion is inevitable.[29] Most genes are patented based on a novel description of how they can be used; in other words, it is the use of the gene which is claimed to be new, not the gene itself. A patent on a use can be made to effectively mean a patent on the gene itself, however, if the gene has the same use in the organisms into which it is implanted as that which it had in the organism from which it was extracted.

While patents may not seem to be a problem for farmers who do not use the new varieties, there are a number of reasons why such patents may even prevent farmers from carrying on with what they have traditionally grown.

First, patents have been granted on the properties of naturally occur-ring plants (for example, the Neem tree in India). The patent-holders can demand licence fees from producers where the patented uses are part of the product (for example, a pesticide based on the Neem tree, which is a traditional product from this native plant).

Second, farmers usually sell some of their crop on the general market. Global trade liberalization, the main purpose of the WTO, has led primary markets to turn to commercial varieties, i.e. those chosen for bulk production and purchase by the major food manufacturers and commodity dealers. Along with the World Bank and International Monetary Fund's Structural Adjustment Programmes and the regional free trade agreements organized between nations, the WTO Agreements on Agriculture have helped to bring about profound changes in the agricultural markets of developing countries. These changes include opening up markets to cheap food imports, limiting or reducing government support for farmers, privatizing farming enterprises, reducing price controls and dismantling marketing boards. In addition, developing countries, especially those with foreign debt, have been encouraged or pressured to produce cash crops for export in order to raise foreign currency to help with repayments.

The conflict between CBD and TRIPs

This section reviews the international controversy over the implementation of the TRIPs agreement and the CBD under four headings: the CDB, TRIPs and plants, the difference between the two treaties, and plants as genetic resources.

The Convention on Biological Diversity (CBD) The objectives of the CBD are 'the conservation of biological diversity, the sustainable use of its components and the fair and equitable sharing of the benefits arising out of the utilization of genetic resources, including by appropriate access to genetic resources and by appropriate transfer of relevant technologies'.[30] At the Rio Summit in 1992, the CBD was opened for signature. But ratification by members has proceeded with mixed success, one of the notable failures being the United States, which signed but has not yet ratified the treaty because its government has concerns about the 'technology transfer' obligation and the scope of the 'equitable sharing' requirement.[31]

In addressing biological diversity[32] conservation, two provisions explicitly recognize the potential value of traditional methods. First, Article 8(j) requires countries to 'respect, preserve and maintain [the] knowledge, innovations and practices of indigenous and local communities embodying traditional lifestyles relevant for conservation and sustainable use'. Second, Article 10 requires countries to 'protect and encourage customary use of biological resources in accordance with traditional cultural practices that are compatible with conservation or sustainable use'.

Some national governments have ratified the convention by enacting legislation to implement these articles as well as Article 11, requiring parties to put in place economic incentives for conservation. These countries are actively involved in implementing reforms to help local communities defend their resources, rights and subsistence agriculture. Some of the most important reforms include the extension of legal recognition to various rights important to indigenous peoples and the protection of traditional systems of property rights, such as communal regulation of access to common resources[33] and local control of land.

TRIPs' treatment of plants As mentioned earlier, TRIPs Clause 27.3 (b) states: 'members [of the WTO] shall provide for the protection of plant varieties either by patents or by an effective sui generis system, or by any combination thereof ... '. As discussed below, many developing countries have enacted legislation and others have projects in progress to draft *sui generis* legislation in an attempt both to meet this requirement and at the same time avoid putting local communities at a severe disadvantage.

The discord between the two treaties Whereas the CBD recognizes the importance of traditional knowledge, sustainable development, fair and equitable sharing of resources and technology transfer, TRIPs focuses on protecting 'varieties', a strictly defined category of plants bred for uniformity and tailored to meet the needs of professional plant breeders.

Neither treaty deals effectively with the existence of the other. Those drafting TRIPs, who, after all, knew of the existence of the CBD, made no provision to protect the traditional knowledge inherent in the development of locally specialized landraces. Under TRIPs, landraces are treated as public knowledge, whereas the CBD promotes their protection as traditional knowledge.

The suspicion of a bias in TRIPs towards developed countries which possess highly advanced biotechnology industries and that were influential in its drafting is reinforced by the objections raised by these same industries against US ratification of the CBD. Sensitivity over this issue has been heightened by the ability of companies and governments owning intellectual property rights to have them enforced through the WTO mechanisms, including by trade sanctions.

Governments of developing countries in the WTO face a dilemma. In order to comply with TRIPs they have to protect plant breeders' rights, but in doing so they could be harming the interests of their own people and working against the objectives of the CBD, to which many are also signatories. The United States has itself introduced the patenting of plants into its own IPR regime and cases such as the hallucinogenic vine, *Banisteriopsis caapi* (patented as 'Da Vine'), and the yellow bean (patented as 'Enola') in 1999 have shown that the US PTO sets quite a low requirement for novelty and distinctiveness, and is not very thorough in checking prior art during patent examination. If developing countries adopt patents on plants, they have to treat applications for recognition of patents issued in the USA in a manner satisfactory to the WTO, or face sanctions. This could mean that local varieties not already patented or otherwise established in admissible public records could become subject to patent protection, with adverse economic results.

It is perhaps not surprising, therefore, that most developing countries have opted for the alternative, a *sui generis* system,[34] although in only a few cases developed to meet local circumstances. While the more developed countries favour modelling a *sui generis* regime on the UPOV conventions, most developing countries are reluctant to join the 1991 UPOV convention, because of the strict eligibility criteria that almost guarantee exclusion of informal local plant varieties from protection. The 1978 convention is less onerous and many countries have joined this as an interim measure, while also working on alternative *sui generis* legislation.

As of 15 January 2004, fifty-eight countries had joined UPOV.[35] Twenty-five nations are parties to the 1978 convention and a further thirty-one to the 1991 convention, while only Spain and Belgium remain with the 1961 version, amended in 1972. A rough count reveals that the membership of developing countries is split approximately 6:1 between the 1978 and 1991 conventions respectively, whereas the bias is reversed for the former Soviet and eastern European states. Among developed countries the split is equal between the two conventions.

Plants as genetic resources A related, although distinct, problem concerns the genetic resources in both wild and cultured plants native to developing countries, particularly those with a high level of biodiversity. The lack of biotechnology in these countries makes it difficult for them to develop new products, such as pharmaceuticals or GM crop plants that can be protected by existing patent regimes, like those in the United States and Europe. Many such countries lack any form of IPR protection for either the genetic material or the traditional knowledge that can provide the key to its commercial exploitation. This imbalance in technology and IPR systems, which favours the products of advanced technology, provides an opportunity for pharmaceutical companies to obtain the unprotected genetic and knowledge resources cheaply and to use the technology they own to develop new products. They can then patent and commercialize these among all WTO member countries, including those from which the original genetic material and knowledge came. There are an increasing number of patent applications before the US PTO for products developed in such circumstances.

Some countries, such as India, with resources that are likely to be exploited in this way, have argued against any protection of IPR concerning plants. Their approach is to rely on the fact that these resources are already in the public domain. This would, in theory, prevent them from being privatized through IPR, by undermining the possibility that inventions based on them could meet the novelty requirement, since no invention already in the public domain can be considered novel.

One of the more difficult tasks for the WTO is to take account of the types of problems mentioned above, in presiding over the implementation of TRIPs within its varied membership.

Developing countries losing control over their PGRs

Legislation to implement the CBD has taken on increased significance in light of the threat posed by TRIPs. Many countries and groups of countries, such as the Andean Community, see the CBD as the only line of defence against an unfair international trade system.[36] A degree of success has already been seen through the use of such legislation: some applications for the protection of varieties in countries with CBD implementing legislation have been rejected because the applicant could not prove compliance with the regulations on access to genetic resources.[37] Unfortunately the power of such measures is limited by national boundaries, because the US IPR regulations, as in most developed countries, require no proof of compliance with the CBD as a condition of IPR being granted.

Biopiracy The activities of some biotechnology companies have been labelled as biopiracy by a variety of NGOs, developing-country governments and grassroots organizations of farmers. The Action Group on Erosion, Technology and Concentration (the ETC Group, formerly Rural Advancement Foundation International [RAFI]) defines biopiracy as 'the appropriation of the knowledge and genetic resources of farming and indigenous communities by individuals or institutions seeking exclusive monopoly control (usually patents or plant breeders' rights) over these resources and knowledge'.[38]

Collection, development and patenting do not necessarily constitute biopiracy. When collectors and developers have no intention of paying the providers for samples, however, or of sharing with them any profits generated from a derived product, then they have taken a resource of potential value without payment or permission from the owners, an act constituting theft. A recent example is the case of Hoodia.[39]

Very few rewards are paid by life-science companies (companies that combine business in pharmaceuticals, agricultural chemicals and products, and food and nutrition) to communities or governments of the countries of origin. ActionAid, a major NGO assisting people suffering poverty and hunger in developing countries, has identified four major indications that biotechnology companies have been, and intend to continue, using their technology and IPR law to exploit the natural resources and people of developing countries, which are:

1) 'Biopiracy' patents claiming genes or gene sequences from crops and plants, including cassava, cocoa, jojoba, millet, nutmeg, rice, rubber, sorghum and sweet potato.
2) Corporate control extending over the world's staple crops through patents on maize, potato, soybean and wheat.
3) Biotechnology patents on genes from cocoa and rubber which could be used as substitutes for the original crops so that they do not need to be grown in developing countries.
4) The corporate race to map the 'genomes' of the staple crops and thereby discover a means by which to patent them.[40]

The threat to food security Poverty reduction is inextricably linked to agricultural growth, a fact recognized by major donors, such as the United States Agency for International Development (USAID) and Britain's Department for International Development (DfID). In 2002, UN Secretary General Kofi Annan stated in his inaugural address to the UN 'World Food Summit: five years later' that food security was then a serious problem for around 800 million people in the world. The problem continues today and is a constant challenge to all member states of the UN that have subscribed to the ICESCR and are committed to defend the right to freedom from hunger, and therefore a right to food, contained in Article 11.

The international community has periodically gathered to examine the issue at the UN. In 1974 the Universal Declaration on the Eradication of Hunger and Malnutrition was adopted by the World Food Conference and in 1996 the World Food Summit took place, resulting in the Rome Declaration on World Food Security and the World Food Summit Plan of Action. Progress was reviewed in 2002 at the 'World Food Summit: five years later'. On each occasion members have reaffirmed 'the right of everyone to have access to safe and nutritious food'.[41] As well as the many NGOs working and campaigning to improve food security, such as ActionAid and GRAIN, many governments of developed countries recognize the problem and provide assistance through aid agencies. For example USAID distributes aid via the Board for International Food and Agricultural Development (BIFAD).

The term 'food security' means slightly different things to different organizations, so there are several working definitions in use. Some of them refer to the universal availability of and access to food, its quality and the intended benefits to the consumers. Others have based their definition on the right declared by the UN. The one determined by USAID in 1992 incorporates the fundamental concepts used at that time by the World Bank, the United Nations Food and Agricultural Organization (FAO) Committee on World Food Security, the USAID Bureau for Africa, the US Development Agency[42] and US law.[43] ActionAid is more specific, saying food security exists when 'the poorest people have the ability to grow, eat, sell and buy sufficient food for themselves and their family'.[44]

Others have added a cultural dimension to the right. The International Union of Nutritional Sciences (IUNS) endorses the 1991 definition from the Life Sciences Research Organization as currently the most universally accepted: food security means 'sustained access at all times, in socially acceptable ways, to food adequate in quantity and quality to maintain a healthy life'.[45] Similar definitions, but with a different emphasis, are used by Oxfam,[46] the UN World Food Summit Plan of Action,[47] the Centre for Studies in Food Security at Ryerson University[48] and the NGO Agroecology.[49] Also, a concept of 'community food security' has been developed by Mike Hamm and Anne Bellows, who include the proviso that a sustainable food system should maximize community self-reliance and social justice.

According to USAID, the improvement and maintenance of food security are dependent on availability, access and utilization, and they have identified detailed meanings and various factors that contribute to and prevent the achievement of each. The following aspects of the USAID analysis relate directly to plant genetic resources issues in farming.

- Availability of food. Excluding imports and donations, food availability relies on domestic production and a means of ensuring that supplies are within reach of the consumer, which means either that food is produced locally or that it is distributed from the site of production. In poorer countries, transport is often slow and expensive, so local production is the main option, and generally entails farming on a small scale for self-sufficiency and local markets. Because this is vital to food security, the rights of farmers to manage seed and land productively need to be carefully protected. Nutritional quality of the food also comes under this heading, as it is basic to the achievement of the intended benefits. Food availability has implications for, among other things, the varieties of plants grown, their productivity, quality, suitability for the growing conditions and resistance to pests and diseases.

- Access, in particular economic access, depends on consumers having 'adequate incomes or other resources to purchase or barter' for food. In addition to the effects that supply and demand may have on prices, the costs of farmers' materials, i.e. seeds and other inputs, can have a significant effect, and must be kept at a level that enables farmers to earn sufficient income to live, while keeping prices affordable.

The issues of cost and control over seeds and other reproductive materials of plants for food have been subjected to much analysis and debate in recent decades. The importance of this type of reproductive material, classified by the UN FAO and other organizations as 'plant genetic resources for food and agriculture', has long been recognized, a fact that is reflected by the many national and international projects and institutions, such as those in the Consultative Group on International Agricultural Research (CGIAR) network, set up to conserve, document and investigate all varieties of agricultural plants.

In 1991, a group of forty-one individuals voiced concern over the loss of numerous varieties in a report widely circulated after a number of international meetings.[50] These views were taken into account in negotiations for the CBD.

Although many institutions[51] have been involved in international efforts to conserve Plant Genetic Resources (PGRs),[52] the FAO has had principal international responsibility. In 1983, it set up the Commission on Plant Genetic Resources (CPGR) as a permanent forum for inter-governmental debate and negotiation, and adopted a formal framework on exploration, use and conservation of PGRs, known as the International Undertaking on Plant Genetic Resources (IU). Together, these were the essential elements of the Global System for Conservation and Utilization of Plant Genetic Resources (the Global System).[53]

The IU was based on a principle of 'common heritage' prevalent at the time, implying that no one should be excluded from access to these resources, and, in fact, in 1983 there was little IPR protection available for genetic and biological resources. The 'common concern' and 'national sovereignty' principles underlying the CBD were developed leading up to the 1992 Earth Summit[54] in response to the realization that not everyone would continue to deal with PGRs on the basis of 'common heritage', since under the 1991 UPOV convention, some PGRs were being absorbed into private ownership through Plant Variety Protection (PVP), depriving the rest of the world of free access to them.

The Global System was, however, recognized as the appropriate framework within which to address outstanding issues in PGRs for food and agriculture,[55] including access to PGRs held *ex situ*[56] prior to the CBD coming into force, and farmers' rights, including those of indigenous and local communities, to share benefits derived from the PGRs they had maintained.

Although the IU was not legally binding, its objective was to ensure that genetic resources of economic and/or social interest, particularly for agriculture, would be explored, preserved, evaluated and made available for plant breeding and scientific purposes.[57] The common heritage basis implied that resources should be 'available without restriction', and the terms under which they could be provided had to be either free of charge, by mutual exchange or on mutually agreed terms.

The FAO, aware that the voluntary nature of the Global System made the collections of PGRs vulnerable to privatization, has made considerable efforts to establish a legally binding treaty governing the conservation and development of PGRs for public use. By November 2001, after seven years of negotiations, the FAO saw its goal achieved as its conference adopted the International Treaty on Plant Genetic Resources for Food and Agriculture, known informally as the International Seed Treaty, which supersedes the IU and entered into force on 29 June 2004. This new instrument will be the basis for an international system backed up by national laws in each ratifying state. Its stated aim is the 'conservation and sustainable use of plant genetic resources for food and agriculture and the fair and equitable sharing of benefits derived from their use, in harmony with the Convention on Biological Diversity, for sustainable agriculture and food security'.[58]

Under the treaty, member states commit themselves to the conservation of PGRs for Food and Agriculture (Article 5) through activities such as surveys and inventories, collection of samples and related information, support for farmers and communities in conserving their landraces, and conservation *in situ*. They must promote sustainable use (Article 6) by encouraging diverse farming systems and plant varieties, and must protect farmers' rights (Article 9) by promoting respect for related traditional knowledge, equal participation in benefits from the use of PGRs and participation in relevant national decision-making, as well as allowing the saving, use, exchange and sale of PGRs. The treaty also requires member states to participate in the 'multilateral system for access and benefit sharing' (Article 12). The system covers an agreed list, currently of sixty-four major crops and forages important to food and agriculture. Participating states agree to provide all other participants and their nationals with access to any PGRs covered by that list, both expeditiously and at zero or nominal cost. For each resource accessed, they need to provide a passport, any useful data that is non-confidential, a Materials Transfer Agreement (MTA), which also applies to all subsequent transfers, and a benefit-sharing agreement.

The seed treaty is an ambitious project that required a degree of compromise and flexibility in the text for all signatories to reach agreement. In addition, many of the central issues remain unresolved and open to interpretation, such as the drafting of the model MTA. So there is uncertainty over both the details of the treaty's implementation and national treatment by the members. Already some NGOs, such as GRAIN, and commentators are pointing out weaknesses and potential pitfalls. For example, when GRAIN interviewed Carlos Correa, consultant to the UN,[59] he made the following points:

- The system lacks a clear conceptual framework of farmers' rights. It seems to have been reduced to 'compensation', or an enhanced 'farmers' privilege'.[60] Also there is no provision for international recognition of these rights.

- Although farmers have contributed approximately half a million seeds to the CGIAR seed banks, they are not involved, even at a representative level, in decisions about what happens to those seeds, except those still under development. States have asserted sovereignty from the fact of possession and lack of other clear individual title. States should not use sovereignty as a device to exclude farmers.

- In Article 12.3 (d),[61] which limits the rights to apply for IPRs over materials received from the Multilateral System, the qualifying phrase 'in the form received' is imprecise enough to allow significantly different meanings. When interpreted in accordance with the Vienna Convention on the Law on Treaties (Articles 31 and 32), the meaning could include minor and trivial changes and modifications that do not essentially alter the material. Each member state, however, has a duty to provide detailed interpretation guidelines to their seed banks and IPR bodies, which they could draft to suit their own interests. Developed countries could follow 'TRIPS plus'[62] standards, allowing IPR protection on forms of PGRs that developing countries would not consider different from that supplied.[63]

There is a further problem in the scope of the treaty. The multilateral system 'only covers 35 food crops and 29 forages, representing a small proportion of the 100 food crops of importance to food security and 18,000 forages of value to food and agriculture'.[64] One reason for this was that developing countries began to lose confidence in the degree to which the benefit-sharing arrangements in the treaty would work, and therefore preferred to retain national sovereignty over certain crops, and protect their PGRs via access controls under the CBD. Although the system is still incomplete, the comments so far indicate that this new treaty could easily fail to prevent further privatization of crop genetic resources or protect farmers' rights.

At the present time, food security is therefore still threatened by patents on plants used for food and agriculture. First, patents decrease farmers' access to affordable seed. Second, public plant breeding efforts are reduced because their value as a public resource is undermined by private interests obtaining patents on derived varieties and their uses. Third, there is a loss of genetic diversity within crops. Finally, traditional forms of seed and plant sharing are prevented. If this treaty fails to achieve its original aim of improving food security, it will have contributed little to the alleviation of poverty in developing countries, and could even lead to worse problems than existed before its creation.

Strategies for developing countries to regain control over their plant genetic resources

In looking for answers, the focus in this analysis has been on law. Under the WTO/TRIPs regime, international law is now heavily influencing law at supranational and national levels. The mandated review of TRIPs Article 27.3 (b) in 1998 required the WTO to consider the impact of the article's implementation on experiences of its member states and to vote on proposals to develop, enhance or amend its contents. At a number of venues, NGOs and pressure groups joined with developing countries to campaign on a range of related issues.

As expressed in Article 65, TRIPs was intended to be implemented in developed countries by 1996, in some developing countries by 2000 and in the least developed countries by 2005. The mandated review of Article 27.3 (b) has been stalled, however, since discussions began in December 1998. While the developed countries wished to expand the scope of TRIPs, developing countries demanded a substantial revision in the light of the problems it has caused them. Amendments proposed by developing countries, however, have largely been given only cursory consideration.

NGOs such as GRAIN have called for more public support to put pressure on the WTO to respond positively to developing countries' proposed amendments. They see three main reasons for urgency. First, this official review is crucial to avoid developing countries being placed in a weaker negotiating position. Second, developing countries that do not comply are now in breach of the TRIPs regulations on implementation, for which the WTO could impose sanctions. Third, as time goes on more patents are being granted that could put these countries at a further disadvantage.

I have therefore examined below some other options for protecting the poorest people in developing countries from biopiracy under TRIPs. There are two areas of the TRIPs agreement to consider, both of which are in Article 27.3 (b): first, the patenting of GM plants, and second, the protection of plant varieties through patents, UPOV or a *sui generis* system. In addition, revisiting commitments to human rights may provide an arena in which to develop possible solutions.

Countering the problems of patents A number of approaches to the problems of patents have been identified:

1. Challenge patents on the grounds of non-novelty (i.e. processes or products previously made public). This action requires significant funding and has had mixed success.
2. Develop strong national legislation on access to genetic resources under the CBD, ensuring that compensation and acknowledgement are built into contracts with biotech companies from the initial research endeavours.
3. Resolve the ambiguity over whether the CBD has primacy over TRIPs, so that the former can prevent the latter from contravening it.
4. Exclude the following from IPR protection:

    a. Non-novel uses of plants or organisms.
    b. Discoveries of naturally occurring entities such as micro-organisms, cell lines, genomes and genes.
    c. Transgenic[65] techniques and constructs, and transgenic plants, animals and micro-organisms.
    d. Nuclear transplant cloning.[66]

5. Place in the public domain, when discovered, the whole genome of any staple crop.
6. Impose a five-year freeze on the patenting of food crops.
7. Publicly fund crop-related genetic research, making such information publicly available, with the option of patenting, so that licences may be granted for large-scale commercialization.[67]
8. Broaden the qualifying evidence of 'prior art' to include foreign prior use or, in specific circumstances, established and trustworthy records, in whatever format, including oral tradition maintained within local communities.
9. Modify the information requirements for patent applications involving

plants or knowledge such that the applicant must state and certify the source.[68]

10. Introduce a system of 'informed consent' whereby communities that have provided or will provide knowledge or materials are informed of the collector's intentions prior to collection and must agree to those intentions and provide certification to that effect.[69]

Countering the problem of Plant Variety Protection Under TRIPs, the subject of *sui generis* systems to protect plant varieties is treated ambiguously. No specific detailed requirements have been set out. The main existing regimes are the UPOV conventions. Joining UPOV is easy, but in the long term can be an expensive and troublesome means of complying with TRIPs.

Many developing countries have raised proposals at WTO meetings in an attempt to have this clause modified: Kenya and the group of least developed countries called for a five-year delay in the implementation deadlines, the group of least developed countries called for flexibility in interpretation of the term '*sui generis*', Malaysia called for clarification of options for *sui generis* systems, India called for TRIPs to be reconciled with and made subordinate to the CBD on this issue, and the African Group produced a 'Common position on the TRIPs review of Article 27.3 (b)', presented to the Council of Ministers at Seattle in December 1999.

There have been a number of strategies proposed for dealing with PVP, including other models on which to base a *sui generis* system. Four general classifications of *sui generis* legal approaches have been identified by Carlos Correa, as set forth below.

PUTTING ALL INFORMATION IN THE PUBLIC DOMAIN The idea behind systematically publishing knowledge on plants and their uses is to place it in the public domain, and thereby defeat the novelty condition for obtaining a patent. Unfortunately this strategy has been largely unsuccessful because, as noted previously, the US patent system, which is most active in plant patenting, does not admit use or sale outside the US as evidence of prior art. Examples of plants, or their uses, that have been the subject of US and European patent applications, despite being in the public domain in other countries, include the Neem tree,[70] barbasco,[71] kava,[72] endod,[73] ayahuasca,[74] quinoa,[75] turmeric,[76] nuña[77] and most recently, yacón[78] and maca.[79]

DEVISING NEW APPLICATIONS OF EXISTING IPR INSTRUMENTS Proposals to apply existing IPR instruments in new ways have looked at indications of geographical origin, trade secrets law, patents and plant breeders' rights legislation. The first might be applied to centres of diversity of certain crops, rather as wines are currently protected, although this would not cover the traditional knowledge associated with the use of a plant. The second can protect holders of knowledge,[80] but the open exchange that prevails in community culture would be a major obstacle. For the third, applications by growers in developing countries are likely to fail, owing to the inability of communities to comply with the novelty requirement. As suggested by Brendan Tobin, however, a requirement could be added to existing regimes requiring all applicants to reveal the source country and ideally provide a certificate of origin for the knowledge or materials used, naming the community and the specific location of supply. The fourth, in the form of the UPOV conventions in their current form, imposes unrealistic conditions of uniformity for informally cultivated or natural varieties to qualify. Correa proposed that a requirement of identifiability be used instead, so that such varieties can also be protected. These four proposals would provide only partial and indirect protection of traditional varieties and knowledge.

NEW IPR APPROACHES Proposals for new solutions within the Western IPR model have been identified but not widely explained. These generally differ from existing models in the products or process covered or in the forms of implementation. An example is the 'Community IPR Proposal', which involves 'public defenders, gene tracking databases and review mechanisms'. Others include a new type of right concerning only unmodified genetic resources or derivatives, although the questions of who should hold the rights and what their extent should be have not yet been clearly articulated.

OPTIONS BEYOND THE IPR MODEL The main approach beyond the IPR model is to create regimes based on 'community intellectual rights', reflecting the culture and value systems of communities, rather than those of the market economy. Its principal proponents have been Guardial Singh Nijar and Twalde Berhan Egziabher. Nijar's model, for example, involves rights that are based on the perpetual custodianship and stewardship of local innovations by local communities, the free exchange of knowledge among communities and an obligation that any other person, organization or corporation that uses the knowledge commercially must pay royalties. Other proposals include treating traditional knowledge as cultural property, the use of traditional resource rights, farmers' rights or discoverers' rights, or the licensed sale of traditional medicinal knowledge and landraces, based on the use of a certificate or 'seal of approval' issued by the community. A GRAIN study of government legislative projects identified four general areas receiving attention: farmers' rights, community rights, CBD provisions, and involvement of local and national stakeholders.

Refreshing national commitments to human rights The UDHR was a landmark agreement establishing an accepted philosophy of the value of people and the rights that every person should ideally enjoy. In Europe, cases concerning human rights can be heard in the European Court of Human Rights and are subject to the European Convention on Human Rights.[81]

THE INTERNATIONAL COVENANT ON ECONOMIC, SOCIAL AND CULTURAL RIGHTS (ICESCR) The ICESCR carries forward many of the fundamental rights embodied in the UDHR, embracing broader aspects of peacetime life, in particular the economic, social and cultural dimensions upon which civil society is founded. By signing this covenant, governments have effectively promised to their citizens and to other nations that they will work towards a balance between rights and duties in which people who fulfil their responsibilities may enjoy economic, social and cultural benefits. These nation-states have also committed themselves to cooperative action internationally to achieve this goal in all countries.

The liberalization of international trade, i.e. the withdrawal of state control from international trade through quotas and import duties, has resulted in a general hands-off approach by many governments, which must now obey the rulings of the world financial and trade institutions. This lack of government intervention in trade is leaving the global organization of markets mainly to the multinational companies, some of which have larger incomes than a small African state.[82]

The lack of government influence amounts to an absence of representation of poorer populations in decisions affecting international trade. This constitutes a weakening of democracy, leaving international trading relations to market forces, subservient to the profit motive of transnational corporations. The result is a lamentable lack of political and democratic influence on global trade and therefore on the flows of wealth upon which the realization of rights depends to a large degree.

Civil action groups have raised this point at numerous gatherings of heads of state, with a notable lack of effect, except in disrupting proceedings. Governments that have signed up to the ICESCR are being reminded of the commitments they have made. It seems that they are being called to account for their actions and failings, not only by their citizens but also by other countries to which they owe a duty of cooperation in pursuance of the ICESCR objectives.

Caroline Dommen has suggested that developing countries could strengthen their hand by bringing to the negotiating table WTO members' commitments under the ICESCR. Developing countries' successful issuing of compulsory licences for production of generic drugs, such as those to treat Aids in South Africa and Brazil, are examples of actions intended to fulfil the promises made under the ICESCR. Similar efforts have been made to protect indigenous knowledge from privatization and to preserve from IPRs farmers' rights to keep and exchange seed in African Group countries, Brazil, Peru, Colombia and India.

IPR, TRIPS AND THE ICESCR Countries arguing that wider human rights considerations should be taken into account in the implementation of TRIPs can find support in both the WTO-TRIPs agreement and the ICESCR. In TRIPs, Articles 7 and 8 introduce welfare and public interest factors into the implementation of the IPR regime. Article 7 states that the agreement should be conducive to social and economic welfare, and should contribute to a balance of rights and obligations. Article 8 allows governments to take into account public health, nutrition and other public interests in formulating IPR laws, and to prevent their abuse.

The ICESCR could be used to reinforce these considerations by arguing that signatories are committed to protecting rights to a minimum standard of living, culture and affordable healthcare. Therefore, actions that may run counter to IPRs but which support these rights are legitimized by the ICESCR and should be allowed by TRIPs under Articles 7 and 8.

AGRICULTURE, THE WTO AGREEMENTS ON AGRICULTURE (AOA) AND THE ICESCR The WTO Agreements on Agriculture also support inclusion of wider considerations. Article 20 states that 'non-trade concerns' and various objectives and considerations mentioned in the preamble should be taken into account. These include food security, rural development, environmental protection and socio-economic issues, including support for marginal and subsistence farmers.

Developed and developing countries have similar issues in this respect, although to different degrees. Developed countries already have protectionist policies, such as the subsidies under the EU Common Agricultural Policy (CAP), which they justify on the basis of maintaining rural communities and environmental protection. Developing countries have been under intense pressure from the WTO to abandon such policies. There is, however, a strong argument supported both by Article 20 of the Agreements on Agriculture and by the ICESCR to allow measures in developing countries to protect domestic food production, particularly in staple foods, and thereby assure a minimum level of food security and accessibility, and to maintain livelihoods among the rural farming poor. There seems to be little substance in the same argument from developed countries where welfare standards are generally much higher. Reform of the CAP has been a notable failure, however, being undermined by France, Spain and Ireland.

Caroline Dommen has suggested using the ICESCR to develop a quantified minimum standard of living in the various aspects of welfare covered in the covenant. In geographical areas where these are not met, she proposes the implementation of a 'development box', in which protection of markets and subsidies are allowed to help raise standards of living to an agreed minimum.

ICESCR INTERNATIONAL COOPERATION The ICESCR includes a commitment that nations will work together to achieve the rights that the covenant contains. This international cooperation aspect should include working towards the fair implementation of other international agreements, such as WTO/TRIPs and the Agreements on Agriculture. If governments fail to cooperate in ensuring that trade agreements do not reduce welfare below acceptable levels, then they have failed in their promises under the ICESCR.

Perhaps it is time to invite the signatories to the ICESCR to recommit to its support, to consider again what this entails today, given the many new international agreements undertaken since 1976, and to form plans of action to adjust any policies that work against the commitments in the covenant. Such a public commitment, along with transparency of action, could produce reform in administration.

Conclusions

The global community needs to realize that nations have responsibilities towards each other that extend beyond military or political dimensions, into trade and other forms of security, in particular those fundamental to human life, such as food. While there may be potential advantages in free trade, that concept cannot be used to justify the undermining of food security in the more vulnerable nations.

The credibility of the WTO and of its aims has been damaged during recent negotiations. Developing countries have become aware of the rights they signed away when they subscribed to TRIPs, and now, with considerable public support in developed countries, are trying to neutralize some of the disadvantages they face, both through *sui generis* Plant Variety Protection legislation and by implementing the provisions of the CBD.

IPRs have been extended, some would argue, into areas for which they were never intended. Opinion in developed countries is split over the ethical arguments for patenting plants and the biotechnology that is enabling the manipulation of genes. Despite their advantages, GM organisms are unpopular in the EU and, it is argued, unproven to be safe – a technology in its infancy.

The root cause of the threat to food security is the profit motive. Private companies need profits to fund research, and they need IPRs to make profits. With doors closing against GM organisms in the European Union, the developing countries are increasingly targeted for GM crop production and marketing. Currently China and Argentina are the only developing countries growing these in commercial quantities, however. Other countries such as Kenya, Brazil and India are taking a more precautionary approach.

It seems likely that developing countries will need all their political skills to protect their food and genetic security, especially in the climate of laissez-faire among developed-world governments when it comes to regulating the tactics of their own industries.

Notes

1 I am grateful to John Taylor for encouragement, information, proof-reading and technical and practical support in the preparation of this chapter. My particular thanks to Professor Bernard Taylor, who found the time to read more than I asked him to. I owe him a particular debt for commenting on drafts, listening attentively and challenging the analyses and arguments.

2 'Developing' refers to countries that not only have low levels of income, but also significant social problems (e.g., illiteracy, high infant mortality, malnutrition) that keep incomes low and unevenly distributed. A developing country may have a diverse industrial base but still have low incomes and significant social problems (e.g., India, Brazil, Argentina, China) (Hurlbut 1994: 382). Developing countries are mainly countries and dependent areas with low levels of output, living standards and technology. Their per capita GDPs are generally below $5,000 and often less than $1,500; however, the group also includes a number of countries with high per capita incomes, areas of advanced technology and rapid rates of growth. It includes the advanced developing countries, developing countries, the Four Dragons (Four Tigers), least developed countries (LLDCs), low-income countries, middle-income countries, newly industrializing economies (NIEs), the South, Third World, underdeveloped countries and undeveloped countries. They are the bottom group in the hierarchy of developed countries (DCs), former USSR/eastern Europe (former USSR/EE) and less developed countries (LDCs) <www.nationmaster.com/kp/less+developed+countries>.

3 Hanmer and Nashchold (2000); IFAD (2001), cited by Peacock (2004: 10).

4 Developed countries are defined as an area of the world that is

technologically advanced, highly urbanized and wealthy, and has generally evolved through both economic and demographic transitions <www.nde. state.nv.us/sca/standards/standardsfiles/social/geoglos.htm>. 'Industrially advanced' refers to countries that have high levels of per capita income and a diverse industrial sector. Thus Germany is an industrially advanced country, Saudi Arabia is not (Hurlbut 1994: 382). This is the top group in the hierarchy of developed countries (DCs), former USSR/eastern Europe (former USSR/EE) and less developed countries (LDCs). It includes the market-oriented economies of the mainly democratic nations in the Organization for Economic Cooperation and Development (OECD), Bermuda, Israel, South Africa, and the European mini-states. It is also known as the First World, high-income countries, the North, industrial countries. These countries generally have a per capita GDP in excess of $10,000, although four OECD countries and South Africa have figures well under $10,000 and two of the excluded OPEC countries have figures of more than $10,000. The thirty-five DCs are: Andorra, Australia, Austria, Belgium, Bermuda, Canada, Denmark, Faeroe Islands, Finland, France, Germany, Greece, Holy See, Iceland, Ireland, Israel, Italy, Japan, Liechtenstein, Luxembourg, Malta, Mexico, Monaco, Netherlands, New Zealand, Norway, Portugal, San Marino, South Africa, Spain, Sweden, Switzerland, Turkey, UK, US. 'Developed countries' is similar to the new International Monetary Fund (IMF) term 'advanced economies', which adds Hong Kong, South Korea, Singapore and Taiwan but drops Malta, Mexico, South Africa and Turkey <www.nationmaster.com/kp/developed+countries>.

5 The term 'biopiracy' was coined in 1993 by the NGO RAFI (Rural Advancement Foundation International), today the ETC Group – Action Group on Erosion, Technology and Concentration (see 'Biopiracy in the Amazon: questions and answers', <www.amazonlink.org/biopiracy/biopiracy_faq.htm>).

6 'Food security exists when all people, at all times, have physical and economic access to sufficient, safe and nutritious food to meet their dietary needs and food preferences for an active and healthy life' (World Food Summit Plan of Action, <www.fao.org/wfs/index_en.htm>).

7 Gustavo Capdevila, 'Poor countries to make their voices heard in Seattle', <www.twnside.org.sg/title/heard-cn.htm>.

8 Action Aid, 'Crops and robbers. Biopiracy and the patenting of staple food crops', November 1999, <www.actionaid.org/pdf/bio.pdf>.

9 <www.unhchr.ch/pdf/report.pdf>

10 International Covenant on Economic, Social and Cultural Rights, op. cit. Article 11: '1. *The States Parties to the present Covenant recognize the right of everyone to an adequate standard of living for himself and his family, including adequate food*, clothing and housing, and to the continuous improvement of living conditions. The States Parties *will take appropriate steps to ensure the realization of this right*, recognizing to this effect the essential importance of international co-operation based on free consent. 2. The States Parties to the present Covenant, recognizing the fundamental right of everyone to be *free from hunger*, shall take, individually and through international co-operation, the measures, including specific programmes, which are needed: (a) to *improve methods* of *production, conservation and distribution*

of food by making full use of technical and scientific *knowledge*, by disseminating knowledge of the principles of nutrition and by *developing or reforming agrarian systems* in such a way as to achieve the most efficient development and utilization of natural resources; (b) taking into account the problems of both food-importing and food-exporting countries, to *ensure an equitable distribution* of world food supplies in relation to need' (emphasis added), <www.unhchr.ch/html/menu3/b/a_cescr.htm>.

11 UPOV has agreed to three conventions: 1961 (as modified by the additional act of 1972), 1978 and 1991.

12 Essentially derived varieties under the UPOV 1991 convention are varieties created by the addition of a single gene to existing varieties, which must be authorized by the breeder of the original plant variety (WIPO 1997).

13 For an inventory of national legislation on patents see Genetic Resources Action International (GRAIN) at <www.grain.org/brl/pat-brl-en.cfm>. For an inventory of national legislation on Plant Variety Protection see Genetic Resources Action International (GRAIN) at <www.grain.org/brl/pvp-brl-en.cfm>.

14 The novelty requirement of US patent law prohibits the patenting of an invention that has been known, used or published in the United States, more than one year prior to the patent application <www.uspto.gov/web/offices/pac/mpep/consolidated_laws.pdf>.

15 Landrace, in plant genetic resources, means an early, cultivated form of a crop species, evolved from a wild population, and generally composed of a heterogeneous mixture of genotypes <www.fao.org/biotech/find-form-n.asp>.

16 Concluded in 1970, amended in 1979 and modified in 1984; open to states party to the Paris Convention for the Protection of Industrial Property (1883) <www.wipo.int/ pct/en/texts/articles/atoc.htm>.

17 <www.wipo.int/pct/en/treaty/about.htm> (paraphrased).

18 The patent offices of Australia, Austria, China, Japan, the Russian Federation, Spain, Sweden, the United States of America and the European Patent Office (situation on 30 June 1999).

19 <www.uspto.gov/web/offices/pac/mpep/consolidated_laws.pdf>.

20 <www.grain.org/publications/wipo-splt-2003-en.cfm>.

21 'Charity fights basmati "biopiracy"', 26 June 2000 <www.bbc.co.uk/hi/english/business/newsid%5F806000/806665.stm>.

22 Genetically Modified Organisms (GMOs) and Genetically Modified Micro-organisms (GMMs) can be defined as organisms (and micro-organisms) in which the genetic material (DNA) has been altered in a way that does not occur naturally by mating or natural recombination. See 'Food and food safety', <europa.eu.int/comm/food/food/biotechnology/gmfood/index_en.htm>. The Cartagena Protocol on Biosafety to the Convention on Biological Diversity defines a 'living modified organism' as one that possesses a novel combination of genetic material obtained through the use of modern biotechnology <www.biodiv.org/doc/legal/cartagena-protocol-en.pdf>.

23 Article 15. Access to Genetic Resources: '1. Recognizing the sovereign rights of States over their natural resources, the authority to determine access

to genetic resources rests with the national governments and is subject to national legislation ... 4. Access, where granted, shall be on mutually agreed terms and subject to the provisions of this article. 5. Access to genetic resources shall be subject to prior informed consent of the Contracting Party providing such resources, unless otherwise determined by that Party ... 7. Each Contracting Party shall take ... measures ... with the aim of sharing in a fair and equitable way the results of research and development and the benefits arising from the commercial and other utilization of genetic resources with the Contracting Party providing such resources. Such sharing shall be upon mutually agreed terms' <www.biodiv.org/convention/articles.asp>.

24 A term used in GMO technology for a transgenic method which genetically sterilizes the progeny of the planted seed, thereby preventing the use of farm-saved seed <www.fao.org/biotech/find-formalpha-n.asp>.

25 FAO, 'Potential impacts of genetic use restriction technologies (GURTs) on agricultural biodiversity and agricultural production systems', Commission on Genetic Resources for Food and Agriculture: Working Group on Plant Genetic Resources for Food and Agriculture, First Session, Rome, 2–4 July 2001.

26 <www.etcgroup.org/article.asp?newsid=394>; <www.guardian.co.uk/gmdebate/Story/0,2763,970123,00.html>.

27 'The company formed today through the merger of the agrochemical divisions of multinational corporations AstraZeneca and Novartis' (GeneWatch UK Press release, 11 October 2000, 'UK calls for Syngenta, the new world leader in GM crops, to abandon terminator and traitor technology', <www.genewatch.org/Press%20Releases/pr17htm>.

28 Ibid.

29 GeneWatch, 'Beginner's guide ...' Meek (2000), p. 1.

30 Convention on Biological Diversity, Article 1.

31 The US did not sign the CBD until 1993 for several reasons, including the requirement of compensation for the use of biological resources and transfer of biotechnology (Sarma 1999, citing Karen Anne Goldman, 'Compensation for use of biological resources under the Convention of Biological Diversity: compatibility of conservation measures and competitiveness of the biotechnology industry', *Law & Policy International Business*, 25 (1994), p. 697.

32 'Biological diversity means the variety among living organisms from all sources including, inter alia, terrestrial, marine and other aquatic ecosystems and the ecological complexes of which they are part. This includes diversity within species, between species and of ecosystems' (Convention on Biological Diversity, Article 2).

33 David Downes put it as follows: 'To help local and indigenous communities share in a greater proportion of the benefits of the sustainable use of genetic resources, as mandated by article 8(j), governments should recognize the legal right of communities to make and enforce commercial contracts for access to resources, so that the communities would have a chance to reap a larger share of the benefits' (Downes 1994: 179).

34 'A unique form of protection tailored to a country's particular needs. Rather than implementing a standard form of protection, i.e. a copyright or patent system, a sui generis system allows a country to develop its own rules to protect a specific subject matter such as plant varieties' (Tansey 1999: 8).

35 The number of countries that have ratified the different UPOV conventions are: 1961/1972: 2; 1978: 25; 1991: 31.

36 Decision 391 of 1996 as modified by 423 of 1997 – Common Regime on Access to Genetic Resources (<www.comunidadandina.org/ingles/treaties/dec/d391e.htm>).

37 For example, in Colombia, the second richest biodiversity country in the world, after eight years of the enactment of Decision 391 of the Andean Community, and fifteen applications submitted, there is not a single contract on access to genetic resources, owing in some cases to rejection for lack of compliance with the legislation, as is the case of BioAndes, and in others to withdrawal on the part of the applicant. For some biodiversity-rich countries, the regime on access to genetic resources has become a perverse incentive to protect and regulate biocultural diversity to an extent that can discourage commercial contracts (Chaves 2003).

38 'Biopiracy in the Amazon: questions and answers', <www.amazonlink. org/biopiracy/biopiracy_faq.htm>.

39 'Hoodia is a succulent plant that grows throughout the semi-arid areas of Southern Africa. The San have traditionally used Hoodia stems to stave off hunger and thirst when on long journeys, as it acts as an appetite suppressant. The active ingredient of the Hoodia succulent cactus was identified by the Council for Scientific and Industrial Research in South Africa (CSIR) and patented. They passed on their work to Phytopharm, a British Company, who patented it as P.57. Phytopharm declared that they had found a potential cure for obesity, with none of the side effects of other treatments because it was derived from a natural product. Their share value rose immediately, and they were soon able to sell the rights to license the drug for 21 million US dollars to Pfizer, the US pharmaceutical giant.' For the full case, see 'Stolen knowledge' at <www.evb.ch/index.cfm?page_id=800>. For more detailed cases of biopiracy see later in this chapter.

40 ActionAid, 'Crops and Robbers ... ', op. cit., p. 3.

41 The 'Rome Declaration' (1996) <www.fao.org/DOCREP/003/W3613E/ W3613E00.HTM>; 'Declaration of the World Food Summit: five years later' (2002), <www.fao.org/DOCREP/MEETING/005/Y7106E/Y7106E09.htm>.

42 'People have "food security" when they have both physical and economic access to enough food to lead a healthy and active life. Food security depends on three elements: adequate food *availability* through agricultural production, imports, and government policies; conditions that give people *access* to food in stores, farmers' markets, and other outlets; and full *utilization* of food through adequate, balanced diet, safe water, sanitation, education, and health care' (emphasis added) (US Development Agency, <www.fas. usda.gov/icd/summit/usactionq&a.html>).

43 The Agricultural Trade Development and Assistance Act of 1990.

44 ActionAid, 'Crops and Robbers ... ', op. cit.

45 <www.iuns.org/features/sciences_for_food_security.htm>

46 'All people, especially the most vulnerable and least resilient, have dignified and unthreatening access to the quantity and quality of culturally appropriate food that will fully support the physical, mental, emotional and spiritual health' (<www.alternatives.com/bfa/secdef1.htm>; <www.oxfam.org.uk>).

47 <famine.tufts.edu/pdf/sphere-nairobi_report.pdf>; <www.fao.org/DOCREP/003/W3613E/W3613E00.HTM>.

48 'A condition in which all people at all times can acquire safe, nutritionally adequate and personally acceptable foods that are accessible in a manner that maintains human dignity. It requires attention to the production and supply of adequate quality and quantity of food, and people's ability to acquire those foods.' This definition is guided by five principles: availability (adequate supplies), accessibility (fair distribution), acceptability (cultural), adequacy (sustainability), and agency (governance and systems for enabling citizen participation), <www.ryerson.ca/~foodsec/centre_03.html>.

49 'The state in which all persons obtain a nutritionally adequate, culturally acceptable diet at all times through local non-emergency sources', < www.agroecology.org/glossary/glossary_e_h.htm>.

50 This was issued by the participants at the Keystone International Dialogue Series, after their third and final plenary session. These meetings on Plant Genetic Resources were initiated in 1988 to promote a strong international commitment to conserving plant genetic resources, through structured, off-the-record, consensus-building dialogue. The third and final report, in 1991, set out a Global Initiative for the Security and Sustainable Use of Plant Genetic Resources. The Keystone recommendations proved influential in the negotiations for the CBD. As a follow-up, in March 1995 the government of Sweden, through SAREC (the Swedish Agency for Research Co-operation with Developing Countries), convened an international 'consultation' of experts, to follow up on the Keystone recommendations 'post-UNCED'. The group concluded that a legally binding, multilateral agreement was needed (Kagedan 1996).

51 The United Nations Food and Agriculture Organization (FAO), the Consultative Group for International Agricultural Research (CGIAR), the International Agricultural Research Centres (IARCs), the International Board for Plant Genetic Resources (IBPGR) – now known as the International Plant Genetic Resources Institute (IPGRI).

52 The IU defined PGRs as 'new products of biotechnology, including commercial varieties and breeding lines; farmers' varieties; wild materials' (Article 2).

53 '... which has developed and evolved to encompass a number of international agreements, technical mechanisms and global instruments, at various stages of development ... each builds on and elaborates the others, in an integrated system for conservation of plant genetic resources. These include: a voluntary International Code of Conduct for Plant Germplasm Collecting and Transfer; a draft Code of Conduct on Plant Biotechnologies; international agreements on genebanks; the World Information and Early

Biodiversity versus biotechnology

Warning System on Plant Genetic Resources, which facilitates information and technology exchanges; international networks of ex situ collections and in situ conservation areas, with complementary basic agreements on genebanks; a periodic publication on the State of the World's Plant Genetic Resources, to assist the CPGR to fulfil its monitoring responsibilities; a Global Plan of Action on Plant Genetic Resources to facilitate the CPGR's coordination role; and an International Fund on Plant Genetic Resources to implement Farmers' Rights' (FAO 1995, Item 5). 'The Global System covers the conservation (ex situ and in situ, including on-farm) and utilization of plant genetic resources (genes, genotypes and genepools) at molecular, population, species and agro-ecosystem level' (ibid.). '144 countries are now formally part of the system, having either adhered to the Undertaking or joined the CPGR, or both. It may be noted that, unlike the Biodiversity Convention, all the FAO activities are limited to plant genetic resources, specifically those of interest to food or agriculture' (Kagedan 1996: 37).

54 United Nations Conference on Environment and Development (UNCED), Rio de Janeiro, 3–14 June 1992. For further details see: <www.un.org/geninfo/bp/enviro.html>.

55 See Resolution 3 of the Nairobi Final Act of the Biodiversity Convention, negotiated and approved along with the Biodiversity Convention.

56 'Ex situ conservation' means conservation outside of a natural habitat (Article 2 of the UN-FAO, CGRFA 'Report of the commission on genetic resources for food and agriculture', Sixth Extraordinary Session, Rome, 25–30 June 2001, CGRFA-Ex 6/01/REP, <www.fao.org/ag/cgrfa/ docsex6.htm>).

57 Article 1, 'Objectives.'

58 <www.fao.org/ag/cgrfa/itpgr.htm#text>

59 GRAIN: 'Interview with Carlos Correa', <www.grain.org/seedling/seed-interview-c-en.cfm>.

60 'Farmers' privilege' is the legal ability to reuse IPR-protected seed <www.grain.org/publications/bio-ipr-fp-june-2003-en.cfm>.

61 Article 12.3 (d) reads: 'Recipients shall not claim any intellectual property or other rights that limit the facilitated access to the plant genetic resources for food and agriculture, or their genetic parts or components, in the form received from the Multilateral System.'

62 For an explanation of 'TRIPS plus' see '"TRIPS-plus" through the back door: how bilateral treaties impose much stronger rules for IPRs on life than the WTO', available at <www.grain.org/publications/trips-plus-en.cfm>.

63 For more detailed discussion of what may or may not qualify for IPR protection under the treaty see Helfer (2003).

64 Mulvany (2001: 20).

65 An experimentally produced organism in which DNA has been artificially introduced and incorporated into the organism's germ line (<www.hyperdictionary.com/dictionary/Transgenic>).

66 This is the moving of a cell nucleus and its genetic material from one cell to another (<www.thefreedictionary.com/nuclear%20transplantation>).

67 An example of this may be seen in the case of bananas (genus *Musa*).

A global consortium of publicly funded institutes, the Global Musa Genomics Consortium, has agreed to cooperate in mapping the genome of a breedable banana variety. The genome will be made public, and members have agreed that any invention developed through the project and protected by patent will be made available to smallholders through a royalty-free licence (Andy Coghlan, *New Scientist*, 21 July 2001. < www.newscientist.co.uk/hottopics/gm/gm.jsp?id=23000700>).

68 Andean Community, *Common Regime on Industrial Property*, Decision 486 of 2000, Article 75 (h).

69 Ibid., Article 26 (h).

70 The use of the Neem tree, i.e. its applications, has been subject to more than forty patents in the US alone and at least 153 worldwide (Leskien and Flitner). In May 2000, after a challenge by India, the Examining Division of the European Patent Office revoked a patent granted to US Grace in 1995 on 'hydrophobic extracted neem oil – a novel insecticide' on the grounds that 'there was no inventive step involved in the claim invention' (*Down to Earth* 2000: 13).

71 'A well-known plant cultivated by Amazonian indigenous people for hundreds of years and used in agriculture and medicine. It is best known as a highly effective poison that stuns and paralyses fish. Conrad Gorinsky, president of the UK's Foundation for Ethnobiology, has patented a barbasco compound and has marketed it to pharmaceutical multinationals Zeneca and Glaxo. Gorinsky's patent claims many uses including, not surprisingly, regulation of muscular activity' (<www.etcgroup.org/documents/occ_out.pdf>).

72 'The basis of the ceremonial beverage of the same name, Kava, is grown in many Pacific countries, including Vanuatu, Samoa, Fiji, Papua New Guinea, Solomon Islands, Federated States of Micronesia, as well as Irian Jaya [Indonesia]. Drug companies are racing to patent Kava's many beneficial uses. French cosmetics giant L'Oreal has patented the use of kava to reduce hair loss' (<www.etcgroup.org/documents/occ_out.pdf>).

73 'Patented by the University of Toledo [US], endod has been selected and cultivated by Africans for many centuries, particularly in Ethiopia. It is used as a soap and shampoo as well as a poison to stun fish. Endod is lethal to snails – a fact discovered by Ethiopian scientists – and may be effective controlling schistosomiasis. After an Ethiopian scientist demonstrated endod's potency to Toledo scientists, they took out a patent, hoping to sell endod as a biological control for the zebra mussel, a pest in the Great Lakes of the US and Canada' (<www.etcgroup.org/documents/occ_out.pdf>).

74 'A medicinal plant cultivated since pre-Columbian times across the Amazon basin ... The International Plant Medicine Corporation (IMPC) took out a US plant patent on a variety of ayahuasca collected from indigenous people in Ecuador. IMPC has ignored requests from indigenous people to give up the patent and is working to develop psychiatric drugs from the plant' (<www.etcgroup.org/documents/occ_out.pdf>). The initial patent on the 'ayahuasca' vine was awarded in 1986. Thirteen years later, in 1999, the US PTO recognized that this should never have been granted. In January 2001, however, the PTO rescinded this decision, thus reinstating the patent (Wiser 2001).

75 Quinoa has been 'a staple food crop for millions in the Andes, particularly for Quechua and Aymara people in Chile, Bolivia, Peru and Ecuador who have bred a multiple [*sic*] quinoa varieties adapted to variable Andean conditions. One of these, Apelawa, has been patented by two professors at Colorado State University [US] because this farmers' variety has genes for male cytoplasmic sterility' (<www.etcgroup.org/documents/occ_out.pdf>).

76 The University of Mississippi Medical Center was awarded a patent in 1995 for this classical 'grandmother's remedy' in India. The claim covered 'use of turmeric in wound healing'. The Council of Scientific and Industrial Research of India (CSIR) challenged the patent on the basis of its absence of novelty, and in 1997 it was revoked (Dutfield 2000: 65). The US Patent and Trademark Office declared invalid such patents on turmeric (Correa 1998: 6).

77 The nuña is an Andean bean that 'hops when it pops', 'flies when it fries', is nutritious, with a faintly peanutty taste and requires little fuel wood to cook. US Patent no. 6,040,503 was granted on 21 March 2000 through Appropriate Engineering and Manufacturing to 'inventors' Mark Sterner and Jeffrey Ehlers of California. The inventors have also received a WIPO (World Intellectual Property Organization) patent (WO99/11115) under the Patent Cooperation Treaty and have indicated that they would apply for patents in as many as 121 countries. The patent gives Ehlers and Sterner exclusive monopoly ownership over nuña crosses with characteristics allowing it to grow outside the Andes. The patent encompasses crosses involving at least thirty-three Andean nuña varieties traditionally bred and developed for centuries in Peru, Bolivia, Ecuador and Colombia (ETC Group, 'Bracing for El Nuña' <www.etcgroup.org/documents/NRNunabean.pdf>).

78 Yacón (*Smallantus sonchifolius*), a native plant of the Andes and a relative of the sunflower, tastes sweet but doesn't make you fat. The human body cannot metabolize the sugar from this plant, so a person could eat a considerable amount without worrying about the consequences. Yacón may replace crops such as the sugar cane and corn fructose in many products, from biscuits to fizzy drinks. The germ plasm of yacón, held in trust by the International Potato Centre (CIP), was given to a Peruvian institute (INRENA), and its director, Josefina Takahashi, later gave the tuber to the ambassador of Peru in Japan (<www.etcgroup.org/article.asp?newsid=176>).

79 Maca is a plant of the mustard family grown by the Andean people for centuries as a food crop and medicinal plant. A member of the radish family, it grows at altitudes up to 4,300 metres, in the intense sun, wind and cold of the barren highlands of the Andes. Maca has also long been valued for its ability to enhance fertility in humans and livestock. Most recently, US and Peruvian companies have extracted the ingredients believed to promote fertility and produced powders and capsules for human consumption. In July 2001, two US patents were granted to Pure World Botanicals Inc. and Biotics Research Corporation, who claim to have 'unlocked maca's chemical secrets' (<www.american.edu/TED/maca.htm#_ftnref1>); see also ETC Group, 'Agricultores y pueblos indígenas del Perú denuncian patentes sobre maca. Un extracto de una raiz andina, patentado por sus propiedades de viagra natural' (<www.etcgroup.org/documents/Genotipo_Maca_julio.pdf>).

80 In *Franklin* v. *Giddins* (1978), an Australian court found that stealing cuttings from a genetically unique nectarine tree was an improper means of acquiring confidential information. Case quoted by Correa (1998: 7).

81 'The Convention for the Protection of Human Rights and Fundamental Freedoms was drawn up within the Council of Europe. It was opened for signature in Rome on 4 November 1950 and entered into force in September 1953. The object of its authors was to take the first steps for the collective enforcement of certain rights stated in the United Nations Universal Declaration of Human Rights of 1948.

'Since the Convention's entry into force eleven Protocols have been adopted. Protocol No. 11 significantly reorganized the Court to deal with an increased case-load. The new European Court of Human Rights came into operation on 1 November 1998' (Information document issued by the Registrar, 'The European Court of Human Rights historical background, organization and procedure', <www.echr.coe.int/Eng/edocs/infodocrevised2. htm#Subsequent%20developments>).

82 Monsanto's revenues as reported in August 2003 were in excess of US$3.3 billion (<www.monsanto.com/monsanto/layout/media/03/10-15-03.asp>). For the African states see < www.clickafrique.com/Reference. asp?param=GNP>.

References

Beckerman, W. (1994) 'Sustainable development: is it a useful concept?', in *Environmental Values 3*, Cambridge: White Horse Press

Chaves Posada, J. (2003) *Problemática de la aplicación de la Decision 391 en Colombia*, Bogotá: Instituto Humboldt

Chen, J. (2001) 'Diversity and deadlock: transcending conventional wisdom on the relationship between biological diversity and intellectual property', *Environmental Law Reporter*, June

CIDSE (2000) 'Biopatenting and the threat to food security', <www.cidse.org/>

Correa, C. (1998) 'TRIPs and the protection of community rights', Paper 5 of *Signposts to Sui Generis Rights*, Barcelona: GRAIN

Crucible Group (1994) *People, Plants and Patents*, Ottawa: International Development Research Centre

Dommen, C. 'The covenant on economic, social and cultural rights: a treasure chest of support for developing countries' concerns in the WTO?', *Bridges*, Jan./Apr., ICTSD, pp. 21–2

Downes, D. (1994) 'The Convention on Biological Diversity: seeds of green trade?', *Tulane Environmental Law Journal*

Down to Earth (2000) 9 (2), June, New Delhi

Dutfield, G. (2000) 'Intellectual Property Rights, Trade and Biodiversity', London: Earthscan

Egziabher, T. B. (1996) 'A case of community rights', in S. Tilahum and E. Sue (eds), *The Movement for Collective Intellectual Rights*, Addis Ababa: Institute for Sustainable Development/Gaia Foundation

Environmental Resource Management (1995) 'Identification of community measures for the implementation of articles 15 and 16 of the Convention of Biological Diversity', Interim report, DG, XI, London: European Commission

FAO (Food and Agriculture Organization) (1995) 'Progress report on the global system for the conservation and utilization of plant genetic resources for food and agriculture', Item 5 of the Provisional Agenda, Commission on Plant and Genetic Resources (CPGR), 6th Session, Rome, 19–30 June, <ftp://ext-ftp.fao.org/ag/cgrfa/cgrfa6/R6W4E.pdf>

Fecteau, L. M. (2001) 'The Ayahuasca patent revocation: raising questions about current US patent policy', *Third World Law Journal*, 69, winter

Fisher, W. W. III (1999) 'The growth of Intellectual Property: a history of ownership of ideas in the United States', <cyber.law.harvard.edu/people/tfisher/iphistory.pdf>

Foreign Policy, (2000) 118, spring, Washington, DC

Hamm, M. W. and A. C. Bellows (2003) 'Community food security and nutrition educators', *Journal of Nutrition Education and Behavior*, 35 (1): 37–43

Hanmer, L. and Nashchold (2000) *Attaining the International Development Targets: will growth be enough?*, ODI working paper

Helfer, L. R. (2003) 'Intellectual Property Rights and the International Treaty on Plant Genetic Resources', part of 'The global conflict over genetic resources', *American Society of International Law Proceedings*, April

Hurlbut, D. (1994) 'Fixing the Biodiversity Convention: toward a special protocol for related intellectual property', *Natural Resources Journal*

IFAD (2001) *Rural Poverty Report: The Challenge of Ending Rural Poverty*, Oxford/Rome: Oxford University Press/IFAD

Kagedan, B. L. (1996) 'The Biodiversity Convention, Intellectual Property Rights and ownership of genetic resources: international developments', Prepared for the Intellectual Property Policy Directorate, Ottawa

Leskien, D. and M. Flintner (1997) 'Intellectual property rights and plant genetic resources', *Issues in Genetic Resources*, 6, Rome: International Plant Genetic Resources Institute

Madely, J. (2000) *Hungry for Trade: How the Poor Pay for Free Trade*, London: Zed Books

— (2001) 'Trade and Hunger', *Seedling*, the quarterly newsletter of GRAIN, February

Meek, J. (2000) 'Beginner's guide to gene patents', *Guardian Unlimited*, 15 November, p. 1, <www.guardian.co.uk/genes/article/0,2763,397385,00.html#article_continue>

Mulvany, P. 'International Seed Treaty: a model for governance of genetic resources?', <http: //ro.unctad.org/trade_env/test1/meetings/plants/INTERNATIONAL%20SEED%20TREATY.doc>

— (2001) 'Global seed treaty hangs in the balance', *Biotechnology and Development Monitor*, 46: 20

Nijar, G. S. (1996) 'In defence of local community knowledge and biodiversity:

a conceptual framework and the essential elements of a rights regime',
Paper 1, Third World Network, Penang

Organization of American States (2001) 'Toward free trade in the Americas.
Regionalism and the Multilateral Trading System'

Peacock, C. (2004) 'Reaching the poor: a call to action – investment in small-
holder agriculture in sub-Saharan Africa', Farm-Africa

Richer, D. (1999) 'Intellectual Property Protection: who needs it?' In *Agricultural Biotechnology and the Poor*, CGIAR conference, 21–22 October

Sarma, L. (1999) 'Biopiracy: twentieth century imperialism in the form of
international agreements', *Temple International and Comparative Law
Journal*, spring

Shrybman, S. 'The World Trade Organization – A guide for environmental-
ists', Vancouver, BC: West Coast Environmental Law, <www.wcel.org/
wcelpub/1999/12757.pdf>

Smith, C. (2000) 'Patenting life: the potential and the pitfalls of using the
WTO to globalize intellectual property rights', *North Carolina Journal of
International Law and Commercial Regulation*, fall

Tansey, G. (1999) 'Trade, intellectual property, food and biodiversity. Key
issues and options for the 1999 review of Article 27.3 (b) of the TRIPs
agreement', Discussion paper commissioned by Quaker Peace & Service,
London, with financial assistance from the Department for International
Development, <www.zen.co.uk/g.tansey/trips-bw.pdf>

Ten Kate, K. and S. Laird (1999) *The Commercial Use of Biodiversity. Access to
Genetic Resources and Benefit-sharing*, London: Earthscan

Tobin, B. (1998) *Protecting Collective Property in Peru: The Search for an Interim
Solution*, Lima: Asociación para la Defensa de los Derechos Naturales

Walden, I. (1995) 'Preserving biodiversity: the role of property rights', in
T. Swanson (ed.), *Intellectual Property Rights and Biodiversity Conservation*',
New York: Cambridge University Press, p. 191

WIPO (World Intellectual Property Organization) (1997) *Introduction to Intellectual Property, Theory and Practice,* London and Boston, MA: Kluwer Law
International

Wiser, G. 'US Patent and Trademark Office reinstates Ayahuasca patent.
Flawed decision declares open season on resources of indigenous peoples',
Washington, DC: Center for International Environmental Law (CIEL)

Websites

ActionAid: <www.actionaid.org>

African group: <www.africaaction.org/docs02/afjn0204.htm>

Agroecology: <www.agroecology.org>

AmazonLink Organization: <www.amazonlink.org>

American University: <www.american.edu>

BBC: <www.bbc.co.uk>

Berkman Centre for Internet and Society at Harvard Law School: <http://cy-
ber.law.harvard.edu/home/>

CIDSE: <www.cidse.org/>

CIEL: <www.ciel.org/>

Comunidad Andina: <www.comunidadandina.org/>

Consultative Group on International Agricultural Research (CGIAR): <www.cgiar.org>

Convention on Biological Diversity: <www.biodiv.org>

Erklarung von Bern: <www.evb.ch/index.cfm?page_id=800>

ETC Group (formerly Rural Advancement Foundation International – RAFI): <www.etcgroup.org>

European Court of Human Rights: <www.echr.coe.int/>

FAO: <www.fao.org/wfs/index_en.htm>

Farm-Africa: <www.farmafrica.org.uk/publications/Call_to_Action_rep.pdf>

GeneWatch: <www.genewatch.org/>

GRAIN: <www.grain.org>

Greenpeace: <www.greenpeace.org>

Guardian Unlimited: <www.guardian.co.uk>

International Cooperation for Development and Solidarity: <www.cidse.org/pubs/tg1ppcon.htm>

International Union of Nutritional Sciences: <www.iuns.org>

Monsanto: <www.monsanto.com>

NationMaster: </www.nationmaster.com/>

Nevada Department of Education: <www.nde.state.nv.us>

New Scientist: </www.newscientist.co.uk>

Organization of American States: <www.sice.oas.org/TUnit/tftr/ftrade4.asp#FT9>

OXFAM: <www.oxfam.org.uk>

Ryerson University: <www.ryerson.ca>

Third World Network: <www.twnside.org.sg>

Ukabc: <www.ukabc.org>

United Nations: <www.un.org>

UPOV: </www.upov.int>

USAID: <www.usaid.gov>

US Patent and Trademark Office: <www.uspto.gov>

West Coast Environmental Law: <ww.wcel.org>

WIPO: <www.wipo.org>

WTO: <www.wto.org>

5 | The right to food: the significance of the United Nations Special Rapporteur

AHMED AOUED

Since the United Nations (UN) Charter turned development into a major social and economic arena for discourse (Article 56), the issue of poverty has become a challenge for the international community. Today we are witnessing the ever increasing impoverishment of the countries and populations of the southern hemisphere, evident through increasing inequalities between nations, as well as between classes within different nations. This phenomenon is most noticeable among the poorest nations, with no prospect for relief given the present international economic system.

Over the past decade, the UN system, through its agencies, namely the UN Economic and Social Council (ECOSOC) and its affiliate, the UN Commission on Human Rights (CHR), has attempted to fashion a right to food (RTF) to ensure 'humanity's freedom from hunger', in the wording of the UN Food and Agricultural Organization (FAO) constitution. The latest of these attempts is the appointment of a Special Rapporteur charged with conducting a comprehensive study on RTF.

This focus on RTF reflects the findings of recent studies documenting the consequences of malnutrition and hunger. In a 1999 report, the World Health Organization (WHO) gave alarming examples of the impact of under-nourishment on disease: over 208 million people are stunted and 49 million are wasted; more than 900 million people suffer from goitre, 16 million are severely retarded and another 50 million suffer other forms of brain damage owing to a deficiency of iodine; 3 million children are at increased risk of infection, blindness and death because they have a vitamin A deficiency.[1] These are only a few samples of a macabre catalogue of diseases and other related threats to life due mainly to malnutrition.

Recent medical findings and scientific research by the WHO Commission on the Nutrition Challenges for the 21st Century of the Administration Committee on Coordination Subcommittee on Nutrition (ACC/SCN) suggest that inadequate access to food and sub-optimal nutritional status may have multiple interacting causes – some of which affect one's whole life and lead to malfunctioning in society. The report summarizes the seriousness and complex interrelationships at work as follows:

The acceptance by the international community that poorly fed adults are economically less effective now needs to be linked to new findings that up to 1 billion adults are malnourished, with a reduced work capacity and an enhanced susceptibility to infections. The remarkably high rates of anemia in children, men and women in many parts of the globe not only impair work capacity but permanently damage the normal brain development of infants ... It is also clear that the commonest form of 'childhood' malnutrition, involving stunted growth, is also closely linked to impaired mental as well as physical development ... Malnourished mothers particularly in Asia are producing low-birth-weight babies ... with a double handicap of physical and mental limitations with new evidence that poor girls grow into malnourished adults who then in pregnancy pass on the long term impact of their own poor development during their fetal life to the next generation ...[2]

Given these dire consequences, the project of addressing malnutrition is central to poverty reduction. The first section of this chapter briefly summarizes the evolution of the issue of poverty within the UN system. The next discusses the importance of the Special Rapporteur and their contribution to the reduction of poverty. Finally, I attempt to place RTF on a normative legal basis and explore the prospect of an independent International Poverty Law (IPL).

The work of the United Nations on poverty reduction

Although the aim of this chapter is not to list the successes and failures of the UN organs in terms of poverty reduction, it is useful to recall that such work formally, although timidly, started with the UN Charter in 1945 and gradually increased through subsequent UN legal instruments dealing with the evolution of the much broader concept of development. This work was especially intense during the 1970s in the wake of the less developed countries' (LDCs) call for a New International Economic Order (NIEO) and the 1980s, with an equally forceful claim for a right to development (RTD). Until the end of the seventies, poverty and development-related issues were measured mainly in terms of economic indicators and data regarding the fulfilment of essential needs of the deprived populations (hence the basic needs theory). With the beginning of the eighties, however, it became clear that poverty should not be restricted to economic factors, but constituted an 'outrage and a violation of human dignity',[3] requiring a broad and innovative legislative framework for its eradication (hence the rights-based approach).

From the basic needs theory to the rights-based approach Briefly, the fundamental assumption of the basic needs theory is that individuals and the satisfaction of their needs lie at the heart of development law's inherent obligations. Development policy should begin with 'the analysis of the precise character of economically and socially underdeveloped groups in order to define a poverty line, and continue to ask why the needs of such people are not met'.[4] An essential aspect of this theory is an investigation and understanding of the root causes of poverty and economic underdevelopment in LDCs, focusing on development as not only economic welfare, but also a more general concept of human betterment. From a legal point of view, the basic needs theory represents an attempt to avoid a fragile and weak legal response to the issue of underdevelopment and poverty. It aims to build a new political consensus around which a transformative law can emerge. In short, it is 'a political theory of justice, expressed through the legal language but mostly without legal substance, due to the severe political and legal constraints placed upon the theory both by the international society and law, and by the social and legal structures of LDCs'.[5] Although this theory has had only limited effect on the advancement of development law, it has contributed significantly to the clarification of the notion of poverty and its appropriation subsequently by the UN organs.

In contrast, the rights-based approach implies that minimum social and economic rights are, indeed, as essential as political rights in all societies. Basic rights, for Shue, 'specify the line beneath which no one is to be allowed to sink'. These rights are *basic* in the sense that no other rights can be enjoyed unless these rights are guaranteed. *Physical security* is the first of such basic rights.[6] The author argues that: '[n]o one can fully, if at all, enjoy any right that is supposedly protected by society if he or she lacks the essentials for a reasonably healthy and active life. Deficiencies in the means of subsistence can be just as fatal, incapacitating, or painful as violating of physical security. The resulting damage or death can at least as decisively prevent the enjoyment of any right, as can the effects of security violations.'[7]

This view is well reflected in the UN official overall human rights policy. In opening the CHR 54th Session, the UN High Commissioner for Human Rights stated that 'By using a human rights entry point, the entire human rights framework is brought into play, civil and political as well as economic, social and cultural rights.'[8] She alluded to and implicitly confirmed the interdependence and indivisibility of the two sets of rights and the need to treat them on the same footing. In addition, such a statement implies a normative legal basis, even if not yet drafted or spelled out in detail.

Approaching all aspects of poverty, including issues related to food and nutrition, from a human rights perspective has various implications. First,

RTF in its narrow sense becomes de facto an inherent part of the law of human rights. Second, RTF emerges as a legal right that operates not only between states but also between states and their citizens. Third, although RTF addresses the individual as subject, it none the less includes a collective component. Moreover, human rights are obligatory for states, which are bound to respect their international commitments to those instruments that they have ratified. This contrasts with UN recommendations that have no legally binding force, but which comprise the bulk of material on RTF, such as that enunciated at such international conferences as the 1995 World Summit on Social Development or the 1996 World Food Summit.[9]

The rights-based approach has, besides its human aspect, the merit of introducing a responsibility and accountability component at different levels of government not found in the basic needs theory. At the national level, the rights-based approach provides a mechanism for more comprehensive implementation of RTF and has the advantage of focusing on the rights of individuals vis-à-vis their states. It more thoroughly describes the role of states and the criteria for good governance in the areas of social and economic rights. In short, the rights-based approach, framed as normative and legally obligatory, requires a legislative response at state level. In addition, it implies that beneficiaries of development are active subjects as 'claim-holders' and stipulates duties or obligations for those against whom such claims can be held (objects or 'duty-bearers'), with the requirement of a corresponding claim or recourse mechanism. At the international level, a rights-based approach implies recognition by the international community that it considers poverty as a violation of human rights. It rests on various grounds capable of freeing the issue of poverty from the sphere of conflicted interests among the haves and have-nots, while requiring international organizations to orient their policies regarding development programmes and aid.[10]

The rights-based approach embraced by the UN and its different organs in their policy programmes for combating poverty triggered a series of changes. Increasingly international civil society, in addition to the traditional UN organizations and inter-governmental regional institutions, became involved with poverty issues. Wealthy countries of the North began to realize that poverty and the constant rhetoric it engenders are threats to social stability. Most of these countries, including the Scandinavian countries, Britain, France, Germany and the United States, have shown some readiness to contribute to the eradication of poverty by taking cosmetic actions, for example wiping out – albeit to an insufficient degree – the debts of financially bankrupt African countries. International tools and instruments designed to effectively combat poverty multiplied and proliferated, while the time and energy devoted to the issue of poverty increased in various international forums. The scope of poverty reduction was extended to other areas such as decent housing, clean water, adequate sewage systems, and the language and terminology used to discuss poverty reduction changed, for example from poverty to extreme poverty, from adequate food to quality and quantity of food. At least in theory, the international community is far more aware of the issues of poverty in general and their implications on individuals than it was a decade ago.

Opponents of the rights-based theory have pointed out that it may be preferable to keep the question of human rights separate and distinct from the question of the duty of developed countries to give economic assistance and preferential treatment to developing countries. They maintain that development issues are domestic preoccupations of a socio-economic nature, which have little to do with law strictly speaking, and should be left to the rule of the free market. The logic of such an argument is not to deny the existence of poverty and hunger and the need to fight these conditions. Rather, this neo-liberal current of thought disregards the ravages that liberalization policies pursued by the industrialized world have inflicted not only on their own people but also on populations of the southern hemisphere. The neo-liberal rules conveyed through the WTO, the IMF and the World Bank are undermining many efforts to promote the emergence of a legally binding RTF and represent a threat to the economic, social and cultural rights that the international community strives to establish as secure and internationally accepted norms.

At the other end of the spectrum, many LDC lawyers argue that, if RTF is primarily cast within a human rights discourse, it adds nothing to the already established law of human rights. The logic of such an argument lies in the notion that RTF is part of the RTD, which is in essence a third human rights generation of solidarity, both collective and individual in nature. Therefore, RTF is not an individual interpretation, but a collective and community approach to poverty, which enables us to identify the real problems involved and the solutions available.

Scope and definition of the right to adequate food in international human rights law The scope and definition of RTF have essentially emerged from the work of the UN organs, namely the CHR and its Sub-commission on the Protection of Human Rights (hereafter the Sub-commission) and, to some extent, a few NGOs involved in the area of poverty reduction. The bulk of such work is rooted in a combination of Article 11 of the 1966 International Covenant on Economic Social and Cultural Rights (ICESCR) and the recommendations of the UN 1996 World Food Summit.

According to Article 11.1 of the ICESCR, states parties recognize 'the right of everyone to an adequate standard of living for himself and his family, including adequate food, clothing and housing, and to the continuous improvement of living conditions'. Pursuant to Article 11.2, states 'recognize that more immediate aud urgent steps may be needed to ensure the fundamental rights to freedom from hunger and malnutrition'. On the basis of such commitments, Objective 7.4 (e) of the 1996 UN World Food Summit Plan of Action urges state participants to:

> invite the UN High Commissioner for Human Rights, in consultation with relevant treaty bodies, and in collaboration with relevant specialized agencies and programs of the UN system and appropriate intergovernmental mechanisms, to better define the rights related to food in Article 11 of the Covenant (ICESCR), and to propose ways to implement and realize these rights ... taking into account the possibility of formulating voluntary guidelines for food security for all.[11]

In response, the UN Committee on Economic Social and Cultural Rights, the think tank of the CHR on development issues, was charged with the task of better defining RTF and identifying the obstacles to its realization. After lengthy studies, in 1999 the Committee adopted General Comment no. 12, which elaborated on Article 11 of the ICESCR and concluded that 'the human right to adequate food is indivisibly linked to the dignity of the human person and is indispensable for the fulfilment of other human rights enshrined in the International Bill of Human Rights'.[12] The Committee specifically recognized the social dimension of RTF, stating that such a right was 'inseparable from social justice, requiring the adoption of appropriate economic, environmental and social policies, at both the national and international levels, oriented to the eradiction of poverty and the fulfilment of all human rights for all'.[13] In its attempt to define RTF, the Committee was strongly influenced by the already existing definition contained in the International Code of Conduct on the Human Right to Adequate Food (hereafter the Code), adopted in September 1997 by three international NGOs.[14] Article 4 of the Code, which was extensively borrowed by the Committee, reads as follows: 'The right to adequate food means that every man, woman and child, alone and in community with others, must have physical and economic access at all times to adequate food or by using a resource base appropriate for its procurement in ways consistent with human dignity. The right to adequate food is a distinct part of the right to an adequate standard of living.'[15]

The UN Committee retained the NGOs' definition because it was heavily inspired by a combination of UN human rights instruments, namely the

Universal Declaration of Human Rights (Article 25), the ICESCR (Article 11) and the Convention on the Rights of the Child (Article 24). In his 1999 Updated Study to the Sub-Commission, former UN Special Rapporteur on RTF Asbjorn Eide reiterated his recommendation that the text contained in the Code should be adopted as a basis for the definition of the content of RTF.[16]

During the work on General Comment no. 12, UN experts particularly stressed two main criteria relating to RTF: adequacy and sustainability. They emphasized that the first criterion was 'to serve to underline a number of factors which must be taken into account in determining whether particular foods ... can be considered the most appropriate ... for the purpose of Article 11 of the Covenant'. The second criterion implies 'food being accessible for both present and future generations'.[17] To clarify further the definition contained in Article 4 of the Code, Mr Eide added that the notion of adequate food could be broken down into at least three elements:

- adequacy of food, which means that the overall supply should cover overall nutritional needs in terms of quantity (energy) and quality (essential nutrients);
- safety, which means food free of toxic contaminants;
- cultural acceptability, which means fit for the prevailing food or dietary culture.[18]

In its 55th Session, the Sub-Commission formally adopted the definition of RTF contained in Article 4 above. In explaining their decision, members of the Sub-Commission stated that General Comment no. 12 'will in the time ahead, stand as the most authoritative document formulated to date regarding the right to food', drafted in the normative context of Article 11 of the ICESCR.[19] The Sub-Commission reaffirmed that '[t]he ultimate purpose of promoting the right to adequate food is to achieve nutritional well being for the individual child, woman and man ... '[20] General Comment no. 12 also proposed ways to implement and realize these rights as a means of achieving the commitments and objectives of the World Food Summit. Briefly, it suggested two ways in which the international community might assist: by intervening when judicious public and community management of natural resources are absent, and by calling on states to refrain from food embargoes or similar measures that endanger conditions for food production and access to food in other countries. It also called on UN agencies to enhance their efforts and cooperate more effectively on the implementation of poverty reduction at national level to ensure that RTF is protected.[21]

Since the 1996 World Food Summit, RTF has become a regularly debated agenda item in the annual sessions of the CHR. Through its resolutions, the CHR has constantly reaffirmed that hunger constitutes an outrage and a violation of human dignity, therefore requiring the adoption of urgent measures for its elimination at national, regional and international level. The CHR routinely articulates as intolerable the fact that millions of people, especially women and children, throughout the world, and particularly in LDCs, do not have enough food to meet their basic nutritional needs.[22] The appointment of a UN Special Rapporteur on the Right to Food in 2000 evidences an effort by the CHR to address this situation and bring a human dimension, as well as a legal approach, to poverty.[23]

The United Nations Special Rapporteur on the Right to Food: limits and conditions

The Special Rapporteur model is one of the CHR's working instruments that has already been used in other areas such as education, housing, torture, disappearances and summary executions. Traditionally, the task of such a body is to undertake fact-finding missions worldwide on a particular topic and subsequently to submit a report to the High Commissioner for Human Rights for consideration and ultimately implementation. In poverty-related issues, this is the third time that the CHR has initiated such a consultation on RTF by appointing Professor Jean Ziegler of Switzerland in April 2000.[24] This third resolution on the RTF is different from the two previous ones in that it expressly recommends that the Special Rapporteur focus 'on implementation mechanisms',[25] i.e. various means through which poverty can be effectively and efficiently reduced before being ultimately eradicated. To that effect, CHR Resolution 2000/10 limits the mandate of the Special Rapporteur to three main axes of intervention: seeking and receiving information, establishing cooperation and identifying issues relating to RTF worldwide. The next sections will address each of these three mandates.

Gathering information Point 9 of Resolution 2000/10 calls on the Special Rapporteur to 'invite all experts from all regions to share their experience' in the identification of mechanisms that might contribute to poverty reduction. This objective is important for two reasons: first, information is particularly difficult to gather on an issue like poverty because of the complexities of the criteria involved, hence the call for assistance from unlimited geographical areas; second, this statement departs from the general assumption that poverty is only an LDC issue and implicitly recognizes that the phenomenon is also a scourge in the most advanced countries of the industrialized world (note the text of Resolution 2000/10, which refers to the 'global dimensions' of poverty and its persistence in some regions). Accordingly, and in the spirit of the above resolution, the poor in Paris, Frankfurt or Los Angeles are regarded as being on the same footing as those of the shanty towns of Bombay, Khartoum or Manila. It is precisely this kind of false parallelism which makes any objective approach to poverty troublesome and difficult to grasp properly.

Such an approach is not new and has been widely contested in the past among lawyers in LDCs, such as Bedjaoui, who wrote as early as 1969 that '[t]he problems of the proletariat within nations in their individual dimension must not make us forget the problems of the proletarian nations of the international community'.[26] The most recent available estimate of the number of the under-nourished (1995–97) illustrates the gap between the poor in the North and their counterparts in the South. Out of the 825 million poor counted worldwide according to FAO criteria, 791 million are in the developing world, of which 180 million are in sub-Saharan Africa with the number constantly rising. East and South-East Asia, with a total of 241 million, and South Asia, with 284 million, have the highest number of under-nourished. The percentage and numbers are relatively stable in the Near East and North Africa, with 33 million, and in Latin America and the Caribbean, with 53 million. The situation appears dire in the eastern European countries in transition, however, where there has been an increase in the number of under-nourished from 20 to 26 million. The poor in the developed countries of the North total 34 million, a marginal figure compared to the 791 million in the southern regions alone. According to the FAO, this number is slowly, but consistently, declining.[27]

Cooperation The Special Rapporteur is charged with coordinating the work of the existing institutions involved in addressing poverty at both national and international levels. Resolution 2000/10 refers to the work previously carried out by other UN bodies, mainly the FAO, which has been very active in poverty reduction since its inception in 1946. Government bodies and institutions are also encouraged to participate, as they are the ones faced with the difficulties of the underprivileged segments of their populations. Particularly important here is the willingness of developed countries to cooperate fully, since no mechanism against poverty can ever work if their governments do not adhere to the idea and manifest their readiness to contribute effectively to the success of the Special Rapporteur's mission. They are quite often reluctant to contribute on the grounds that they also have their poor, and since assistance comes from public funds, i.e. tax-payers' money, they cite the popular slogan 'charity begins at home'. Such arguments are detrimental to LDCs' chances of reducing hunger on the one hand, and on the other hand reinforce the belief that the developed states remain the masters of the game in any anti-poverty programme outside their national boundaries. It appears that the developed countries will cooperate only if, *inter alia*, their interests are preserved or at least not jeopardized, and only if their political will and the philosophy they propagate coincide with such interests. In this context, given the present state of international economic relations and recent developments regarding world globalization, it remains doubtful that the international collective efforts declared during the World Food Summit to halve the number of under-nourished worldwide by the year 2015 will ever materialize.

NGOs are the other potential partners relied upon in the RTF resolution to assist the mission of the Special Rapporteur. As recipients of all UN resolutions dealing with poverty, on the same footing with governments, NGOs' participation in data collection and fieldwork is crucial for the Special Rapporteur's report. As noted earlier, NGOs have played a significant role in clarifying the definition of RTF through the International Code of Conduct on the Human Right to Adequate Food and other intellectual work. In addressing a number of the challenges that globalization presents to the implementation of the ICESCR, particularly with respect to Articles 11 and 15, NGOs constitute a reservoir of information and provide valuable expertise to the Special Rapporteur. Thus their inclusion in Commission Resolution 2000/10 is not incidental but rather intentional.

Identification The Special Rapporteur is charged with the critical task of identifying the structural causes of poverty, which have a serious impact on the human rights conditions of millions of people worldwide. These conditions are largely determined by a number of systemic factors such as inequitable economic relations, a slowdown in financial assistance and foreign investment, weakness in commodity prices, debt burden and the reluctance of the Western world to reduce its trade barriers to LDCs' goods. Most critics in the South point to these factors as being the cause of the poor's misery, but fail to mention the internal dysfunctioning of many poor countries, which adversely affects their own economic development. Indeed, it would be wrong to attribute poverty and nutrition deficiencies exclusively to international structures or external factors, and thereby lose sight of factors related to domestic policies and practices, for example internal constraints of various kinds, such as poor leadership, corruption or prevarication on the part of local officials. These factors often play a substantial part in national underdevelopment and result in malnutrition and hunger among vulnerable segments of the populations in the LDCs.

Given the severe consequences of malnutrition and hunger noted earlier, identifying emerging issues related to RTF is essential to understanding the nature and complexities of the problem, and may also help to identify the corresponding national and international obligations of states. One possible avenue for accomplishing this goal is to envisage a separate corpus of law dealing solely with poverty issues (within which RTF is incorporated), motivated by the belief that the great inequalities of wealth between and within states are widening and the conviction that law can be used to bring about change towards greater justice among nations.

The right to food as the basis of an International Poverty Law (IPL)

From a legal point of view, the idea of an autonomous corpus dealing only with poverty at international level may well seem attractive. The growing awareness of and concern for development inequalities have deeply affected traditional international law. Quite naturally the poor countries were the first to welcome such an initiative because they are the most affected by the scourge of misery and desperately need relief. For most of these countries, present international law is not suited to dealing with poverty claims and issues, for at least two reasons. First, as previously mentioned in connection with RTD, contemporary international law may not be designed or equipped to intervene legitimately and effectively in domestic dealings between states and their nationals. Second, inter-state practices may emerge as an obstacle between the formulation of RTF and the attribution of liability, as is typical of the international system and its structures. Even if traditional international law is showing promising signs of a progressive transformation, the inherent logic of a right to be free from hunger claimed by the individual against the international community falls short. At the very least, this right currently cannot be practially effective, owing to the lack of mechanisms for its implementation and supervision.

The purpose of an IPL as discussed in this chapter is not to create a new legal system that would reduce the poor countries to constantly applying officially for public charity and favours, or to legitimize the existing conflict between the rich and the poor based on an assumed impotence of classical international law to deal with poverty issues. The idea of an IPL cannot either be conceived as a simple formalization of the present order, or, to paraphrase Guy Feuer, as an 'instrument to transform that order in favor of three quarters of the population of the world'.[28] The aim, often reiterated by LDCs, is to persuade the developed world to review several aspects of the current mechanisms in international economic relations, as well as the functioning of a number of international institutions, namely the World Bank, the IMF and the WTO. The LDCs do not want to sink again into the rhetoric of the 1970s aid policy, which was regarded more as charity or tied aid, perpetuating the LDCs' status as constantly assisted populations. In essence, the claims to international social justice and equity elaborated in the new emerging context of RTF are the same as those elaborated during the decades of the NIEO in the seventies and RTD in the eighties. It is perhaps time that the claims made by LDCs during these decades cease to be characterized as statements of policy objectives and vague promises of a unilateral kind rather than contractual obligations. Like poverty, apathy and contempt are morally devastating and constitute a blow to the dignity of the human race. The role of a new corpus of IPL is precisely to reposition RTF within a more human context and ensure a smooth transition from a basic needs discourse, which has demonstrated its limits, to a rights-based approach. In short, IPL may move RTF claims from the realm of ideology and politics into the normative sphere of law.

The problem of the 'lawness' of IPL is connected to the classical issues encountered in traditional international law, namely the capability of the legal community to envisage a new law at international level without elucidating certain preliminary and classical questions such as: Is IPL a compartment of international law or a reincarnation of it in another dimension? Or is it a reinterpretation or rereading of the whole conspectus of present international law? What should be, if any, the relation between the new IPL and traditional international law? These are questions of prime importance which need to be answered if any new law is to be discussed by the international community, especially by conservative Western legal scholars. LDCs must keep in mind that their attempt in the seventies to establish an international law of development failed mainly because they presented the new corpus as merely an offshoot, with rather uncertain legitimacy, of international economic law, itself a branch of international law. Therefore, on its most basic level, it is important to consider the development of a future IPL within questions of form as well as substance. Another major obstacle is the nature of the content to be attributed to RTF within a new IPL. Some may consider placing both RTF and international law into IPL as a subversion of law for ideological or humanitarian purposes; those who accept the purposive role of international law, however, and indeed all law, would view the non-neutrality of the expression RTF and, by extension, IPL as simply indicative of the purposiveness of all legal choices. The debate is both philosophical and technical.

Even given the debates regarding the sites of legitimacy within international law, it would be wrong to assume that LDCs have rejected international law as a site for the development of transformative law.[29] Their attitude has been determined by the incapability of public international law in its classical form to respond to their needs given the demands generated mainly in the current social and economic fields. Being unable to change existing international law, the LDCs resort to new methods of creating their own corpus of law in order to circumvent the old barriers built by centuries of international law development. But Western legal scholars are often resistant to abandoning the distinction between law now in force (*lex lata*) and law that one desires to establish (*lex ferenda*). As Slinn warned: 'The anxiety here is that the blurring of the distinction between what is and what is not a current, binding rule of international law creates an uncertainty which threatens the integrity of the international legal system and encourages confusion between law, morality and ideology.'[30]

While it is too early to predict the fate of IPL, prior attempts of LDCs may assist in anticipating the future of any new undertakings. The North–South Dialogue initiated during the NIEO and its legal basis, the Charter of Economic Rights and Duties of States (1979), initially intended to serve as a forum for negotiation, turned into a North–South confrontation. Likewise, the international law of development upon which the Third World countries placed so much hope in the eighties was reduced to a simple right to development, still in sterile discussions at the Geneva CHR annual session under Agenda Item no 7. Last, but not least, UN General Assembly Resolution 2626, which sought to impose on privileged nations of the North a precise obligation to contribute through a defined percentage of GNP to development aid and therefore to reduce poverty, was soon buried and shelved indefinitely.

These rather pessimistic experiences should not, however, be viewed as major obstacles for the emergence of a new IPL if the political will of Western politicians comes into play. In the following sections, it will be argued that from the legal technical point of view all the necessary components for envisaging a new corpus of law are available: including the sources of IPL, the subjects of IPL, and the justiciability of IPL.

The sources The most significant constraining factor to the development of IPL emanates from the sources of international law. A background principle is that sovereign states have the independence and power to veto the emergence of any new corpus outside of existing public international law. The founding text relied upon as source of the new IPL consists in large measure of the general principles of Article 55 of the UN Charter regarding the promotion by the UN of higher standards of living, full employment and conditions of economic and social progress and development. The force of that article is strengthened by Article 56, under which all members pledge to take joint and separate action in cooperation with the UN for the achievement of the purposes set forth in Article 55. These UN commitments are further taken up in Article 25 of the 1948 Universal Declaration of Human Rights (UDHR), which calls for a general right to an adequate standard of living, summing up the main concern underlying all economic and social rights. In addition to these main UN instruments, there are 'soft' poverty laws, for example Article 2 (3) of the 1993 Declaration to the Right to Development and Objective 7a of the 1996 World Food Summit and the rhetoric that emerged during the World Conferences on Food (1974) and Nutrition (1992). Various provisions of the ICESCR, however, deal more comprehensively than any other instrument with RTF, especially, as already discussed, its Articles 2 (1), 11, 15, 22 and 23, which impose an obligation on state parties to take steps, including legislative measures, to procure the full realization of the rights created by the Covenant, including 'continuous improvement of living conditions'. In their present formulation, however, the above ICESCR provisions do not necessarily provide a solid foundation for the development of IPL, since they do not constitute 'hard' law and therefore lack the necessarily binding legal force, and since their realization depends on resources (which are not always available) at national level and on the good will of states (which is aleatory) at international level.

Nevertheless, there may be a valid avenue to escape this impasse. Since RTF has been incorporated into the international law of human rights and has been adopted as such by the UN General Assembly or its organs, i.e. ECOSOC and its progeny, the CHR and the UN Sub-commission, the old and long-standing Western argument that the UN resolutions have no legal force should simply become irrelevant.[31] Moreover, human rights, as represented by the two international covenants, including the ICESCR, are norms of positive international law largely accepted by the international community, including the Western rich countries. Accordingly, human rights aspects of poverty may be envisaged as rules of law, particularly since RTF, on which IPL rests, is recognized as part of the ICESCR, that is to say a legally binding treaty, even if such legal force is at present contested by Western scholars.

The subjects RTF, sometimes also called the right to adequate food or the right to freedom from hunger, is a fundamental right that is closely linked to the very right to life, in that no other right can be enjoyed unless this right is guaranteed by the state. It implies, indeed mandates, that states have an obligation to ensure at a minimum that people within their territorial jurisdiction do not starve, but rather have physical and economic access at all times to food, *ideally* in such quantity and quality to allow for a healthy and active life.

There are, however, two limits to such an assumption. First, individuals are the active subjects of RTF, in the sense that they are the ones who are concerned with ensuring livelihoods for themselves and their dependants through their own efforts, provided that opportunities exist. All resolutions of the CHR uphold this premise, i.e. that RTF does not mean an unequivocal right to be provided for by the state. But there is a widely accepted agreement that states can do much to create conditions under which people are able to take care of their own needs, including obtaining food. Second, the principal 'duty-holder' of RTF, and, indeed of all human rights is the state, which has to comply with its obligations derived from human rights conventions. In particular, the state is obliged to *respect*, *protect* and *fulfil* enumerated rights for all citizens. In so doing, notes Windfuhr, expert for FIAN International, 'a State does not necessarily have to be rich or extraordinarily prosperous, but it has to prove – according to Article 2 of the ICESCR – that it is using the maximum of its available resources for that endeavor'.[32]

Therefore, primary responsibility for the realization of RTF lies with states, which should take all necessary steps towards the goal of full enjoyment of such a right. Under Article 11 of the ICESCR, states have the responsibility to create, protect and facilitate the use of needed opportunities. The same obligations are articulated in Article 2 of the declaration on RTD – that states have not only the right but the duty to formulate appropriate national development policies that aim at the constant improvement of all individuals' and the entire population's well-being. This duty must be disassociated from exceptional circumstances such as natural catastrophe or emergency relief.[33] Here again, it is important to note that a minimum of conditions both nationally and internationally is necessary for states to provide such opportunities. It is not sufficient to declare that states must comply with their human rights obligations towards their citizens in implementing RTF, if individuals do not possess the necessary tools to claim and eventually obtain the full and effective enjoyment of such a right.

Justiciability Since RTF is a fundamental human right firmly established in international law, subjecting such a right to judicial supervision is essential to ensure real accountability of the 'duty-bearers' (the state) towards the 'claim-holders' (the individuals). The Geneva Commission on Human Rights has recently considered adopting an Optional Protocol Covenant on Economic, Social and Cultural Rights (hereafter the Optional Protocol) providing for a system of individual and group complaints.[34] Advocates of the Optional Protocol argue that such an instrument would ensure that individuals have access to an effective remedy at international level

The right to food

for violations of their most basic economic, social and cultural rights. They point out that the adoption of the Optional Protocol would give any person or group that is victim of a violation of RTF access to effective judicial remedies. The Optional Protocol would also permit the development of a significant body of jurisprudence that would assist in defining and interpreting the normative implications and operational requirements of economic, social and cultural rights.[35] Thus advocates maintain that individual pursuit of the RTF vis-à-vis the state will ultimately strengthen the state's effort to consolidate its structures for combating poverty and, simultaneously, contribute to reinforcing the state's effort to secure food for its citizens.

Opponents of such a mechanism argue that violations of RTF are particularly hard to define because state sovereignty is still framed in traditional political terms.[36] Moreover, the nature of RTF, as a derivative of the overall rights contained in the ICESCR, relies chiefly on economic resources that might not be available in many countries of the South. In such a case, if a complaint procedure were established at national level, in judicial, quasi-judicial or administrative bodies, what kind of redress would be available to individuals? In the poorest countries, where poverty is pervasive and assumed to be natural, what kind of claim could be made against the state? In practice, it is hard to see how an individual or group of individuals could seek redress for and obtain compensation (and, if so, in what amount) for an alleged non-performance of any of the duties imposed by RTF. This is particularly true in non-democratic authoritarian political systems, which paradoxically form the majority of poor states.

At international level, it is the UN human rights machinery, primarily the Committee on Economic, Social and Cultural Rights, which has the task of monitoring the realization and, consequently, violations of the RTF. But how would the principle of justiciability be applied to UN institutions and other international agencies that have failed to fulfil their engagements towards the poor countries or are implicated in the creation of poverty and hunger in these same countries? As discussed earlier, poverty in many countries is due partially to external factors over which states are powerless; in such cases, would the same principle of justiciability be invoked to seek reparations? In other words, can states that are themselves victims of the injustice of the current world economic system be given the opportunity to challenge international organizations, namely economic and financial entities, that have failed to implement anti-poverty programmes, and what kind of remedies might these states obtain?

From the foregoing fragile premises, the question arises as to whether it will be possible to envision a corpus of international norms under IPL that will deal with poverty reduction and eradication. In light of the current opposition, mainly from the Western conservative countries, the notion of an IPL may appear unacceptable as long as RTF continues to be regarded as pure legal formalism, devoid of any scientific content. In the eyes of many Western lawyers and politicians alike, a great deal of what is included in RTF is not legal in the technical sense of the word. Rather, RTF is viewed as essentially goal-oriented, providing a dynamic perspective on the law-making process and an instrument designed to transform through the IPL the existing order in favour of the disadvantaged majority of the world's population. It is this perception of international law which is a matter of controversy between those who see the international legal system as a set of neutral rules to be impartially applied without regard to the policy imperatives or consequences and those who see international law as *'le droit applicable à la société internationale'*.[37]

While legal scholars in wealthy nations theorize on the content of RTF, more than 800 million people throughout the world, and particularly in the under-privileged countries, do not have enough food to meet their basic nutritional needs. As former ICJ judge Bedjaoui remarked: 'The situation cannot endure. International law cannot be, nor can it remain, indifferent to the dignity of man; it cannot be reduced to a collection of dry techniques when the question of food is putting at risk the basic moral values of the human race.'[38] The international community must realize that any anti-poverty programme is a two-way enterprise in which both rich and poor nations contribute within their own spheres and according to their own abilities towards a collective effort. Although much of the burden lies on the rich North as the main supplier of capital and technology necessary for the eradication of underdevelopment in general and poverty in par-ticular (including the specific RTF), sacrifices also have to be made by the Southern countries in critically related areas such as good governance and population planning. Only then can IPL emerge as a new legal instrument in the fight against poverty

Conclusion

The concept of a specific RTF was initially absent from the UN docu-ments drafted before and during the seventies, which constitute the back-bone of international development law. It was rather diluted in the much broader and vaguer concept of development set out in a few UN General Assembly resolutions aimed at international redistribution of wealth and power rather than specifically tackling the issue of poverty. It was not until the beginning of the 1990s that RTF became an important subject first discussed within the more general framework of extreme poverty during the CHR sessions in Geneva and then incorporated into the general legal framework of human rights. Since the 1996 World Food Summit in Rome, the concept of RTF has rapidly developed and acquired a sort of *vivendus* which in turn gave it a legal 'flavour', albeit not without controversy.

One possibility suggested in this chapter to overcome present disagreement over poverty reduction is to elaborate a new corpus of international law, which would serve as a catalyst in addressing chronic poverty in economically deprived countries. But in the present international economic and political climate, the task seems insurmountable unless the international community interjects morality and humanism, i.e. the concept of international solidarity, not charity, into policy development.

If a new poverty law discourse is ever to emerge, it must be the expression of a new international order, which would impose on the wealthiest states a duty to contribute to the alleviation of underdevelopment of the poor nations in a spirit of human solidarity, different from previous so-called aid programmes, which, instead of eradicating poverty by its roots, contributed to its regeneration and generalization among a large number of LDCs.

Pope John Paul II quite poignantly captured the underlying concepts that must drive the development of IPL:

> It is not just a question of giving one's surplus to those in need, but of helping the entire peoples presently excluded or marginalized to enter into the sphere of economic human development. For this to happen it is not enough to draw on the surplus goods which in fact our world abundantly produces, it requires above all a change of lifestyles, of models of production and consumption, and of established structures of power which today govern societies. (John Paul II, encyclical letter *Centisiumus Annus*, 58)[39]

Notes

1. Reported in E/CN: 4/1998/21 para. 2, p. 2. See also CHR Resolution 1997/8.

2. P. T. Muchlinski (1987) '"Basic needs" theory and development law', in F. Snyder and P. Slinn (eds), *International Law of Development: Comparative Perspectives*, London: Professional Books.

3. Ibid., p. 237.

4. Sanbrook R. (1999) 'Citizenship, rights and poverty. Narrowing the gap between theory and practice', Paper presented at the IDEA Democracy Forum 2000, University of Toronto.

5. Ibid.

6. Doc. E/CN.4/1998/21, p. 3.

7. For a discussion on the legal binding force of UN resolutions, see Guy Feuer (1987) 'The role of resolution in the creation of general rules in the

international law of development', in Snyder and Slinn, *International Law*, pp. 137–44.

8. See in particular the UNDP paper on 'Human Rights and Development', UNDP Publications, January 1999.

9. Objective 7.4 (e) in World Food Summit Plan of Action, Rome, November 1996. Subsequently the CHR endorsed this request in its resolutions 1997/8, 1998/23 and 1999/24. (See Doc. E/CN.4/2000/48, Summary of Reply, para. 6, p. 3.)

10. General Comment, para. 3 in E/C/12/1999/5, p. 3.

11. Ibid.

12. The three international NGOs at the origin of Article 4 of the International Code of Conduct on the Human Right to Adequate Food are: FIAN (Food First Information and Action Network), WANAHR (World Alliance for Nutrition and Human Rights) and Institut Jacques Martin International. The Code was adopted in September 1997.

13. See the written statement submitted by the World Alliance of Reformed Churches, a non-governmental organization in general consultative status, and very active in CHR activities, in Doc. E/CN.4/2001/NGO/4.

14. Doc. E/CN.4/Sub.2/1999/12. For a discussion of the definition of RTF by NGOs, see Doc. E/CN.4/2001/NGO/4; also Doc. E/CN.4/2000/48, para. 44, p. 10.

15. Doc. E/C.12/1999/5, para. 7, p. 3.

16. Doc. E/CN.4/1999/45, p. 3.

17. Doc. E/CN.4/Sub.2/1999/12, paras 44–50, pp. 13–14.

18. Ibid.

19. Doc. E/CN.4/1999/45, pp. 9–10.

20. World Food Summit Plan of Action, Rome, November 1996. See also Doc. E/CN.4/2000/48, para. 33, p. 7.

21. The resolution on RTF was adopted by a roll-call vote of 49 to 1 with 2 abstentions; Doc. E/CN.4/RES/2000/10.

22. The personality of the Special Rapporteur is not fortuitous. The appointee, Prof. Jean Ziegler of Geneva University, is a moderate left-wing figure known for his opposition to Western capitalist ideology.

23. See particularly point 9 of the RTF Resolution of 2000. There were previous UN consultations on the right to food in 1977 and 1988 initiated by the same Geneva-based Commission on Human Rights.

24. Mohamed Bedjaoui (1987) 'Some unorthodox reflections on the "Right to Development"', in Snyder and Slinn, *International Law*, p. 92.

25. Doc. E/CN.4/2000/48, paras 33 and 34, p. 7.

26. Reported in 'The substance and politics of a human rights approach to food and nutrition policies and programmes', WHO Symposium held at the Palais des Nations in Geneva, 12 and 13 April 1999.

27. 'Ending malnutrition by the year 2020', Report by the Commission on the Nutrition Challenges for the 21st Century of the Administration Committee on Coordination Subcommittee on Nutrition, March 1999.

28. Feuer, 'The role of resolution', p. 7.

29. As long ago as the Bandung Conference in 1956, respect for international law was proclaimed as one of the ten principles of peaceful coexistence.

30. Snyder and Slinn, *International Law*, p. 33.

31. Ibid.

32. Doc. E/CN.4/1999/45, p. 5. FIAN International is the acronym for Food First Information and Action Network, one of the three NGOs that endorsed the International Code of Conduct on the Human Right to Adequate Food. See note 12 above.

33. In cases of emergencies, states have obligations not only with regard to their own inhabitants, but also, under the UN Charter, to cooperate in solving problems of a social and humanitarian nature. This is a moral obligation to share the burden of providing food aid and other measures of relief to affected populations in special circumstances, which is different from the ongoing discussion of RTF as an emerging basic human right applicable in all circumstances.

34. Doc. E/CN.41997/105; Doc. E/CN.4/2000/9. See also the Workshop on the Justiciability of Economic, Social and Cultural Rights, with particular reference to an Optional Protocol to the Covenant on Economic, Social and Cultural Rights (Palais Wilson, Finland, 5–6 February 2001).

35. Doc. E/C.12/1999/5, p. 8.

36. See note 34 above on the Workshop on the Justiciability of Economic, Social and Cultural Rights.

37. Peter Slinn (1987) 'Differing approaches to the relation between international law and development', in Snyder and Slinn, *International Law*, p. 33.

38. Bedjaoui, 'Some unorthodox reflections', p. 87.

39. Reported in Doc. E/CN.4/2001/NGO/4. See the written statement submitted by the World Alliance of Reformed Churches, 16 January 2001.

6 | South African poverty law: the role and influence of international human rights instruments

MARIUS OLIVIER AND LINDA JANSEN VAN RENSBURG

In per capita terms South Africa is an upper-middle-income country, but despite this relative wealth, the experience of most South African households is that of outright poverty or of continuing vulnerability to being poor. In addition, the distribution of income and wealth in South Africa is among the most unequal in the world, and many households still have unsatisfactory access to education, healthcare, energy and clean water, as well as to wealth-generating assets and opportunities.[1] Addressing these poverty-related problems is one of the main priorities of the South African government. There is, however, little substantial and developing jurisprudence available in South Africa on the scope and core content of socio-economic rights, and especially poverty rights. Taking into account the lack of substantial jurisprudence in this regard, Section 39(1)(b) of the Constitution of the Republic of South Africa 108 of 1996 (the Constitution) compels a court, tribunal or forum, when interpreting the Bill of Rights, to consider international law. The Constitution further provides for special social, economic and cultural rights as justiciable fundamental rights in the Bill of Rights.

A recent and laudable jurisprudential development in the area of poverty law in South Africa is the Constitutional Court case of *The Government of the Republic of South Africa and Others* v. *Grootboom and Others*, 2001 (1) SA 46 (CC) (hereafter *Grootboom*). In this case the court recognized the importance of international law and especially the International Covenant on Economic, Social and Cultural Rights (ICESCR) and the General Comments of the United Nations Committee on Economic, Social and Cultural Rights (UNCESCR) in the interpretation of socio-economic rights. The court further noted that the Constitution obliges the state to act positively and progressively to ameliorate the plight of the hundreds of thousands of people living in deplorable conditions throughout the country. It must provide access to housing, healthcare, sufficient food and water, and social security to those unable to support themselves and their dependants.

The aim and purpose of this chapter are to analyse the linkage between international instruments (such as the ICESCR, the Convention on the Rights of the Child and the African Charter on Human and Peoples' Rights) and the South African policy and legal (inclusive of constitutional) framework in order to make concrete suggestions as to how these can be employed to eradicate and alleviate poverty in the unique circumstances of South Africa. Specifically this chapter focuses on the social security dimension of addressing poverty in the South African context, from the perspective of human rights protection in general, and international human rights instruments in particular.

Background on poverty in South Africa: a principled, factual and legal perspective

A principled perspective: poverty, social exclusion and social security
Although it is evident that social security (including both social insurance programmes based on employment status and social assistance means-tested schemes) has as one of its primary aims addressing and redressing poverty, it is increasingly recognized that social security has to deal with a frame of deprivation that goes farther than mere poverty. It is, therefore, necessary to distinguish between poverty (the outcome of the process of impoverishment, according to Berghmen) and the wider notion of social exclusion (the process leading to multi-faceted deprivation), and to consider the role that social security has to play with respect to both.

While poverty has traditionally been associated with a lack of resources, the recent concept of social exclusion views poverty through a more comprehensive lens. In fact, poverty (referring to a lack of disposable income) can be seen as part of the multi-dimensional and dynamic concept of social exclusion (referring to multi-faceted deprivation). Social exclusion, therefore, can be understood with reference to the failure of any one or more of the following: (i) the democratic and legal system (civic integration); (ii) the labour market (economic integration); (iii) the welfare state system (social integration); and (iv) the family and community system (interpersonal integration). Conversely, social participation, being the positive counterpart of social exclusion, is to be determined with reference to all four systems.[2] Or, as a recent ILO/UNDP study remarks, the notion of social exclusion links both social rights and material deprivation. It encompasses not only the lack of access to goods and services, which underlies poverty and basic needs satisfaction, but also exclusion from security, from justice, from representation and from citizenship. It concerns inequality in many dimensions – economic, social, political and cultural. Berghman concludes: 'so the conceptual differences become somewhat clearer: there is the traditional concept of poverty, which by now is restricted to denoting a lack of disposable income; and there is the comprehensive concept of social exclusion that refers to a breakdown or malfunctioning of the major societal systems that should guarantee full citizenship. Poverty then is part of – a specific form of – social exclusion. The latter is broader and should not necessarily always encompass an element of poverty.'[3]

Poverty in the traditional sense and social exclusion are therefore related but not synonymous: the presence of one does not automatically imply the presence of the other.[4] This has major implications for the development of social security law, which has to direct its attention not only at the cross-sectional incidence of income poverty, but also at a multi-dimensional set of living conditions. An interpretation of (both domestic and international) human rights provisions that recognizes the interrelationship between socio-economic rights, on the one hand, and civil and political rights, on the other hand, could be instrumental in ensuring that poverty in its multi-dimensional setting is effectively addressed.

Moreover, the wider role entrusted to social security also implies that the traditional perception of social security as being aimed at only (mere) income protection is too restrictive. For example, an increasingly accepted aim of social security is now to contribute to the reintegration, not only in the labour market sense of the word but also socially and otherwise, of the individual beneficiary of social security.[5] In a similar vein, preventative measures aimed at employment protection and at avoiding the occurrence of particular risks have also become part of the social security policy frame-work. The wider role of social security thus allows one to adopt a more holistic and integrated approach towards dealing with issues of exclusion – an approach that takes into account the different spheres of exclusion and what needs to be done cross-sectionally to ensure integration, restoration and participation. One could, therefore, say that income security and social participation are both goals to strive for in any social security system.

This wider role of social security also implies that merely extending coverage when someone is not covered by the social security protective regime is not always the panacea that will solve all the ills associated with exclusion. Dealing with exclusion becomes much more than clinically determining one's eligibility for social security. As Rodgers articulates, it requires identifying and analysing the root causes of the exclusion, the processes that bring the exclusion about, the affected categories of people, and the role of actors involved in the process of exclusion. Social exclusion must be addressed through a multi-dimensional approach:

- linking social rights and welfare arrangements;

- intervening in the labour market (for example, by encouraging and regulating reintegration);
- introducing measures that would strengthen the links between social security and labour market incentives (such as job-seeking assistance, financial incentives to employ, and skills training);
- focusing on targeted involvement with particularly vulnerable groups (for example, through specifically targeted programmes reaching certain excluded groups, such as rural women or the young unemployed);
- ensuring multi-actor involvement (i.e. the state, trade unions, non-governmental and community-based organizations, enterprises, and other social security stakeholders);
- managing market mechanisms in order to widen access; and
- balancing passive and active policies, and introducing both reactive and pro-active measures (inclusive of affirmative action measures) against exclusion.

It is, however, especially in dealing with (the more restricted area of) impoverishment and poverty that social security is of major importance and effect. The potentially dramatic impact of the receipt of the aggregate of the entire social security transfer (i.e. more than formal minimum protection schemes) on poverty incidence and the reduction of the pre-transfer poverty gap has been well documented in, among other places, Europe,[6] and is, at least as far as its effect on the poverty incidence, certainly confirmed by the South African experience. This is, of course, particularly true if social security makes available above-minimum earnings-related protection that would serve as a brake preventing one from sliding back into poverty. The payment of pension benefits to the (historically poor) elderly certainly has had this effect.[7] As Berghman notes: 'Thus, although the fight against poverty and social exclusion – or, to put it the other way round, the fight for income security and social participation – requires much more than the mere provision of minimum income protection, the latter role on the part of the traditional social security schemes retains its full relevance in this context.'[8]

The role of social security in successfully reducing poverty can never be seen in isolation, however, as this would not be possible without the complementary effect of labour market policies. In fact, where labour markets do not function well, in particular owing to a shortage of labour demand, too many social security beneficiaries may put the social security system under unbearable strain.

The factual perspective: the poor, the structurally unemployed and the informally employed The limited nature of protection in terms of the South African social security system has affected the poor, particularly the informally employed and structurally unemployed among them. This stems from the fact that the social insurance system, notably unemployment insurance and compensation for work injuries and diseases, does not provide coverage to those outside formal employment. Social assistance measures seldom operate to the direct advantage of the poor and the informally employed among them. Owing to the targeted nature of both social services and programmes and of the various social grants (notably the old age grant, the disability grant and the recently introduced child support grant), many if not most of the persons falling within the categories mentioned remain part of the population excluded from the social security system. While approximately 6.8 million South Africans are beneficiaries under the present grant system, the level of income support is extremely low (for example, the value of the old age grant is R700 per month), particularly since on average the benefits have to provide subsistence for five additional household members in African communities. In addition, the financial means tests created in order to access these grants have tended to promote a poverty trap syndrome.

All this is aggravated by the exceptionally high levels of unemployment and poverty in South Africa. Structural unemployment hovers between 25 and 30 per cent of the economically active population of South Africa, making it extremely unlikely that large pockets of the rural and urban poor will successfully enter the labour market in the near future.[9] Approximately 45 per cent of the informally employed in rural areas receive an income that is below the MLL (Minimum Living Level). It is also estimated that 45 per cent of the South African population, i.e. 18 million people, live in abject poverty – they are mostly African, females and children, and rural residents.[10] The categories of the poor and informally employed mentioned (in particular the rural poor) fall at the lower end of the income inequality spectrum, contributing significantly to the Gini coefficient of 0.58, which is the third highest in the world.[11] Informal employment activities among the poor are as a rule restricted to economic survival. Furthermore, although the new democratic government has had some success in enhancing accessibility to resources such as housing, water, land and electricity, these programmes and initiatives are often not well coordinated, are sometimes not comprehensive, and have failed to deliver as expected.[12] These figures are even more forceful given the fact that the government has not yet put forward an integrated strategy for reducing poverty and inequality. Therefore, the present South African social security system is hugely deficient in providing a true safety net for the rural and urban poor and the informally employed and structurally unemployed, operating within a paradigm where a consistent model for the alleviation of extreme poverty has yet to develop.

In recent years, however, the formal social assistance system has to some extent been modified to reach more of the poor and needy. For example, in 1993 parity between the black and non-black beneficiaries of the means-tested old age grant was established. The child support grant intended to replace the state maintenance grant also has as its aim to target poor families in particular, extending monetary assistance on a means-tested basis to larger households with children under the age of nine years.[13] By making childcare support accessible to the primary care-giver (and no longer merely the legal parent of the child), this grant gives recognition to a peculiar characteristic of many African households, namely that the person caring for a young child in an extended family context is often not the parent of the child. In a similar vein, the expansion of the definition of a marriage vis-à-vis eligibility for a social grant to include a marriage recognized in terms of South African law, or concluded in accordance with customary law or a system of religious law, underscores the more sensitive approach adopted towards the reality of family relationships among large numbers of the poor and needy in South Africa.[14]

The legal perspective: exclusion and marginalization

THE EXISTING SOCIAL SECURITY FRAMEWORK: AN OVERVIEW The social security system in South Africa is characterized by a strict distinction between social assistance and social insurance. In the area of social insurance, the Unemployment Insurance Fund (Unemployment Insurance Act 63 of 2001, hereafter UIA) pays out benefits to contributors and their dependants in the event of unemployment, illness, maternity and adoption. Employers and employees contribute on an equal basis to the fund with almost no state contribution. Compensation for employment injuries and diseases is paid to employees and their dependants out of the Compensation Fund, to which employers contribute on the basis of industry-based risk assessments (Compensation for Occupational Injuries and Diseases Act 130 of 1993, hereafter COIDA). For historical reasons, however, some of the categories traditionally covered under social insurance are not regulated on a public insurance fund basis at all, but rather are covered through private mechanisms – in particular retirement and health.[15]

The state social assistance system rests on two pillars: the provision of various kinds of social services and the payment of social grants. No universal coverage exists, as a needs-based and categorical approach is followed. The main social grants, i.e. the child support grant, the disability grant and the old age grant, regulated and paid out in terms of the Social Assistance Act 59 of 1992, are all means-tested. They are of a non-contributory nature, as payments are made from the state budget, based on an annual budgetary allocation. Additional categorical requirements provide that the beneficiary must be both a resident in and citizen of South Africa. From the viewpoint of a South African constitutional and international human rights instruments approach, the concept of social assistance in the applicable legislation is unrealistically narrow in terms of addressing issues of poverty. In its first two annual Socio-Economic Rights Reports (1997–98 and 1998–99), the South African Human Rights Commission (SAHRC) was fairly critical of social assistance, noting that the social assistance concept adopted for purposes of the Social Assistance Act restricts the term to an income replacement grants system. It would have been more appropriate if the concept also encapsulated transfers in kind and transfer of services, as these logically and conceptually form part and parcel of what social assistance is designed to achieve. SAHRC also noted that the Department of Social Development needed to justify the fact that there were (at that stage) only 3 million grant recipients, while 49 per cent of families remain poor. According to SAHRC, minimum standards for defining the right to access to social security must still be developed and the impact of policies and other measures regarding previously marginalized and vulnerable groups should be evaluated.

Healthcare for the bulk of the population is quite limited, with free primary healthcare and free hospital care accessible only to women with young children and the aged. For a selected part of the rest of the population, medical services are covered by private schemes, which are increasingly subjected to regulation.[16] In the absence of a national pensions scheme, private pension funds (regulated under the Pension Funds Act 24 of 1956) and more recently also provident funds have mushroomed. Around 74 per cent of formal sector workers are covered.[17] There are, however, several problems with the present regulations, which tend to cause and entrench poverty in South Africa. First, workers are allowed to and often do withdraw provident funds before they have matured. At retirement, many of these workers, who will have spent their savings, will become impoverished and will consequently end up drawing a state social grant. Second, there is no obligation to belong to a pension or provident fund. Thus, many workers, particularly the informally and self-employed, later become dependent on state social grants for the elderly. Furthermore, in practice, retirement contributions are often not transferable when an employee changes employment.

The social security debate in South Africa has been significantly enhanced by the constitutional entrenchment of social security rights. Interpreting and enforcing rights associated with social security, as is the case with other socio-economic rights,[18] and giving effect to statutory entitlements that have accrued in this regard,[19] emphasizes the importance of undertaking a proper legal analysis of the nature, content and ambit of the right to (access to) social security. The way in which the law deals with social assistance issues in particular is a reflection of the poor and inefficient administration and the flagrant disregard of basic legal tenets. The courts have not hesitated to intervene and assist beneficiaries when statutory entitlements to social assistance grants, as well as constitutional requirements and principles of administrative law, have been denied. In several cases, the courts have found that the unilateral suspension or withdrawal of grants is unlawful and invalid. For example, in 2000 the Eastern Cape High Court ordered the reinstatement of disability grants in a class action, with some retroactive awards going back to1996.[20]

This is not to say that the constitutional imperative has been the only or perhaps even the primary driving force behind the current interest in social security. It is evident that the more sensitive approach to matters of socio-economic concern since the democratic elections of 1994, the wider international context of the social security paradigm and the commitments that South Africa may incur in this regard,[21] as well as the need for a much more coherent approach in this area, are all playing a decisive role. More importantly, it is the very plight of those who are (still) excluded from the formal framework of social security, in particular the vast majority of the poor and needy who enjoy virtually no entitlement,[22] which has caused concern and already brought about some reconsideration of the fundamental characteristics of the system.[23]

In conclusion, the lack of a coherent approach in South African social security is clearly discernible and needs to be researched properly and rectified. In a sense, the present system suggests an archaic and rigid distinction between social insurance and social assistance – it lets those who are or have been in formal employment benefit from a fairly well-developed social insurance coverage (in particular unemployment insurance and workers' compensation coverage), while social assistance, in particular the grant system, remains restricted in coverage, as it is mainly based on a categorical, means-tested approach which provides meagre protection against the occurrence of a limited number of social risks. There is, therefore, little social solidarity in the system, apart from state-mandated budgetary flows (through the tax system) to social assistance. This is exacerbated by the fact that those in formal employment are usually in a position to expand their own protection by occupationally based and/or private coverage against risks such as sickness, health, disability and old age. Glaring disparities between the relatively rich and the poor are therefore prevalent, reinforc-ing and perpetuating not only the ever present inequality, but also abject poverty in this country.

EXCLUSION AND MARGINALIZATION IN SOUTH AFRICAN SOCIAL SE-CURITY AFFECTING THE POOR Thus many categories and groups are excluded from social security, for example the unemployed (both in the temporary and structural sense), excluded employees (for example farm and domestic workers), the self-employed, the informally employed and other atypically employed categories, many rural and urban poor, the aged dependent on social assistance and non-citizens. Some of the categories do overlap, while not all persons belonging to a particular category or group could be said to be in need of reliance on a public system of social security (for example, many professional self-employed people). For present purposes, we focus on the following non-exhaustive categories:

<u>Statutorily excluded workers</u> i) Persons who do not fit the 'employee' con-cept: South African social security laws extend social security protection only to those who legally qualify as 'employees', or a similar term used in the event of a particular piece of legislation (such as 'contributor' in Section [1] of the Unemployment Insurance Act 63 of 2001 [UIA]). Even though the statutory definitions might sometimes go farther than what in common law is understood under the term 'employee', the respective definitions and/or the case law nevertheless make it clear that major categories, such as independent contractors, are excluded.[24] From this it follows that the self-employed, the informally employed and several other categories of the atypically employed are for all legal and practical purposes excluded from vast areas of the social insurance system in South Africa, notably compensation for workplace injuries and diseases, and unemployment insurance.

It is true that in some limited instances the notion of 'employee' has purposely been extended, so that more employees,[25] and in one instance also persons who are not themselves employees, have become entitled to social security benefits.[26] Generally speaking, however, social security leg-islation in South Africa has not yet mirrored the widening of the employee concept in the labour laws of South Africa.

ii) Persons deliberately and specifically excluded from the 'employee' concept: one of the curious characteristics of South African social legisla-tion remains the exclusion of certain categories of persons from the ambit of the definition of 'employee' (or a similar term) contained in the relevant laws, even though these persons would otherwise perfectly fit the notion of being employees. The most telling example is perhaps the exclusion of domestic employees of private households from the COIDA. The COIDA also does not cover persons employed outside South Africa, while the UIA further specifically excludes employees whose remuneration exceeds a certain monetary ceiling, migrant workers who have to be repatriated at the termination of their service, employees who are remunerated on a purely commission basis, casual employees working fewer than eight hours per week, and civil servants.

In the South African context many of these exclusions, apart from being archaic in nature, have a distinct racial and/or gender flavour: because of the country's history of employment-based racial and gender hierarchy, these groups are most likely to be African and/or women. Given the preponderance of Africans and women in many of these categories, and given the absence of a reasonable justification for their exclusion, it might well be that the disparate treatment meted out can be regarded as a form of indirect discrimination. It is, therefore, to be hoped that the recommendation contained in both the ILO Country Review and the Labour Market Commission Report, that coverage extensions (including the self-employed also) be introduced, will be enacted.

<u>Dependants</u>   A dependant of a deceased employee can also qualify for a benefit under these laws. The definition of 'dependant'[27] in the various social security laws is normally linked to the employee/contract of service concept, in the sense that coverage is extended to dependants of deceased employees or persons who rendered services on the basis of a contract of employment. Even though the definition of 'dependant' makes provision for live-in partners and partners in an indigenous marriage to be beneficiaries as well, however, satisfactory recognition of extended families, religious marriages and unconventional unions is often still lacking. Furthermore, it would appear that a spouse married to the deceased employee in terms of customary or religious law would sometimes not qualify as a beneficiary if there was also a civil law marriage with another wife existing at the time of the employee's death.[28] It is doubtful whether the exclusion from these categories of de facto dependants will eventually pass constitutional and equality muster, given the constitutional prohibition on unfair discrimination based on marital status, religion and sexual orientation.[29]

In essence, then, the effect of relying on the 'employee' and 'contract of service' notions (or similar notions employed by the legislature) in order to signify coverage is that large categories of those who work atypically, as well as those specifically excluded, effectively do not enjoy social security protection.

The Constitution of the Republic of South Africa 1996

The Constitution contains a Bill of Rights that addresses civil and political, as well as socio-economic, rights. No reference is made in the Bill of Rights to the traditional division[30] between first-, second- and third-generation rights. Social rights have exactly the same status as other civil and political rights.[31] The notion of not differentiating between these apparent 'categories' of rights places emphasis on the fact that all rights are interrelated, interdependent and indivisible.

Social rights and specifically those rights pertaining to the alleviation of poverty are contained in different sections of the Bill of Rights. Section 27(1)(c) states that 'everyone has the right to have access to social security, including, if they are unable to support themselves and their dependants, appropriate social assistance'. Apart from Section 27(1)(c), which makes direct reference to the right to access to social security, other provisions in the Bill of Rights make indirect reference to this concept. Section 26 grants everyone the right to access to adequate housing, Section 27(1)(a) provides for the right to access to healthcare services, including reproductive healthcare, and Section 27(1)(b) provides for the right to access to sufficient food and water. These sections are all subject to the phrase that the state must take reasonable legislative and other measures, within its available resources, to achieve the progressive realization of these rights: Section 26(2) and 27(2). Section 28 specifically addresses the social rights and special needs of children and does not contain a similar qualification as contained in Sections 26 and 27 concerning 'progressive realization'. Section 28(1)(c) grants every child the right to shelter, basic nutrition, basic healthcare services and social services.

Before analysing the content and meaning of these social rights pertaining to the alleviation of poverty in South Africa, however, it is important to examine the role and function of international law, in particular from a constitutional perspective.

A South African perspective towards international law
REASONS WHY INTERNATIONAL LAW MUST BE CONSIDERED There are several reasons why international human rights law must be taken into account when social rights contained in the South African Constitution are interpreted. First, South Africa has indicated its intention to become a party to and be legally bound by the obligations imposed by relevant international treaties. International conventions applicable to social rights that have been ratified by South Africa are the United Nations Convention on the Rights of the Child, the African Charter on Human and People's Rights and the African Charter on the Rights and Welfare of the Child.

South Africa is in the process of ratifying the primary international document regulating social rights, the United Nations International Covenant on Economic, Social and Cultural Rights (ICESCR).

Second, even in those instances where South Africa is not legally bound by obligations under a treaty, Section 39(1)(b) of the Constitution compels adversarial bodies when interpreting the Bill of Rights to consider international law.[32] Section 39(1) reads as follows: 'When interpreting the Bill of Rights, a court, tribunal or forum – (a) must promote the values that underlie an open and democratic society based on human dignity, equality and freedom; (b) must consider international law; and (c) may consider foreign law.' The Constitution thus compels the courts and other adjudicative bodies in South Africa to consider international law whether it is binding or not binding when the courts interpret the above-mentioned social rights. This section emphasizes the special role international jurisprudence has to play in the field of interpreting social rights, which can be interpreted as an 'international-friendly approach'. International agreements and customary international law thus provide a framework within which the Bill of Rights can be evaluated and understood. For this purpose, decisions of tribunals dealing with comparable instruments, such as the United Nations Committee on Human Rights, the Inter-American Commission on Human Rights, the Inter-American Court of Human Rights, the European Commission on Human Rights and the European Court of Human Rights, and in appropriate cases reports of specialized agencies such as the International Labour Organization, may provide guidance in interpreting particular provisions of the bill. In *S* v. *Makwanyane and Another*,[33] the Constitutional Court's emphasis that non-binding international law must be taken into consideration implies that soft law must also be considered. Soft law consists of imprecise standards, generated by declarations adopted by diplomatic conferences or resolutions of international organizations, which are intended to serve as guidelines to states in their conduct, but which lack the status of 'law'. The court further held that, although the judiciary must take into consideration, and may be assisted by, public international law, it is in no way bound to follow it.[34]

Third, there is substantial and developing jurisprudence available on the scope and core content of socio-economic rights, for example General Comments of the UNCESCR, the Limburg Principles of 1987 and the Maastricht Guidelines of 1997. The latter instrument contains official commentary of the International Commission of Jurists on the nature, application and duties of state parties towards the ICESCR.

Fourth, international cooperation requires that international human rights as well as social and labour policy must be considered. As Jenks states: 'In this new world of interdependence full recognition and effective respect of human rights assume far greater importance than in a society where, over a wide range of conduct, individual and national freedom are affected relatively little by the conduct of others; *labour standards become a necessary corollary of human rights; and both human rights and labour rights tend to become increasingly international in character*'.[35]

CONSTITUTIONAL PROVISIONS PERTAINING TO INTERNATIONAL LAW
Common law recognizes customary international law as part of South African law. This is confirmed by Section 232 of the Constitution, which grants customary international law legal force in the Republic unless it is inconsistent with the Constitution or an Act of Parliament.

Section 231 of the Constitution deals with international agreements (or treaties), and the signing, ratification and transformation thereof. In order for an international agreement to become law in the Republic, it has to be signed by the national executive, approved by parliament (ratified) and enacted into law by national legislation (transformed). Certain exceptions are also dealt with in this section. An agreement of a technical, administrative or executive nature, as well as an agreement that does not require ratification or accession, will not have to be ratified before it becomes law in the Republic.

Section 231(4) provides for the possibility that a self-executing treaty or a self-executing provision in a treaty, which has been approved by Parliament to be law in the Republic without having to be ratified, will be binding unless it is inconsistent with the Constitution or an Act of Parliament. An agreement or provision in an agreement is self-executing if existing legislation is of such a nature that it allows the Republic to carry out its international obligations without the need for additional legislation. An agreement that has been signed and ratified, but not yet transformed, is still binding on South Africa within the international arena.

A common-law presumption that requires a court to interpret legislation consistently with international law was incorporated into Section 233 of the Constitution. This section provides that when interpreting any legislation, a court must give preference to any reasonable interpretation of the legislation that is consistent with international law over any alternative interpretation that is inconsistent with international law.[36]

THE COMMITTEE ON THE RIGHTS OF THE CHILD In January 2000, the Committee on the Rights of the Child (CRC) considered South Africa's first report and adopted concluding observations on South Africa's compliance with the United Nations Convention on the Rights of the Child. The CRC noted that South Africa has not yet ratified the ICESCR. The CRC stressed that the ratification of this international human rights instrument would strengthen the efforts of the state party to meet its obligations in guaranteeing the rights of all children under its jurisdiction and encouraged the state party to reinforce its efforts to finalize the ratification. The CRC also made certain observations regarding social rights of children aimed at alleviating poverty, criticizing the South African government on the following:

- the lack of coordination between those ministries responsible for the implementation of the Convention;
- insufficient efforts made to ensure the adequate distribution of resources allocated for children's programmes and activities;
- the phasing out of the State Maintenance Grant and the potential economic impact on disadvantaged women and children who currently benefit from the programme;
- the continuing threat to the survival and development of children within the state party by early childhood diseases such as acute respiratory infections and diarrhoea;
- the high incidence of child and infant mortality as well as maternal mortality, the high rate of malnutrition, vitamin A deficiency and stunting, the poor condition of sanitation, insufficient access to safe drinking water, especially in rural communities; and
- inadequate legal protection, programmes, facilities and services for children with disabilities, particularly mental disabilities.[37]

While South Africa failed to comply with the provisions in the Convention on the Rights of the Child in major respects, the CRC is assisting South Africa in addressing these problems through its recommendations. Thus international supervisory bodies can play an important role in assisting countries to implement international poverty law.

Aims Owing to the devastating effects of the apartheid regime on the quality of life of many people in South Africa and their enjoyment of socio-economic rights, the overarching aims of the Constitution are to heal the injustices of the past, to ensure social justice, to improve the quality of life for all South African citizens (*inter alia* by alleviating poverty and suffering) and to free the potential of each citizen.[38]

In various sections of the Constitution,[39] as mentioned above, reference is made to fundamental values that underpin the objectives and aims of the Constitution. As noted, Section 39(1) compels courts, tribunals and forums to promote the values that underlie an open and democratic society based on human dignity, equality and freedom when interpreting the Bill of Rights. Since providing food, clothing and shelter is essential to human dignity, freedom and equality, affording socio-economic rights to all people enables them to enjoy the other rights enshrined in the Bill of Rights. The realization of these socio-economic rights is also key to the advancement of race and gender equality and the evolution of a society in which men and women are equally able to achieve their full potential. The universal aim and basis for the existence of social security rights and other social rights pertaining to poverty is to protect a person's right to human dignity,[40] considered a fundamental constitutional value[41] as well as a fundamental right[42] contained in the Bill of Rights.[43]

One of the aims of a well-structured social security system is to give effect to the principle of solidarity. A spin-off of solidarity is the prevention of social exclusion. Social security measures and other measures aimed at the alleviation of poverty can place a person in a position to fulfil his/her role in society with dignity.[44] The ILO describes the importance of solidarity as follows: 'It is not possible to have social security, worthy of the name, without a consciousness of national solidarity and perhaps – tomorrow – international solidarity. The effort of developing social security must therefore be accompanied by continuous effort to promote this crucial sense of shared responsibility.'[45] For a variety of reasons, the consciousness of solidarity, which should support all our efforts towards social security, has tended to become weaker as the role of social security has widened. The aims of social security and other measures targeted at the alleviation of poverty and social exclusion cannot be achieved if those who benefit from social security do not play an active role in its development. It is essential for them to participate voluntarily in this process of change and to accept responsibility for the agencies created to assist them.

Ubuntu[46] and nation-building within the South African perspectives can contribute to a sense of shared responsibility. Mokgoro describes *ubuntu* as a metaphor for group solidarity where the group is dependent on limited resources. Mokgoro further states: 'People are willing to pool community resources to help an individual in need. This is captured in some of the African aphorisms such as "a botho ba gago bo nne botho seshabeng" which, literally translated, means, "let your welfare be the welfare of the nation".'[47] The White Paper on Social Welfare describes the importance of *ubuntu* as follows: 'The principle for caring for each other's well-being will be promoted, and a spirit of mutual support fostered. Each individual's humanity is ideally expressed through his or her relationship with others and theirs in turn through a recognition of the individual's humanity. Ubuntu means that people are people through other people. It also acknowledges both the rights and the responsibilities of every citizen in promoting individual and societal well-being.'[48]

Thus group solidarity is not a foreign principle within South African society. The respect for and promotion of the principle of *ubuntu* can play a key role in guaranteeing the success of a comprehensive social security system and other measures aimed at the alleviation of poverty and social exclusion in South Africa. This in turn also emphasizes the importance to be given to group protection in the fight against poverty and deprivation. In fact, upon analysing the recent Constitutional Court judgment in *Grootboom*, and comparing that judgment with previous judgments of the Constitutional Court on the enforcement of socio-economic rights in the domain of social security, it appears that the courts will more readily offer assistance when they are presented with the position of historically deprived and disadvantaged groups rather than cases of individuals claiming assistance.

Limitations on social rights In certifying the 1996 Constitution, the Constitutional Court acknowledged that socio-economic rights are in fact enforceable even if they give rise to budgetary considerations.[49] Indeed, Section 7(2) places a duty on the state to respect, protect, promote and fulfil the rights in the Bill of Rights and consequently the social rights pertaining to poverty. On a primary level, the duty to respect requires negative state action and the courts will only expect the state not to unjustly interfere with a person's fundamental rights. This is known as negative enforcement by the courts.

The duties to protect, promote and fulfil place a positive duty on the state that requires positive action from the courts. On a secondary level, the state is obligated to protect its citizens from political, economic and social interference with their stated rights. This obligation does not require that the state distribute money or resources to individuals, but requires setting up a framework wherein individuals can realize these rights without undue influence from the state.

At the tertiary level, Section 7(2) requires that the state promote and fulfil everyone's rights. The beneficiary has the right to require positive assistance or a benefit or service from the state. The nature and scope of these state obligations, however, depend on the exact wording or phrasing of the fundamental right, as well as on the external and internal limitations of this right.[50]

EXTERNAL LIMITATIONS Section 7(3) refers to external limitations, stating that the rights in the Bill of Rights are subject to the limitations contained in or referred to in Section 36 or elsewhere in the bill. In the case of *S v. Zuma*,[51] the Constitutional Court stated that constitutional analysis contains two phases.[52] First, the applicant must show that there was an infringement on the duty to respect, protect, promote and fulfil the rights in the Bill of Rights. Second, the respondent must show that the infringement was justifiable and that the right was legitimately restricted in accordance with the general limitation clause contained in Section 36 of the Bill of Rights.

Current social assistance legislation (which provides a safety net for categories of vulnerable people in South Africa) includes the Social Assistance Act 59 of 1992, Special Pensions Act 69 of 1996, Demobilization Act 99 of 1996 and the Promotion of National Unity and Reconciliation Act 34 of 1995. If a provision of this social assistance legislation infringes upon social rights addressing poverty issues, such an infringement will be justifiable only if the limitation falls within the ambit of Section 36(1) of the Constitution. Section 36(1) determines that the rights in the Bill of Rights may be limited only in terms of law of general application to the extent that the limitation is reasonable and justifiable in an open and democratic society based on human dignity, equality and freedom, taking into account all relevant factors, including the nature of the right, the importance of the purpose of the limitation, the nature and extent of the limitation, the relation between the limitation and its purpose and less restrictive means to achieve the purpose.

INTERNAL LIMITATIONS

Similarity between Sections 26(2) and 27(2) of the South African Constitution and Article 2(1) of the ICESCR The state's duty to respect, protect, promote and fulfil the social rights pertaining to the alleviation of poverty is further qualified by the phrasing of Sections 26(2) and 27(2), both of which state that the state must take reasonable legislative and other measures, within its available resources, to achieve the progressive realization of each of these rights. The inclusion of these qualifications is an acknowledgement that the social rights cannot be fulfilled by the state immediately and completely.

Almost the same formulation and phrasing are found in Article 2(1) of the ICESCR, and the comments on the document can serve as a valuable source for interpreting the South African provisions, utilizing an 'international-friendly' approach. In the *Grootboom* case, the Constitutional Court interpreted the meaning of Sections 26(2) and 27(2) and articulated the manner in which the courts are prepared to enforce socio-economic rights.[53]

<u>Reasonable legislative and other measures</u> The UNCESCR is of the opinion that each state has a duty to realize rights to the 'maximum of their available resources'.[54] If the state is a developing country or is experiencing some economic difficulties, it must at least realize minimum core obligations. The UNCESCR makes the following statement with regard to minimum core obligations: 'The Committee is of the view that a minimum core obligation to ensure the satisfaction of, at the very least, minimum essential levels of each of the rights is incumbent upon every State Party.'[55] The UNCESCR further states that 'If the Covenant were to be read in such a way as to not establish such a minimum core obligation, it would largely be deprived of its *raison d'être.*' The failure by the state to provide for the basic subsistence needs of the population may be considered as a prima facie violation of the Covenant.

The South African Constitutional Court noted that the General Comment of the UNCESCR does not specify precisely the meaning of 'minimum core'.[56] The court further stressed that the minimum core obligation is determined generally by having regard to the needs of the most vulnerable group that is entitled to the protection of the right in question. It is in this context that the concept of minimum core obligations must be understood in international law. The court argued that it is not possible to determine the minimum threshold for South African purposes owing to the fact that, unlike the UNCESCR, the court does not have comparable information. The court mentioned that the UNCESCR developed the concept of 'minimum core' over many years of examining reports by reporting states. The court therefore concluded that the real question in terms of the South African Constitution is whether the measures taken by the state to realize social rights are reasonable. The court further indicated that it is not in any event necessary to decide whether it is appropriate for a court to determine in the first instance the minimum core content of a right.

The court then went further and interpreted the relevant limitation by considering reasonableness. First of all the court stated that it would not enquire whether other more desirable or favourable measures could have been adopted, or whether public money could have been better spent. The question would be whether the measures that have been adopted are reasonable. It is necessary to recognize that a wide range of possible measures could be adopted by the state to meet its obligations. Many of these would satisfy the requirement of reasonableness. Once it is shown that the measures do so, this requirement is met. The court stressed further that the policies and programmes must be reasonable both in their conception and their implementation.

The court stated further that:

Reasonableness must also be understood in the context of the Bill of Rights as a whole. A society must seek to ensure that the basic necessities of life are provided to all if it is to be a society based on human dignity, freedom and equality. To be reasonable, measures cannot leave out of account the degree and extent of the denial of the right they endeavour to realise. Those whose needs are the most urgent and whose ability to enjoy all rights therefore is most in peril, must not be ignored by the measures aimed at achieving realisation of the right. It may not be sufficient to meet the test of reasonableness to show that the measures are capable of achieving a statistical advance in the realisation of the right. Furthermore, the Constitution requires that everyone must be treated with care and concern. If the measures, though statistically successful, fail to respond to the needs of those most desperate, they may not pass the test.[57]

In a prior case, *Soobramoney* v. *Minister of Health (KwaZulu-Natal)*,[58] the Constitutional Court made no mention of reasonableness. In *Soobramoney*, the court held that the judiciary should be slow to interfere with rational decisions taken in good faith by the political organs and medical authorities whose responsibility it is to deal with such matters. Thus before the judgment in the *Grootboom* case, many assumed that socio-economic rights could be enforced, but that courts would be reluctant to interfere with the functions of the legislative and executive branches of government. The state thus has the discretion about when and how these rights should be realized. After the judgment in the *Grootboom* case, however, it appears that the court will not investigate the rationality and bona fides of the executive and the legislature, but will rather ask whether the socio-economic programme and the implementation thereof were reasonable.

The ICESCR phrase 'by all appropriate means, including particularly the adoption of legislative measures'[59] has been interpreted to mean that states have a degree of discretion in choosing the measures of implementation.[60] In principle a state may choose between legislative, administrative, judicial, social, educational or other methods to undertake the realization of the rights. The UNCESCR commented that:

The phrase 'by all appropriate means' must be given its full and natural meaning. While each state party must decide for itself which means are the most appropriate under the circumstances with respect to each of the rights, the 'appropriateness' of the means chosen will not always be self-evident. It is therefore desirable that State parties' reports should indicate not only the measures that have been taken but also the basis on which they are considered to be the most 'appropriate' under the circumstances.

However, the ultimate determination as to whether all appropriate measures have been taken remains one for the Committee to make.[61]

In some cases, however, the enactment of legislation might be essential, for example where the existence of a law contravening the provisions of the Covenant would oblige the state concerned to enact annulling legislation.[62] The attitude of the UNCESCR with regard to the enactment of legislation can be summarized as follows: 'in many instances legislation is highly desirable and in some cases may even be indispensable … '[63] Legislation must be accompanied by effective and accessible enforcement procedures.[64]

<u>Progressive realization</u> The UNCESCR summarizes the position of the 'progressive realisation' of socio-economic rights as follows: 'On the other hand, the phrase must be read in the light of the overall objective, indeed the *raison d'être*, of the Covenant which is to establish clear obligations for State parties in respect of the full realisation of the rights in question. It thus imposes an obligation to move as expeditiously and effectively as possible towards the goal.' The UNCESCR further mentions that 'any deliberately retrogressive measures … would require the most careful consideration and would need to be fully justified by reference to the totality of the rights provided for in the Covenant and in the context of the full use of the maximum of available resources'.[65] It then states that the ultimate objective of the Covenant is the 'full realisation'[66] of the rights. The fact that the 'full realisation' is subject to the condition of progressiveness is merely recognition of the fact that the full realization of all socio-economic rights will generally not be able to be achieved in a short period of time.

In the *Grootboom* case, the court drew on the UNCESCR's interpretation of the phrase 'progressive realisation'. The court stated that 'progressive realisation' implies that rights cannot be realized immediately, but that the goal of the Constitution is for the basic needs of all in our society to be effectively met; the requirement of progressive realization means that the state must take steps to achieve this goal.

<u>Within available resources</u> The court referred to the judgment in *Soobramoney*, which interpreted the meaning of the phrase 'available resources' as follows:

What is apparent from these provisions is that the obligations imposed on the state by sections 26 and 27 in regard to access to housing, health care, food, water and social security are dependent upon the resources available for such purposes, and that the corresponding rights themselves are limited by reason of the lack of resources. Given this lack of resources and the significant demands on them that have already been referred to, an unqualified obligation to meet these needs would not presently be capable of being fulfilled. This is the context within which section 27(3) must be construed.[67]

In the *Grootboom* case, the court further stressed that there is a balance between goal and means. The measures must be calculated to attain the goal expeditiously and effectively, but the availability of resources is an important factor in determining what is reasonable. Thus the availability of resources is only one of the factors that have to be considered when determining whether there was an infringement of a right. Following the reasoning of the *Soobramoney* case, the *Grootboom* court stated: 'The state has to manage its limited resources in order to address all these claims. There will be times when this requires it to adopt a holistic approach to the larger needs of society rather than to focus on the specific needs of particular individuals within society.'[68]

'Right to access to ... ' Sections 26(2) and 27(2) refer to the 'right to access to ... ' and not purely to the 'right to ... '[69] In the *Grootboom* case, the court reached the conclusion that the 'right to access to' can be interpreted more broadly than the 'right to':

> The right delineated in section 26(1) is a right of 'access to adequate housing' as distinct from the right to adequate housing encapsulated in the Covenant. This difference is significant. It recognises that housing entails more than bricks and mortar. It requires available land, appropriate services such as the provision of water and the removal of sewage and the financing of all of these, including the building of the house itself. For a person to have access to adequate housing all of these conditions need to be met: there must be land, there must be services, there must be a dwelling. Access to land for the purpose of housing is therefore included in the right of access to adequate housing in section 26. A right of access to adequate housing also suggests that it is not only the state who is responsible for the provision of houses, but that other agents within our society, including individuals themselves, must be enabled by legislative and other measures to provide housing. The state must create the conditions for access to adequate housing for people at all economic levels of our society. State policy dealing with housing must therefore take account of different economic levels in our society.[70]

Applying the court's opinion to social rights pertaining to the alleviation of poverty, it appears that 'access to' means more than a pure 'right to',[71] suggesting that the state will have to provide, by way of legislative and other measures, that everyone has access to those social rights.[72]

Recommendations to alleviate poverty contained in other recent international documents

As already indicated, one of the main policy priorities of the South African government is to address poverty-related problems. The United Nations Poverty Report recommends that countries develop a formal plan aimed at the eradication and alleviation of poverty, which must be comprehensive and contain much more than a few projects targeted at the poor.

Different state departments in South Africa currently run separate projects aimed at alleviating poverty, for example the Department of Labour's Social Plan, the Department of Social Development's 1998 Programme on Children and Youth at Risk, the 1996 Flagship Developmental Programme for Unemployed Women with Children under 5 Years, the National Restructuring and Development Programme and different public work programmes. We suggest, however, that, consistent with the UN Poverty Report recommendations, a national anti-poverty plan must be developed integrating all the above measures by setting viable targets, timetables, budgets and organizations. The success of such a plan is of course dependent on effective implementing and monitoring bodies.

The World Bank indicates that actions at the global level can further contribute to national action plans. The World Bank recommends the following key areas where international action may be of assistance to national anti-poverty plans:

- expanding market access in rich countries for developing countries' goods and services;
- reducing the risk of economic crises;
- encouraging the production of international public goods that benefit poor people;[73] and
- ensuring a voice for poor countries and poor people in global forums.[74]

The United Nations Poverty Report suggests that, in a world of increasing economic integration, the success of countries' poverty reduction programmes depends critically on their economic and financial policies. It is therefore important that such programmes aimed at the alleviation of poverty be linked to these international policies. It further suggests that debt relief be linked to poverty reduction. Because of external debt, poorer countries are inhibited in spending on social services.

Conclusion

Poverty law is, strictly speaking, not a separate branch of law in South Africa. Yet given that it is a broad area of law that regulates, permeates and directs the alleviation of poverty, there is much to be learned from the developments reflected in authoritative international documents and in international human rights instruments.

As indicated in this chapter, in South Africa, for various reasons, the most important international instrument is perhaps the ICESCR. First, it is significant that the wording of Sections 27(1)(c) and 27(2) of the South African Constitution largely parallels ICESCR provisions, even though the Constitutional Court in *Grootboom* emphasized certain distinctions.[75] Second, South Africa signed the Covenant in 1994 and ratification is apparently imminent. Legally speaking, South Africa has incurred an international obligation to refrain from acts that would defeat the object and purpose of the treaty and is supposed to review all domestic law and policy to ensure compliance with the obligations imposed by the treaty on the date of ratification.[76] Third, since its inception in 1985 the UNCESCR has in the course of its supervisory and monitoring role (as mandated by the UN Economic and Social Council) issued several General Comments, serving as an authoritative source of interpretation of the ICESCR. These comments are important for South African purposes, as they serve as guidelines for addressing poverty questions from a socio-economic rights perspective in general and a social security context in particular. It would also appear that, despite the criticism expressed in the *Grootboom* case regarding these comments, the essence of the jurisprudential developments in South Africa is largely in agreement with the process and purpose spelled out in the comments.

Several of the General Comments have either a direct or an indirect impact on the interpretation of the right to social security contained in Article 9 of the ICESCR and its role in addressing poverty issues, notably General Comments nos 1 (1989), 3 (1990), 4 (1991), 5 (1994) and 6 (1995), and must, for the reasons stated above, be viewed as important in interpreting both the material and procedural content and ambit of the fundamental right to access to social security.

General Comment no. 6, which also deals with the social security rights of older persons, defines social security with reference to 'all the risks involved in the loss of means of subsistence for reasons beyond a person's control'.[77] General Comment no. 1 requires state parties to undertake a comprehensive review and regular monitoring in order to determine to what extent a right such as the right to social security is enjoyed by all individuals, and to give special attention to specific groups or sub-groups that appear to be particularly vulnerable. On the basis thereof, clearly stated and carefully targeted policies (which also set priorities) have to be elaborated, involving a constructive domestic dialogue with non-governmental organizations. General Comment no. 3 stipulates the so-called obligations of conduct and obligations of result which the ICESCR imposes on a state party. A state party is expected to take all appropriate measures within a reasonably short time to ensure compliance with the rights enshrined in the Covenant. The principal obligation of result is to achieve progressively the full realization of the various rights, even though it might take some time. It is incumbent upon states bound by the ICESCR to satisfy, at the very least, a minimum essential level of, for example, the right to social security, bearing in mind factors and priorities such as whether a significant number of individuals are deprived of the right in question (i.e. the excluded and the marginalized) – even in times of severe resources constraints. In fact, the Committee has interpreted Article 11(1) of the ICESCR as requiring state parties to give 'due priority to those groups living in unfavourable conditions by giving them particular consideration'. It has also held that ' ... policies and legislation should correspondingly not be designed to benefit already advantaged groups at the expense of others'.[78]

Building on this international human-rights-friendly approach, it is possible to foresee the incremental and systematic development of international poverty law in a unique South African context.

Notes

1 Poverty and Inequality in South Africa Report (1998: 1).

2 Berghman (1997: 6) refers to the comment by certain European researchers that 'one's sense of belonging in society depends on all four systems'. Compare Commins (1993: 4), which continues as follows: 'Civic integration means being an equal citizen in a democratic system. Economic integration means having a job, having a valued economic function, being able to pay your way. Social integration means being able to avail oneself of the social services provided by the state. Interpersonal integration means having family and friends, neighbours and social networks to provide care and companionship and moral support when these are needed. All four systems are therefore, important ... In a way the four systems are complementary: when one or two are weak the others need to be strong. And the worst off are those for whom all systems have failed ... ' For a similar appreciation of the distinction between the (narrower) income-related poverty concept and the (wider) multi-dimensional social exclusion concept, see Rodgers (1994: 2–3, 8).

3 Berghman (1997: 6).

4 One can be poor in the traditional sense of the word, but not necessarily deprived (in the sense of being socially excluded). Conversely, some of those who are not poor can still be deprived in other than income terms, as is

evident from the European experience: see the remarks by Berghman (1997: 7) in respect of certain Netherlands data.

5 To the extent, of course, that reintegration is possible and appropriate. Among others, labour demand is one of the factors that would dictate meaningful reintegration.

6 Berghman (1997: 13–14). He remarks that evidence for some countries and regions (referring to the second half of the 1980s) indicates that the poverty incidence that would exist without interference from the social security system (before) is intensively reduced by the existing schemes (after). Even the least effective European country, Greece, was doing much better than the US system. As far as the reduction of the poverty gap is concerned, he refers to evidence that indicates that over the same period Belgium apparently managed to reduce the poverty gap by 95.9 per cent and Greece by 64.3 per cent, whereas the USA could reduce same only by 64.3 per cent.

7 See Berghman (1997: 7). 'Whereas traditionally a large part of the poor consisted of elderly persons, the gradual maturation of pension schemes has resulted in a relative decline in the numbers of elderly poor people. Although for some of them new problems arise with respect to dependency and the (financial) burden of intensive cure and care this yields, in general the newer cohorts of retired persons can certainly rely on adequate pension schemes' (ibid.: 15).

8 Ibid.: 12.

9 See the government-commissioned Poverty and Inequality in South Africa Report (hereafter referred to as PIR) (1998: 82).

10 Ibid.: 45. Ten million live in ultra-poor households earning less than R193.77 per month (UNDP 2000: 55).

11 PIR (1998: 2, 23–4): here it is noted that this places South Africa in the second-highest position after Brazil. In the meantime Guatemala has moved in, placing South Africa in the third position (UNDP 2000: 63).

12 For example, only 1 per cent of land has been redistributed through the land reform programme (ibid.: 59–60).

13 Section 4 of the Social Assistance Act 59 of 1992, as amended; GN R656 of 8 May 1998.

14 Reg. 1 of GN R882 of 26 June 1998.

15 In these areas, public provision covers those without sufficient means – such as the state old age social grant and public health services (in particular primary healthcare and public hospitals). Conceptually, in the South African context, this must be seen as part of the social assistance system.

16 Under the Medical Schemes Act 131 of 1998, medical schemes may, as a rule, no longer refuse membership or differentiate between members of a scheme on the basis of age or medical history. Certain core medical services have to be covered by these schemes.

17 The assets of these funds account for a whopping 73 per cent of GDP. There has been massive growth in membership of these funds: over the past thirty-five years the growth rate has been 7 per cent per annum (Van der Berg 1997: 481, 485, 489).

18 For two recent examples, see *Soobramoney* v. *Minister of Health (KwaZulu-Natal)* 1998 (1) SA 765 (CC) (in respect of the right to medical treatment) and *Jooste* v. *Score Supermarket Trading (Pty) Ltd* 1998 BCLR 1106 (CC) (where the court upheld the constitutional validity of the statutory provision that substitutes the liability of the compensation fund for the common-law liability of the employer in the event of a workplace injury or illness suffered by the employee).

19 In *Bacela* v. *MEC for Welfare (Eastern Cape Provincial Government)* 1998 (1) All SA 525 (E). The decision of the MEC to suspend payment of arrear pensions, payable in terms of the Social Assistance Act 59 of 1992, owing to budgetary constraints, was successfully challenged. See also *Ngxuza & others* v. *Secretary, Department of Welfare, Eastern Cape Provincial Government & another* 2000 BCLR 1322 (E); *Bushula & others* v. *Permanent Secretary, Department of Welfare, Eastern Cape Provincial Government & another* 2000 BCLR 728 (E); and *Rangani* v. *Superintendent-General, Department of Health and Welfare, Northern Province* 1999 (4) SA 385 (T).

20 *Ngxuza & others* v. *Secretary, Department of Welfare, Eastern Cape Provincial Government & another* 2000 BCLR 1322 (E), upheld by the Supreme Court of Appeal in *The Department of Welfare, Eastern Cape Provincial Government* v. *Ngxuza* 2001(4) SA 1184 (SCA).

21 The provisions of the important International Covenant on Economic, Social and Cultural Rights, adopted by the United Nations in 1966, are particularly relevant.

22 See, in particular, PIR, which highlights, among other things, the lack of a coherent strategy on the part of government to deal comprehensively and effectively with the plight of the poor.

23 For example, the recent introduction of the child support grant, at the expense of the long-existing state maintenance grant, is a clear indication of a commitment on the part of government to let more and larger families in the impoverished section of the community benefit from state social assistance measures.

24 See, for example, Section 1 of the Basic Conditions of Employment Act 75 of 1997 and the Employment Act 55 of 1998 respectively; *Smit* v. *Workmen's Compensation Commissioner* 1979 (1) SA 51 (A); *Niselow v Liberty Life Association of Africa Ltd* 1998 *ILJ* 752 (SCA); *Liberty Life Association of Africa Ltd* v. *Niselow* 1996 *ILJ* 673 (LAC); *SABC* v. *McKenzie* 1999 *ILJ* 585 (LAC); *MASA* v. *Minister of Health* 1997 *ILJ* 528 (LC); *Oosthuizen* v. *Mining & Engineering Supplies CC* 1999 *ILJ* 910 (LC).

25 See Schedule 4 of COIDA, as amended from time to time. For example, all employees, regardless of level of income, are now covered by COIDA (in contrast with the preceding legislation, which restricted applicability to employees who earned less than a maximum annual amount, fixed from time to time). A monetary ceiling on the amount of remuneration to be taken into account for purposes of calculating benefits is, however, still applicable.

26 So, for example, does the definition of 'employee' in Section 1 of the COIDA provide for the inclusion of the dependants of a deceased employee.

27 The statutory method providing for the coverage of dependants dif-

fers: in some cases the definition of 'employee' is widened so as to include dependants (see Section 1 of COIDA); in other cases a specific definition of 'dependant' is added to the legislation (Sections 30–32 of the UIA, and Section 1 of the Pension Funds Act 24 of 1956).

28 See, for example, para. (b) of the definition of 'dependant' in COIDA.

29 See *Langemaat* v. *Minister of Safety & Security* 1998 *ILJ* 20 (T). Recently, for purposes of the public traffic injury insurance scheme, the Constitutional Court found that the right of a widow to support if married in terms of Islamic law is worthy of public recognition and protection by the law: *Hafiza Ismail Amod (born Peer) & Commission for Gender Equality* v. *Multilateral Motor Vehicle Accidents Fund* 1998 (3) SA 1 (CC).

30 Traditionally, a distinction has been made between first- (civil and political), second- (socio-economic) and third-generation rights. The United Nations perpetuated this distinction between first-, second- and third-generation rights by introducing two separate covenants. The first covenant contains only first-generation rights and the second covenant contains second- and third-generation rights. Underlying the decision to draft two separate covenants was the assumption that second- and third-generation rights imply legal obligations and enforcement that differ substantially from first-generation rights. The same distinction is noticeable within the European regional system of human rights where a separate European Social Charter contains provisions for the realization of economic, social and cultural rights (Morphet 1992: 78; Liebenberg 1995: 360–61; De Vos 1997: 69; Scott 1999: 633).

31 Compare with India, where socio-economic rights are contained in the constitution as directive principles of state policy.

32 The following constitutional cases are examples where the South African Constitutional Court considered binding as well as non-binding international law when interpreting the Bill of Rights: *S* v. *Williams* 1995 (3) SA 632 (CC); *Ferreira v Levin NO* 1996 (1) SA 984 (CC); *S* v. *Rens* 1996 (1) SA 1218 (CC); *Coetzee* v. *Government of South Africa* 1995 (4) SA 631 (CC); *Bernstein* v. *Bester* 1996 (2) SA 751 (CC); *In re Gauteng School Education Bill 1995* 1996 (3) SA 165 (CC); *Grootboom*, para. 26. It is important to note that in the *Grootboom* case the court expressed concern about the difficulty of determining the core content of socio-economic rights.

33 *S* v. *Makwanyane and another* 1995 (3) SA 391 (CC), 1995 (6) BCLR 665 (CC) para. 35; *Grootboom*.

34 See *Prince* v. *The President of the Law Society, Cape of Good Hope* 1998 (8) BCLR 976 (C) 984–986, 988–989. In *Grootboom*, the court states as follows: 'The relevant international law can be a guide to interpretation but the weight to be attached to any particular principle or rule of international law will vary. However, where the relevant principle of international law binds South Africa, it may be directly applicable.'

35 Jenks (1960: 4–5). See also Valticos (1998: 394) (emphasis added).

36 *The Azanian Peoples Organization (AZAPO) and others* v.*The President of the Republic of South Africa* 1996 (4) SA 671 (CC); Dugard (2000: 62–4); Blake (1998: 670, 680–81).

37 Committee on the Rights of the Child, *Concluding Observations* 2000 CRC/C/15/Add.122 paras 11, 12, 15, 24, 29, 32.

38 The Preamble of the Constitution of the Republic of South Africa states that the Constitution as the supreme law of the Republic aims to heal the divisions of the past and establish a society based on democratic values and to improve the quality of life of all citizens and free the potential of each person.

39 Section 1 of the Constitution states that the Republic of South Africa is one sovereign democratic state founded on the values of human dignity, the achievement of equality and advancement of human rights and freedoms, non-racialism and non-sexism. Section 7(1) further states that the Bill of Rights is the cornerstone of democracy in South Africa. It enshrines the rights of all people in our country and affirms the democratic values of human dignity, equality and freedom.

40 Van Langendonck (1986: 2); Von Maydell (1998: 5, 7); Ben-Israel (1995: 146); *Grootboom* para. 23.

41 Sections 1 and 7(1) of the Constitution.

42 Section 10 of the Constitution reads as follows: 'Everyone has inherent dignity and the right to have their dignity respected and protected.'

43 Notably, the South African courts have consistently stated that there is close correlation between the right to equality and the protection of a person's dignity: *Hoffmann* v. *SA Airways* 2000 (21) *ILJ* 2357 (CC); *Walters* v. *Transitional Local Council of Port Elizabeth & another* 2001 BLLR 98 (LC).

44 Compare Van Langendonck (1986: 1).

45 International Labour Organization (1984: 115).

46 Justice Langa describes *ubuntu* in *S* v. *Makwanyane* 1995 (3) SA 391 (CC), 1995 (6) BCLR 665 (CC) para. 224 as follows: 'The concept is of some relevance to the values we need to uphold. It is a culture which places some emphasis on communality and on the interdependence of the members of a community. It recognises a person's status as a human being, entitled to unconditional respect, dignity, value and acceptance from the members of the community such person happens to be part of. It also entails the converse, however. The person has a corresponding duty to give the same respect, dignity, value and acceptance to each member of that community. More im-portantly, it regulates the exercise of rights by the emphasis it lays on sharing and co-responsibility and the mutual enjoyment of rights by all.'

47 Mokgoro (1997: 52).

48 Chapter 2, para. 24.

49 *Certification of the Constitution of the Republic of South Africa, 1996* 1996 (4) SA 744 (CC) paras 76–7. See also *Grootboom* para. 20.

50 Internal limitations are limitations contained within the fundamental right itself and are aimed to confine the scope and application of the specific fundamental right. External limitations refer to the general limitation clause in the Bill of Rights.

51 1995 (4) BCLR 401 (CC) 414.

52 Compare De Waal et al. (1999: 142).

53 This case raises the state's obligations under Section 26 of the Constitution, which gives everyone the right of access to adequate housing. Sections 26(2) and 27(2) have similar wording. Therefore, the judgment of the court will also be applicable to Section 27.

54 Sections 26(2) and 27(2) of the South African Constitution state that the state must realize the rights 'within its available resources', as opposed to the language of the Covenant, which states 'to the *maximum* of its available resources'.

55 General Comment no. 3 at 86 para. 10. Compare also Craven (1995: 141); Henckaerts (1996: 23); Robertson (1994: 702); Guideline 9, 'The Maastricht Guidelines'; Leckie (1998: 100); De Villiers (1997: 306).

56 *Grootboom* para. 30.

57 Ibid., para. 44.

58 1997 (12) BCLR 1696 (CC) para. 29.

59 See Article 2(1) of the ICESCR. Sections 26(2) and 27(2) of the South African Constitution stipulate that 'the state *must* take reasonable legislative and other measures'. It is suggested that the enactment of legislation is compulsory but that the state will still be able to take other measures if it can show that these measures are the most appropriate.

60 Principles 17 and 18, 'Limburg Principles'; Dankwa and Flinterman (1987: 139); Craven (1995: 115); Häusermann (1992: 54); Bruno and Zöckler (1995: 74); Leckie (1998: 106).

61 Craven (1995: 115); Sybesma-Knol (1995: 81). General Comment no 3 (1990) UN Doc E/1991/23 Annex III UNESCOR supp. at 84 para. 4.

62 Principles 17 and 18, 'Limburg Principles'; Dankwa and Flinterman (1987: 139); Craven (1995: 126).

63 General Comment no. 3 (1990), UN Doc. E/1991/23.

64 Principle 19, 'Limburg Principles'; Dankwa and Flinterman (1987: 139); Craven (1995: 126); Alston and Quinn (1987: 168).

65 General Comment no. 3 at 85 para. 9.

66 Sections 26(2) and 27(2) of the South African Constitution stipulate that the state must 'achieve the progressive realisation of each of these rights' and not the *full realization* of these rights.

67 *Soobramoney* v. *Minister of Health (KwaZulu-Natal)* 1997 12 BCLR 1696 (CC) para. 11. As quoted in *Grootboom* para. 46.

68 *Grootboom* para. 31 (emphasis added).

69 Majola remarks that there is still uncertainty as to what is meant by 'access to' and that the core content of this right must still be interpreted by the courts (Majola 1999: 6). Davis et al. (1997: 345) further remark that the distinction can be understood as an attempt to avoid an interpretation that this section creates an unqualified obligation on the state to guarantee free housing on demand for everyone. See also Du Plessis (1997: 186); Du Plessis (1996b: 13–14); Du Plessis (1996a: 293); Du Plessis and Gouws (1996: 35).

70 *Grootboom* para. 35.

71 This approach of the court places a heavier burden on the resources

of the state. It implies that the state will have to create effective policies to achieve the maximum output.

72 An example is to create the necessary infrastructure in rural areas for the elderly poor to enable them to collect their old age pensions.

73 By controlling infectious diseases, boosting agricultural yields and safeguarding the interests of poor people in the intellectual property rights regime (World Bank 2000/2001: 182–5).

74 By strengthening the capacity of poor countries to represent their interests and building global networks of poor people's organizations (ibid.: 185–8).

75 Article 9 and Article 2(1) respectively.

76 See the Vienna Convention on the Law of Treaties of 1969, Articles 18, 26 and 27; Liebenberg (1995: 371–2).

77 Para. 26.

76 General Comment no 4, para. 11.

References

Alston, P. (1995) 'Disability and the International Covenant on Economic, Social and Cultural Rights', in T. Degener and Y. Koster-Dreese (eds), *Human Rights and Disabled Persons: Essays and Relevant Human Right Instruments*, Dordrecht

Alston, P. and G. Quinn (1987) 'The nature and scope of state parties' obligations under the International Covenant on Economic, Social and Cultural Rights', *Human Rights Quarterly*

Andreassen, B., A. G. Smith and H. Stokke (1992) 'Compliance with economic and social human rights: realistic evaluations and monitoring in the light of immediate obligations', in A. Eide and B. Hagtvet, *Human Rights in Perspective: A Global Assessment*, Oxford

Arambulo, K. (1999) *Strengthening the Supervision on the International Covenant on Economic, Social and Cultural Rights: Theoretical and Procedural Aspects*, Antwerp

Ben-Israel, R. (1995) 'Social security in the year 2000: potentialities and problems', *Comparative Labour Law Journal*

Berghman, J. (1997) 'The resurgence of poverty and the struggle against exclusion: a new challenge for social security?', *International Social Security Review*, 50

Blake, R. C. (1998) 'The world's law in one country: The South African Constitutional Court's use of public international law', *South African Law Journal*

Bruno, S. and M. Zöckler, 'Social Protection by International Law: Law-Making by Universal Organisations (especially the United Nations)', in B. Von Maydell and A. Nussberger (eds), *Social Protection by Way of International Law*, Berlin

Castermans-Holleman, M. C. (1995) 'The protection of economic, social and cultural rights within the UN framework', *Netherlands International Law Review*

Commins, P. (1993) *Combating Exclusion in Ireland 1990–1994: A Midway Report*, Brussels: European Commission

Craven, M. C. R. (1995) *The International Covenant on Economic, Social and Cultural Rights: A Perspective on Its Development,* Oxford

Dankwa, E. V. O. and C. Flinterman (1987) 'Commentary by the rapporteurs on the nature and scope of states parties' obligations', *Human Rights Quarterly*

Dankwa, E. V. O., C. Flinterman and S. Leckie (1998) 'Commentary to the Maastricht guidelines on violations of the International Covenant on Economic, Social and Cultural Rights', *Human Rights Quarterly*

Davis, D., H. Cheadle and N. Haysom (1997) *Fundamental Rights in the Constitution – Commentary and Cases*, Kenwyn: Juta

De Villiers, B. (1997) 'The protection of human rights in developing countries', in R. Blanpain (ed.), *Law in Motion*, The Hague

De Vos, P. (1997) 'Pious wishes or directly enforceable human rights?: social and economic rights in South Africa's 1996 Constitution', *South African Journal of Human Rights*

De Waal, J., I. Currie and G. Erasmus (1999) *The Bill of Rights Handbook*, Kenwyn: Juta

Donnelly, J. (1989) *Universal Human Rights in Theory and Practice,* Ithaca, NJ

Dugard, J. (2000) *International Law: A South African Perspective,* Kenwyn: Juta

Du Plessis, L. M. (1996a) 'Evaluative reflections on the final text of South Africa's bill of rights', *Stellenbosch Law Review*

— (1996b) 'The bill of rights in the working draft of the new Constitution: an evaluation of aspects of a constitutional text *sui generis*', *Stellenbosch Law Review*

— (1997) 'Menseregte in die skadu's en skanse van die ivoortoring', in akademiese waardering van enkele fasette van menseregtebeskerming in Suid-Afrika se finale Grondwet)', *Stellenbosch Law Review*

Du Plessis, L. M. and A. Gouws (1996) 'The gender implications of the final constitution with particular reference to the bill of rights', *South African Public Law*

Feyter, K. (1995) 'De juridische gevolgen van de internationaal en nationale erkenning van economische, sociale en culturele rechten', *Mensenrechten*

Gomez, M. (1995) 'Social economic rights and human rights commissions', *Human Rights Quarterly*

Häusermann, J. (1992) 'The realization and implementation of economic, social and cultural rights', in R. Beddard and M. H. Dilys (eds), *Economic, Social and Cultural Rights: Progress and Achievement*, London

Henckaerts, J. (1996) 'Het internationaal verdrag inzake economische, sociale en culturele rechten: de kinderschoenen ontgroeid?', *Mensenrechten*

International Labour Organization (1984) *Into the Twenty-first Century: The Development of Social Security*, Geneva: ILO Publications

Jenks, C. W. (1960) *Human Rights and International Labour Standards*, London

Kartashkin, V. (1982) 'Economic, Social and Cultural Rights', in K. Vasak (ed.), *The International Dimensions of Human Rights*, vol. I, Paris

South African poverty law

Klabbers, J. (1996) *The Concept of Treaty in International Law*, The Hague

Leckie, S. (1998) 'Another step towards indivisibility: identifying the key features of the violations of economic, social and cultural rights', *Human Rights Quarterly*

Liebenberg, S. (1995) 'The International Covenant on Economic, Social and Cultural Rights and its implications for South Africa', *South African Journal of Human Rights*

Lund, F. (1993) 'State social benefits in South Africa', *International Social Security Review*

Majola, B. (1999) 'A response to Craig Scott: a South African perspective', *Economic and Social Rights Review*, 4 (1)

May, J., J. Govender and D. Budlender (1998) *Poverty and Inequality in South Africa*, Report prepared for the Office of the Executive Deputy President and the Inter-Ministerial Committee for Poverty and Inequality, Pretoria: Government Printers, 13 May

Mokgoro, Y. (1997) 'Ubuntu and the law in South Africa', in *Seminar Report: Constitution and the Law*, organized by the Faculty of Law, Potchefstroom University for Christian Higher Education, 31 October, Johannesburg: Konrad-Adenauer-Stiftung

Morphet, S. (1992) 'Economic, social and cultural rights: the development of governments' views, 1941–88', in R. Beddard and M. H. Dilys (ed.), *Economic, Social and Cultural Rights Progress and Achievement*, London

Olivier, M. (1998) 'Extending labour law and social security protection: the predicament of the atypically employed', *ILJ*, pp. 669–85

O'Regan, K. (1999) 'Introducing socio-economic rights', *Economic and Social Rights Review*, 4 (1)

Pronk, J. (1995) 'Communicating complaints about violations of social-economic human rights', in F. Coopmans and F. Van Hoof (eds), *The Right to Complain about Economic, Social and Cultural Rights*, Utrecht

Ramcharan, B. G. (1979) 'A critique of the Third World response to violations of human rights', in A. Cassese (ed.), *UN Law/Fundamental Rights: Two Topics in International Law*, Alphen aan den Rijn

Robertson, E. R. (1994) 'Measuring state compliance with the obligation to devote the "maximum available resources" to realizing economic, social and cultural rights', *Human Rights Quarterly*

Rodgers, G. (1994) *Overcoming Social Exclusion*, A contribution to the World Summit for Social Development, International Institute for Labour Studies, ILO

Scott, C. (1999) 'Reaching beyond (without abandoning) the category of economic, social and cultural rights', *Human Rights Quarterly*

Standing, G. et al. (1996) *Restructuring the Labour Market: The South African Challenge*, ILO country review

Steiner, H. J. and P. Alston (1996) *International Human Rights in Context*, Oxford

Sybesma-Knol, N. (1995) 'Het internationaal verdrag inzake economische, sociale en culturele rechten', *Mensenrechten*

UNDP (2000) *South Africa: Transformation for Human Development 2000*, Pretoria

Valticos, N. (1998) 'International labour standards and human rights: approaching the year 2000', *International Labour Review*

Van der Berg, S. (1997) 'South African social security under apartheid and beyond', *Development Southern Africa*

Van Langendonck, J. (1986) *Söciale Zekerheid Wat is dat Eigenlijk?*, Antwerp

Von Maydell, B. (1997) *Human Rights and Social Security*, XVth World Congress of Labour and Social Security, 22–26 September, Buenos Aires: Peeters

Ziskind, D. (1982) 'Labor laws in the vortex of human rights protection', *Comparative Labor Law*

South African court cases

The Azanian Peoples Organization (AZAPO) and Others v. *The President of the Republic of South Africa* 1996 (4) SA 671 (CC)

Bacela v. *MEC for Welfare (Eastern Cape Provincial Government)* 1998 (1) All SA 525 (E)

Bernstein v. *Bester* 1996 (2) SA 751 (CC)

Bushula & others v. *Permanent Secretary, Department of Welfare, Eastern Cape Provincial Government & another* 2000 BCLR 728 (E)

Certification of the Constitution of the Republic of South Africa, 1996 1996 (4) SA 744 (CC)

Coetzee v Government of South Africa 1995 (4) SA 631 (CC)

Ferreira v. *Levin NO* 1996 (1) SA 984 (CC)

The Government of the Republic of South Africa and others v. *Grootboom and Others* 2000 (11) BCLR 1169 (CC)

Hafiza Ismail Amod (born Peer) & Commission for Gender Equality v. *Multilateral Motor Vehicle Accidents Fund* (Case no 444/98 of 29 September 1999) (CC)

Hoffmann v. *SA Airways* 2000 (21) *ILJ* 2357 (CC)

In re Gauteng School Education Bill 1995 1996 (3) SA 165 (CC)

Jooste v. *Score Supermarket Trading (Pty) Ltd* 1998 BCLR 1106 (CC)

Langemaat v. *Minister of Safety & Security* 1998 *ILJ* 20 (T)

Liberty Life Association of Africa Ltd v. *Niselow* 1996 *ILJ* 673 (LAC)

MASA v. *Minister of Health* 1997 *ILJ* 528 (LC)

Ngxuza & others v. *Secretary, Department of Welfare, Eastern Cape Provincial Government & another* 2000 BCLR 1322 (E)

Niselow v. *Liberty Life Associaton of Africa Ltd* 1998 *ILJ* 752 (SCA)

Oosthuizen v. *Mining & Engineering Supplies CC* 1999 *ILJ* 910 (LC)

Prince v. *The President of the Law Society, Cape of Good Hope* 1998 (8) BCLR 976 (C)

Rangani v. *Superintendent-General, Department of Health and Welfare, Northern Province* 1999 (4) SA 385 (T)

S v. *Makwanyane and another* 1995 (3) SA 391 (CC), 1995 (6) BCLR 665 (CC)

S v. *Rens* 1996 (1) SA 1218 (CC)

S v. *Williams* 1995 (3) SA 632 (CC)

SABC v. *McKenzie* 1999 *ILJ* 585 (LAC)

Smit v. *Workmen's Compensation Commissioner* 1979 (1) SA 51 (A)

Soobramoney v. *Minister of Health (KwaZulu-Natal)* 1995 3 SA 391 (CC), 1995 6 BCLR 665 (CC)

Walters v. *Transitional Local Council of Port Elizabeth & another* 2001 BCLR 98 (LC)

South African legislation

Basic Conditions of Employment Act 75 of 1997

Compensation for Occupational Injuries and Diseases Act 130 of 1993

The Constitution of the Republic of South Africa 108 of 1996

Demobilization Act 99 of 1996

Employment Act 55 of 1998

Medical Schemes Act 131 of 1998

Pension Funds Act 24 of 1956

Promotion of National Unity and Reconciliation Act 34 of 1995

Social Assistance Act 59 of 1992, as amended; GN R656 of 8 May 1998

Special Pensions Act 69 of 1996

Unemployment Insurance Act 30 of 1966

White Paper on Social Welfare General Notice 1108 in *Government Gazette* 18166 of 8 August 1997

International documents

The Maastricht Guidelines on Violations of the International Covenant on Economic, Social and Cultural Rights

Committee on Economic, Social and Cultural Rights, *General Comments* no. 1, 1989, UN Doc. E/1989/22

Committee on Economic, Social and Cultural Rights, *General Comments* no. 2, 1990, UN Doc. E/1990/23

Committee on Economic, Social and Cultural Rights, *General Comments* no. 3, 1990, UN Doc. E/1991/23

Committee on Economic, Social and Cultural Rights, *General Comments* no. 4, 1991, UN Doc. E/1991/23

International Covenant on Civil and Political Rights adopted by the General Assembly Resolution 2200A (XXI) of 16 December 1966 999 (entered into force on 23 March 1976)

International Covenant on Economic, Social and Cultural Rights adopted by the General Council Resolution 2200 (XXI) of 16 December 1966 993 (entered into force on 3 January 1976)

Limburg Principles on the Implementation on the International Covenant on Economic Social and Cultural Rights

United Nations Convention on the Rights of the Child adopted by the General
Assembly Resolution 44/25 of 20 November 1989 (entered into force on 2
September 1990)

United Nations Development Programme (2000) *Poverty Report – Overcoming
Human Poverty*, New York: UNDP

Vienna Declaration and Programme of Action adopted by the World Conference on Human Rights on 25 June 1993, UN-Doc.a/CONF.157/23 of 12 July
1993

World Bank (2000/2001) *World Development Report – Attacking Poverty*, Oxford:
Oxford University Press

7 | Child labour in India and the international human rights discourse[1]

DEBI S. SAINI

This chapter addresses the connections between poverty, illiteracy and child labour through the lens of international human rights discourse, particularly assessing the debate between the developed countries and the lesser developed countries (LDCs) over incorporating a 'social clause' articulating waged worker rights into international trade agreements.

Poverty, often viewed simply as lack of income, is now being approached through the broader perspective of lack of opportunities, albeit usually based on income, asset and power deficits. The United Nations *Human Development Report* (HDR) of 1997 conceptualized human poverty as 'the denial of opportunities and choices most basic to human development – to lead a long, healthy, creative life, to enjoy a decent standard of living, freedom, dignity, self-esteem and respect for others'.

One of the most basic opportunities necessary for poverty alleviation is the availability of education, and especially primary education. It is often impossible, or certainly more difficult, for illiterate and semi-literate people to understand, demand and secure their civil, political, social, economic, cultural and human rights, which are essential for human development in general and for increasing one's power to fight exploitation in particular. Many discourses regarding the welfare state and social justice acknowledge the importance of enhancing the competencies of the poor both as individuals and as collectives so as to enable them to access social protection against poverty, destitution, indignity, exploitation and denial of human rights.

The problem of child labour is intimately connected with illiteracy, in that children who are required or expected to perform substantial work often do not have access to or resources for education. Thus, any reform agenda relating to child labour abolition must be grounded in the concept of poverty as lack of opportunity.

Advocates of social welfare and justice, who have traditionally relied on governmental programmes to address poverty, increasingly find themselves in a state of considerable despair in the contemporary globalizing world. Mainstream economists posit that economic growth, resulting from a 'free' globalized market, will reduce poverty. Thus the alleviation of poverty should be addressed only through the 'trickle-down effect' of market-led gross domestic product (GDP) growth. But market growth does not always facilitate poverty reduction; indeed, it often increases inequality (Bardhan 2001).[2]

Economic discourse, parading as scientific rationality, may be oblivious to prevailing social and cultural infirmities, the rent-seeking potential of certain actors in the economic system, restrictions on the free flow of information, and the susceptibilities of the poor and powerless in the political power dynamics. These issues form the context in which the market mechanism works, and therefore will influence its outcomes. Market mechanisms always suffer from imperfections; they do not address people not having economic power. Thus, governments and independent rights groups cannot assume that the market will alleviate poverty and relinquish their responsibility for addressing basic human values, human rights and social protection of the poor.

Since the Second World War, various international institutions have enacted conventions that address human rights and dignity and provide guidance for state actions and programmes that might enrich people's lives. These international prescriptions have been accepted and endorsed in various degrees by many countries, often resulting in legal changes on a state or local level.

There are tensions, however, about the mechanisms through which these standards should be implemented. Perhaps one of the most controversial issues in this regard is the attachment of a 'social clause' to world trade agreements by the World Trade Organization (WTO). In the era of globalization, many social justice advocates, particularly in the developed countries, fear a steep diminution in labour standards. Specifically, they fear that workers' rights to free speech and association will be censured and that employers may use more child and forced labour in an attempt to minimize labour costs. Yet many LDCs and, indeed, human rights advocates in the LDCs view some of the standards advocated by developed countries as onerous and particularly resist the adoption of sanctions for human rights employment violations attached to trade agreements with the developed world. They argue that the concept of a social clause is inimical to the political sovereignty of nations and especially to the economic sustenance of LDCs in the competitive world business environment. Thus, while the social clause is being viewed by the developed world as an important instrument with which to fight world poverty and violations of human rights, many in the LDCs question the genuineness of the developed world's intentions.

This chapter does not deal with all aspects of the debated social clause, but rather examines the structural framework of this body of law and its potential to promote human rights and poverty alleviation in the sphere of child labour eradication. In the next section, I provide a critique of the traditionally perceived causes of child labour and illiteracy in India. The third section documents the extent of child labour and lack of school attendance in India. In the fourth, I articulate the evolution of India's statutory and constitutional legal response to child labour and illiteracy, recognizing the state failure in implementing the constitutional proclamations and other legal rights. In the fifth and sixth sections, I describe widely ratified International Labour Organization (ILO) and United Nations (UN) poverty directives that address child labour and illiteracy. It is argued that while these directives, at least in India, have put considerable pressure on the government, they have not resulted in the desired changes envisaged by the directives. The final section then importantly examines the contents of and motivation behind the social clause as part of trade agreements and assesses the contribution of the emerging international poverty law (IPL) to the issue of child labour and universal primary education.

Child labour, illiteracy and poverty in India: linkage and causes

Traditionally, children worldwide learned occupational skills in a family environment with the view that they would use those skills as 'positive assets in adulthood' (Schildkrout 1980: 480); for example, they would work with their parents as farm labourers in family-owned fields. This was believed to be a normal way of living one's childhood. But both the production process and the family structure have changed substantially since the Industrial Revolution, resulting in urbanization and more mechanized production. These developments have dissociated children's work from the family context. As primary education became widespread, particularly in the developed countries, child labour was largely minimized or eliminated. In a large part of the developing world, however, effective attempts to abolish child labour were not made for various reasons.

India falls into the category of those countries where little or no progress has been made in the abolition of child labour. Previously, within the caste system in India, the practice of child labour for poor children in a family context was not viewed as demeaning enough to deprive the children of their childhood. The illiteracy of children, however, regardless of caste (although the incidence of child labour and illiteracy is much higher among lower castes), is now viewed as a more serious problem than before (Gupta and Voll 1999). The lack of access to education ensures the perpetuation of such children's poverty owing to the failure to develop competencies that are necessary to exercise one's economic, social and cultural rights.

Especially, primary education is the sine qua non of social development; it enables the powerless to appreciate the framework of empowerment and the anti-poverty policies of the state. It is also considered a basic foundation of good citizenship, 'the primary vehicle for imparting cultural values in children, and making them adjust to the fast-changing environment around them' (Saini 2001). Therefore, some scholars have argued for expanding the definition of child labour to include even children's work performed in family contexts, when such work deprives the children of education. Some have gone to the extent of suggesting that all out-of-school children should be treated as child labourers for purposes of planning and resource allocation (Burra 2001: 481).

Child labour is dangerous not just from the viewpoint of perpetuating poverty. Industrial work particularly can be traumatic to children's human development and cause their physical and moral degradation. It may result in 'decreasing self-esteem among children and their descent to a sub-human level' (Sinha 1994: 2694). Child labour takes away the beauty of living one's childhood. Even if lived in poverty, childhood can be perhaps the most wonderful phase of one's life. Its psychological importance lies in its ability to evoke nostalgic reminiscence during adulthood (Saini 1998). The loss of childhood due to child labour, I believe, is as important as the impoverishing impact on the economic, social and moral aspects of child labourers. Thus, child labour, especially during the early years, may prove devastating to the tender feelings of childhood, lowering the self-esteem of the child and eventually adversely affecting his or her developmental potential.

Why there are child labourers in India is a controversial issue. Some posit that poor parents subject their wards to child labour so that they can be the main or supplemental contributors to family income. Following this line of thinking, most analysts – including government officials – attribute this practice to the high incidence of poverty in the country (Government of India 2000: 169). Thus, child labour is seen as a natural reality associated with poverty, which has come to be known as 'the harsh reality theory' of child labour.

The most tangible impact of child labour, whatever its causes, is the denial of education and the possibility of a dignified career to the child. Likewise, the causes of this issue are not free from debate. The choice of whether to attend school is often popularly believed to be that of the parents; the children, rarely asked or allowed to participate, simply acquiesce in decisions that keep them illiterate. But employers also have a vested interest in the perpetuation of child labour owing to cost advantages resulting from children's reduced wage. Often scholars and journalists

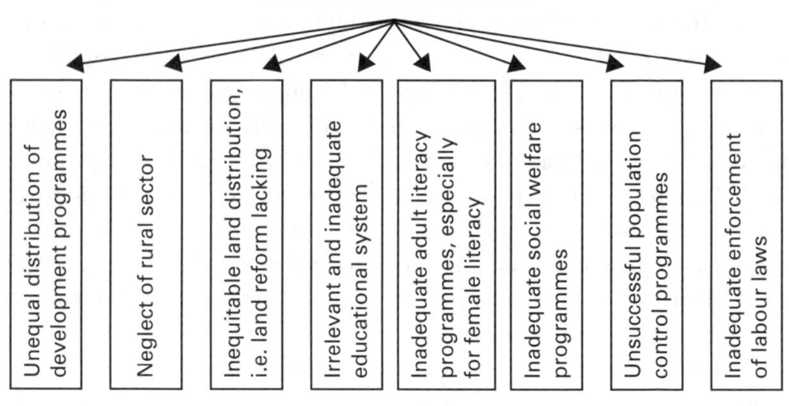

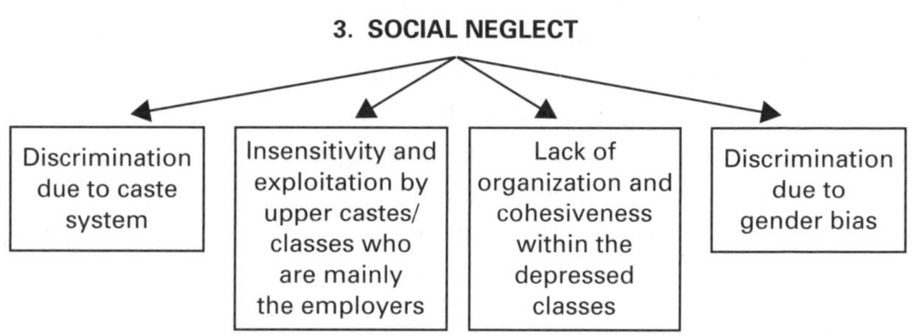

4. PARENTAL APATHY

Mind-set that children must contribute to family income

FIGURE 7.1 Hierarchy of causes of child labour
Source: Gupta and Voll (1999)

uncritically accept as necessary the existence of this linkage between child labour and poverty. They also opine that economic growth in a nation will trickle down, resulting in a more equitable distribution of the pie through greater employment opportunities or skill enhancement, thereby increasing the economic status of the parents. They argue that parents will thus desire a better quality of life for their children and place greater value on education for their children. Based on this analysis, the government finds it much easier to blame the 'poverty syndrome' as the cause of high illiteracy rates, and, in effect, eschew any ability to significantly alter this situation.

Recent writings have, however, questioned the assumption that poverty is the sole or even the main cause of child labour and school drop-outs. As shown in Figure 7.1, Gupta and Voll (1999) identify four sets of causes that perpetuate the problem in India. Their hierarchical order puts governmental neglect as the main cause of the problem. This is followed by a related one, i.e. lack of political will. Social neglect and parental apathy towards education and belief that children should work are the third and fourth in order of importance. They also pertinently identify the exploitative caste-surcharged Indian social order as being responsible for the lack of sufficient awareness of the importance of education among low-caste parents. Furthermore, bias against and apathy towards girls' education is rampant among the urban poor and both the rural rich and poor. This conditioning is strengthened by the absence of pro-active governmental initiatives; state agencies lack the political will to deal with the issue with a sense of urgency. A host of factors, including a bureaucratic style of government, insufficient allocation of resources for primary education and general neglect of the powerless rural sector, among others, reduce the efficacy of the government's basic education programme. Inefficiency and corruption in labour law enforcement are also known to be rampant in India (Saini 1999, 1995b). And trade unions do not have child labour abolition on their priority agenda for legal action (Ramaswamy 1999).

A significant study was conducted by a Public Report on Basic Education (PROBE) team of the Centre for Development Economics (a part of the Delhi School of Economics, University of Delhi) in late 1996 (Dreze 1998). This is perhaps one of the few major empirical studies exploring the causal roots of child labour and out-of-school children in India. The PROBE team surveyed 188 randomly selected villages in Bihar, Madhya Pradesh, Rajasthan and Uttar Pradesh – the four Indian states that account for over half of India's out-of-school children. They researched data in all school facilities and interviewed 1,221 households in the villages in this regard. The study's findings explode several myths about child labour and poverty in India, with important implications for implementing a compulsory and effective primary education agenda. Its findings are consistent with and validate the causes discussed in the above paragraph.

First, the study found that despite the claim of the government, elementary education is not free; indeed, the cost is not even negligible. The average annual cost of elementary education is Rs 300 per child (which includes the cost of books, slates, clothes, fees, etc.). This is a large amount of money for a poor north Indian family. Second, the survey explodes the myth that Indian (read poor) parents have little interest in children's education. Rather, it found that an overwhelming majority of parents, including those from the lower castes, highly value education. Ninety-eight per cent of the respondents said they would like their children to receive at least eight years of school education; and 63 per cent that they would even like their daughters to receive a similar level of education. This study significantly undermines the bureaucracy's argument about lack of parental concern and motivation as the key obstacle to the success of any universal programme of elementary education. Third, the study debunks the belief that economic dependence on child labour is the key reason for poor families' inability to send their children to school. Out-of-school children were found performing only two hours of extra work per day compared with the school-going children.

The PROBE study recognizes that sending a child to school requires major parental effort, including overseeing the child's sustained attendance and progress in school. PROBE found, however, that what discourages parents from taking on this endeavour is the poor quality of education that their children would receive. The study found that little real learning occurred in the badly organized school systems, which lacked adequate rooms and furniture, a sufficient number of teachers, an appropriate school curriculum and teaching methods, and any atmosphere of seriousness in imparting education. The study discovered that a number of students were not able to read and write even after remaining in school for several years.

The findings of the PROBE study impart important lessons for policy-makers. While not denying the linkage between child labour and poverty, the study points to a reverse chronology of linkages as also articulated by Gupta and Voll (1999), showing that poverty is the result and not the cause of an unsuccessful universal primary education programme. The official chronology, as is well known, claims that child labour is perpetuated mainly by poverty. We need additional such studies, perhaps involving greater sociological rigour than those just based on opinions and perceptions, to unravel the complex causes of child labour and illiteracy more compre-hensively and convincingly. But the current research certainly underscores a lack of seriousness on the part of the Indian government in designing and executing an appropriate primary education programme that could be put into effect in the Indian socio-politico-economic milieu. The PROBE study will make it more difficult for government officials to plead their helplessness in dealing with child illiteracy owing to the lack of parental motivation. Just as Gupta and Voll (1999) find governmental neglect and the lack of political will to be the main causes of child labour and lack of school attendance, the PROBE study finds the determinant cause to be the failed elementary education agenda, with poverty resulting therefrom.

Thus the state needs to take effective steps to increase children's propensity for school attendance by making the primary education system more attractive and purposive, reducing its costs, providing a more comprehensive midday meal system, and making essential educational items available to poor children free of charge. Most importantly, it must improve the syllabuses, pedagogy and quality of education. It appears that it is not just employers who have a vested interest in children's illiteracy and poverty, but also an indifferent state with its covert bureaucratic apathy towards the grave issue of child labour (see Burra 2001 for similar observations). Thus, a central issue in child labour abolition in India is compelling the state to effectively discharge its obligation of imparting compulsory primary education.

The magnitude of the problem

India has the second-highest national population in the world – according to the 2001 census, 1,027 million. The literacy rate among the population aged seven years and above stands at 65.38 per cent. The corresponding figures for males and females are 75.85 and 54.16 per cent respectively. This slow progress in improving literacy is despite the constitutional proclamation in 1950 that primary education would be compulsory for all by 1960. The Indian population at the time of the 1991 census[3] was 846 million, of which 297 million were children in the 0–14 age group and 203 million were in the age group 5–14. Scholars divide the child population into three sub-sets: those attending school, those employed on a full-time basis, and those who participate in household activities without being in economic employment. The latter category of children is very large; it is also referred to as 'nowhere children' (Chaudhri 1997a: 793), children who are neither in paid employment nor in school. The official statistics include only the second-category children as child labourers. The 1991 census data reported that 112 million children were enrolled in the formal school system and about 7 million were in non-formal education. Non-formal education includes those studying at home on their own or in non-recognized organizations. The national literacy rate at the time of the 1991 census for the population aged seven years and above was estimated to be 52.21 per cent. The country today has more than 300 million illiterates. Approximately 83 million children in the age group 5–14 (45 per cent) do not attend school. This age group also has a very high drop-out rate – 54 per cent, of which 59 per cent are girls. Since the country's population has risen past the 1 billion mark, according to the 2001 census, all these figures must have gone up. Unlike developing countries such as China, primary education has not been a priority on the agenda of the Indian state. India has been spending a very low portion of its gross national product (GNP) on children's education for the last fifty years, which is a mere 0.8–1 per cent (*Economic Times* 2001: 2). The government's education agenda has set a goal of 6 per cent of GDP to be spent on education (at all levels), but actual expenditure is far below this dream.

According to estimates for the year 1999/2000, 26.10 per cent of Indian people live below the poverty line.[4] The percentage living in rural areas is higher, at 27.09 per cent, while the figure in urban areas is 23.62 per cent. In terms of total numbers, 260.2 million people in the country live below the poverty line (*Times of India* 2001: 1). Using a different measure of poverty, Gupta and Voll (1999: 87) estimate that 'about 40 percent of the [Indian] people live below the poverty line'. They argue that the poverty line in India was defined in 1995 at Rs 11,000 per annum (equivalent to US$300), which was based on certain minimum calorific human consumption needs.

The 1991 census child labour data were available only in 1997 after being compiled by the Registrar General of Census Operations (Government of India 1997) over a period of six years. The data show that, out of the total workforce of 314 million in the country in 1991, 11.28 million were children. The data also indicate that the state with the highest child labour popula-tion is Andhra Pradesh (AP), having 1.66 million working children. Other major states employing child labour are Madhya Pradesh, Maharashtra and Uttar Pradesh (UP). These states have child labour populations of more than 1 million each. The 1991 census data also reveal that 90 per cent of the child labour in the country is employed in agriculture and allied employments such as cultivation, ancillary agricultural labour, livestock, forestry and fisheries. Comparative child labour data from the 1971, 1981 and 1991 censuses shows that, although there is a decline in child labour in nearly all states and union territories since the 1981 census, there is a significant rise in its incidence in the state of West Bengal, with the figure increasing from 0.6 million in 1981 to 1.18 million in 1991 (Government of India 2000). The second round of the National Sample Survey (NSS) data had projected the country's child labour population for the year 1990 and 2000 as 18.17 and 20.25 million respectively (Mehta 1991; Saini 1995a). Economists believe that census data generally underestimate (Mehta 1991: 135; Patel 1991). The Indian Ministry of Labour has estimated that there are 17 million child labourers in the country, of which 2 million work in hazardous occupations (Ramachandran 2000).

The estimates above do not include child labourers employed in home-

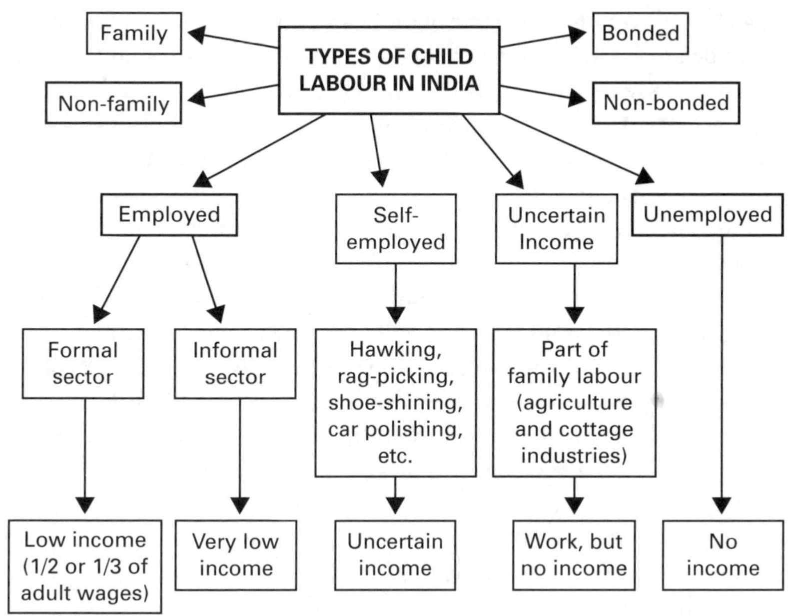

FIGURE 7.2 Types of child labour in India
Source: Gupta and Voll (1999)

based work. Also, several scholars believe that the estimates grossly under-estimate the real incidence of child labour. Some non-governmental studies estimate the number of working children in India as somewhere between 40 and 100 million (Ashraf 1999: 222; Pankaj 1995: 2980; Sahoo 1990: 2529).[5] A study by Gupta and Mitra (1997: 847) reveals that 34 per cent of the children in their sample were working either at home or outside the home. They argue that 'based on the poverty criterion, this percentage could be as high as 65 per cent'.

Some well-known industries that employ a large number of child labourers include matches, fireworks and explosives in Sivakasi (Tamil Nadu), glass and bangles in Ferozabad (UP), bidi in Nizamabad (AP) and North Arcot District of Tamil Nadu, carpets in Bhadoi, Varanasi and Mirzapur (UP), carpet weaving in Jammu and Kashmir, lock-making in Aligarh (UP), gem polishing in Jaipur (Rajashthan), slate mines in Markkapur (AP), leather units in Agra and Kanpur (UP), diamonds in Surat City (Gujarat), and tea gardens in Darjeeling (West Bengal). The key motive of employers in employing child labour is to minimize costs through lower wages and thus maximize profits. In certain industries (for example, carpet weaving) the 'nimble finger' argument is articulated as an additional factor.

As Figure 7.2 indicates, some of those who work outside family units are in bonded or forced conditions. A large number of Indian child labourers work in family settings, however, and have been described as 'nowhere children'. While often not visibly employed, they constitute the largest number of child labourers, working mostly on family farms.

Similar to the gender discrepancy in educational expectations noted earlier, there is a gender bias in Indian child labour. A large majority of rural girls work in the agricultural sector. Also, according to the 1991 census, of the 109 million male children, 56.6 per cent were in schools, whereas of the 101 million female children, 44.2 per cent were in schools. The country needs a substantial number of schools to accommodate the 'nowhere children' and the child labourers, who should be freed from work and required to attend school. If we continue at the current pace of development of the coverage and level of basic education, India is going to face serious problems in the near future. Some economists estimate that by 2010 India will have the dubious distinction of having the largest aggregate number of illiterate workers across castes and classes; and that the Indian workforce will not be competent to handle the demands of technology (Chaudhri 1997a: 807). It is necessary for our culture and our government to focus on the question of compulsory primary education and the role of child labour (Saini 1998). No doubt the pressure for child labour abolition coming from various quarters will contribute to the realization of the wider goal.

The national policy framework of child labour abolition in the pre-internationalization era

The history of the child labour abolition agenda in India is replete with instances of absence of political will, bureaucratic inertia and indifference, and purely symbolic legal measures.

One of the earliest Indian laws relating to child labour was the Children (Pledging of Labour) Act, 1933, which prohibited parents and guardians from pledging the services of children. Such practices were being followed mostly in bidi industries in southern India and Karnataka (Saini 1995a). This legislation was followed by enactment of the Employment of Children Act, 1938 (ECA). The ECA had a restricted scope in that it prohibited only the employment of children below fourteen years of age in occupations such as the transport of passengers by rail and handling goods within the limits of any port. The act was found not to be responding to all problems of child labour, and the need was felt for a law that permitted the employment of children subject to certain safeguards in terms of working conditions and provisions related to prohibition in certain areas of work. This led to its replacement in 1986 with the Child Labour (Prohibition and Regulation) Act (CLPRA).

Box 7.1 chronologically delineates the evolution of Indian child labour policy. The constitution of India, which came into force on 26 January 1950, 'commands law for production of policies and programmes of action for empowering the poorer and disempowered sections of society' (Saini 2001). In Chapters III and IV,[6] it contains several provisions that have implications for the prohibition and regulation of child labour, and provide for, among other things, compulsory primary education (initially a non-enforceable provision). The constitutional philosophy and provisions related to the protection of children, at least technically, reflect the important position that children's rights enjoy in India. These can be seen as symbolic of a systematic attempt to carve out certain concrete goals to pursue regarding the development of children.

The constitution enunciates three specific fundamental rights of children in Chapter III. Article 24 prohibits the employment of children under fourteen years of age in factories, mines and hazardous occupations; Article 23 prohibits all forms of *begar* (working under duress without pay) and bonded labour, whether for children or adults; and Article 15(3) empowers the state to make laws providing special protection to women and children.

Chapter IV of the constitution contains general guidelines for the state in administering social justice to Indian citizens and articulates non-enforceable rights for poorer, powerless and vulnerable sections of society. But the Supreme Court has held that these directives are nevertheless fundamental to the governance system. The rights envisaged in this chapter include the right to work, maternity relief, social security and a living wage. This chapter also provides that the state shall ensure that the 'tender age of children is not abused' (Article 39[e]) and that children should be given opportunities and facilities to develop in a healthy manner and in conditions of freedom and dignity, and that childhood and youth should be protected against exploitation and moral and material abandonment (Article 39[f]). Perhaps the most significant constitutional provision (though only through a directive principle) that might restrict the practice of child labour is Article 45, which provides that '[t]he state shall endeavour to provide *within a period of 10 years* (from the commencement of the Constitution [i.e. 26 January 1950]) *free and compulsory education* for *all children* until they complete the age of *fourteen years*' (emphasis added). Ironically, the Indian state has not yet enforced this article; even after fifty years, there is no national provision for compulsory primary and basic education. The failure to put into effect this constitutional directive signifies the state's indifference to the

Box 7.1 Evolution of India's child labour policy

1. Enactment of Children (Pledging of Labour) Act, 1933	Feb. 1933	Pledging of labour of children prohibited and penalty for parents/ guardians pledging child labour prescribed.
2. Enactment of Employment of Children Act, 1938	1938	Employment of children below fourteen years prohibited in certain occupations.
3. Adoption and Enactment of Constitution of India Act by the Constituent Assembly	1949	Prohibition of employment of children below fourteen years of age in factories, mines and hazardous employments in terms of a fundamental right; Directive Principles laid down against the abuse of the 'tender age of children' until fourteen years of age; and free and compulsory education of children up to fourteen years within ten years.
4. Ratification of No. 5 Minimum Age (Industry) Convention, 1919, of ILO	Sept. 1955	Employment of children under fourteen years of age in any public or private industrial undertaking prohibited.
5. Report of the National Labour Commission	1969	Recommended combination of work with education and flexible employment hours that should not inhibit education.
6. Report of Gurupadswamy Committee, 1979	1979	Recommended setting up of Child Labour Advisory Boards; fixation of minimum age of entry to any establishment; strengthening of enforcement machinery.
7. Establishment of the Central Child Labour Advisory Board with Labour Minister as chairman	Mar. 1981	To review implementation of existing laws; to suggest legislative and welfare measures for working children; to review progress of welfare measures.
8. Enactment of Child Labour (Prohibition and Regulation) Act, 1986	Dec. 1986	Employment of children below fourteen years of age prohibited in specified occupations and processes; regulation of working conditions

		of children in non-prohibited employments provided for; penalties for violation of the law provided for; and uniformity in definition of 'child' in related laws provided for.
9. Adoption of the National Child Labour Policy, 1987	Aug. 1987	Provided for a legislative action plan; focusing of general development programmes for the benefit of working children; and formulation of project-based action plan in areas of high concentration of child labour.
10. Report of the task force on child labour set up under the chairmanship of Dr L. M. Singhvi.	Dec. 1989	Recommended amendments to child labour laws and national policy on child labour.
11. Report of the National Commission on Rural Labour	Jul. 1991	Recommended enactment of compulsory primary education acts by the state; creation of non-formal education centres; enhancement of outlays for elementary education; guaranteed waged employment for parents of working children; universal prohibition of child labour.
12. Prime minister's declaration	15 Aug. 1994	Elimination of child labour in hazardous occupations by the year 2000; estimated 2 million as the number of child labourers in health-hazardous industries.
13. Establishment of the National Authority for the Elimination of Child Labour under the chairmanship of the Union Labour Minister	1 Oct. 1994	1. To lay down the policies and programmes for the elimination of child labour, particularly in hazardous employments. 2. To maintain the progress of the implementation of programmes for the elimination of child labour. 3. To coordinate the implementation of the child labour elimination projects of various ministries of the government of India. 4. To originate plan of action for the convergence of services and schemes of the central and state governments to be implemented at district level.

Sources: Government of India (2000); Voll (1999)

problems of child labour and universal primary education. One of the key reasons for this failure in implementation may be 'the presence of acutely hegemonic groups in our society where people exploit others due to their superior power of money, muscle, rank or position' (Saini 2001). India is one of the highest-ranking countries in the world in terms of bureaucratic corruption. It needs to rapidly increase its literacy level so that it can build a countervailing power of people to fight hegemony and corruption. Some states have successfully overcome the power of such societal elements over child education. For example, the state of Kerala claims to have achieved 100 per cent literacy, which has 'sent the incidence of child labour plummeting during the 1970s' (Chaudhri 1997a: 793). Other states, such as Tamil Nadu, Himachal Pradesh and Punjab, have also achieved impressive results in primary education and reduction of child labour. Even though these states still need to improve the quality of their primary educational system, their experiences provide hope that greater state determination can help fight the opposing vested interests.

In the last two decades, the Indian higher judiciary has increasingly made laws through its judicial power of constitutional interpretation and public interest litigation (PIL) when it finds that the executive and legislative branches of government have failed to act on a constitutional principle. Using this power, the Supreme Court of India, in a significant 1993 judgment,[7] declared that Article 45 should be interpreted as containing a fundamental right to primary education, which means that citizens can now enforce it in a court of law, and that the state is obliged to provide primary education throughout the country. In addition, the constitution was amended in 2002 to provide for a right to education up to matriculation as a fundamental right for every citizen (a fuller discussion of this is contained in the penultimate section of this chapter). But this right has yet to be put into operation, and basic education is neither universal nor compulsory in actuality. It is well known that many Indian laws relating to state obligations to the poor and powerless remain merely symbolic (Saini 1995b); it remains to be seen how long it will take for this law to become fully operational.

Article 24, as noted above, guarantees the prohibition of employment of children in factories, mines, plantations and 'hazardous employment'. But the term 'hazardous employment' in this constitutional provision has not been defined. Following the Bhopal disaster, the Factories Act of 1948 was amended in 1986 to include provisions protecting workers involved in hazardous processes. The amended Factories Act does define the term 'hazardous process' for the purpose of that act. But this definition has not been applied to the constitutional guarantee in Article 24. Some constitutional experts opine that all labour undertaken by children is hazardous in that it deprives them of their childhood. They argue, therefore, that Article 24 should be interpreted to prevent employment of children in any activity (Baxi 1994). Such an analysis calls into question the underlying premises of a law like the CLPRA, whose comprehensive framework is directed at regulating, rather than abolishing, child labour, and thus perhaps merely perpetuates the problem.

Even though the CLPRA replaced the ECA, it re-enacted the ECA's Schedules A and B. Part II of the CLPRA prohibits the employment of children under fourteen for the jobs delineated in Schedules A and B. Part III regulates the employment of child labour in those establishments in which children above fourteen years of age can work, i.e. those that do not involve the occupations or processes articulated in Schedules A and B.

But in effect, the CLPRA does not make any major departure from its predecessor as far as child labour abolition is concerned. Perhaps the key difference between the two laws is that the CLPRA restricts the definition of the family to only parents and children as opposed to a much wider definition of family provided in the ECA, although neither statute bans child labour in the defined family. Table 7.1 sets out some of the principal features of the CLPRA. One major loophole in this law is that an employer's activities carried out with the aid of the child's 'family' is outside the purview of this legislation. Thus, the CLPRA permits the employment of children even in hazardous processes where the process is carried out within the family unit. As a result, many clever employers have installed looms for carpet weaving in children's homes or employed children to roll bidis in their homes.

Even with its limitations, the CLPRA, the main and, perhaps, the only key instrument for abolishing and regulating child labour in India, is enforced quite lackadaisically. When the author was intensively involved in training labour inspectors at the National Labour Institute (Noida), he witnessed various problems in the enforcement of this law. The inspectors themselves did not appear convinced that there was any real need for a law on child labour prohibition given the massive poverty in India. They also viewed 'hazardous' as attributable only to physical harm, and did not appreciate the 'hazards' inherent in the emotional and educational deprivation of children. Some of the inspectors openly admitted making extra income through employer bribes for permitting violations of various labour laws, including the CLPRA.

Before adopting the New Economic Policy (NEP) globalization programme in July 1991, Indian industrial policy emphasized small-scale industry, which in a way exacerbated child labour by enabling small

Child labour in India

TABLE 7.1 Employment of children – protective legal provisions

No.	Name of enactment	Protective provisions for children
1.	The Children (Pledging of Labour) Act, 1933	Any agreement to pledge the labour of children is void.
2.	The Factories Act, 1948	Employment of children under fourteen years of age prohibited, under the law at Sl. nos 1 to 5.
3.	The Mines Act, 1952	
4.	The Motor Transport Workers Act, 1961	
5.	The Bidi and Cigar Workers (Condition of Employment) Act, 1966	
6.	The Child Labour (Prohibition and Regulation) Act, 1986	Except in a family-based context or recognized school-based activities, children not permitted to work in occupations concerned with: • Passenger, goods, mail transport by railway • Carpet weaving • Cinder picking, cleaning of ash pits • Cement manufacturing • Construction • Cloth printing • Dyeing, weaving • Manufacturing of matches, explosives, fireworks • Catering establishments in railway premises or within port limits • Bidi-making

		- Mica cutting, splitting - Abattoirs - 'Hazardous Process' and 'Dangerous Operation' as defined/notified in Section 2(cb) and Section 87 of the Factories Act, 1948, respectively - Wool cleaning - Printing, as defined in Section 2(k) of the Factories Act, 1948 - Cashew and cashewnut descaling and processing - Soldering processes in electronic industries In occupations and processes other than the above-mentioned, work by children is permissible only for six hours between 8 a.m. and 7 p.m. with one day's weekly rest. Occupier of establishment employing children to give notice to local inspector and maintain prescribed register.
7.	The Plantations Labour Act, 1951	Children/adolescents are allowed to work twenty-seven hours a week. Child work is not allowed during the night, i.e. from 7 p.m. to 6 a.m. Children permitted to work in plantation only where certificate of fitness is granted by certifying surgeon. On completion of fifteen days' work, one day's leave with wages is to be allowed.
8.	Minimum Wages Act, 1948	

Source: Government of India (2000)

employers to minimize wage costs through the employment of children. The adoption of the NEP jolted small-scale industries by delicensing reserved items in the small-scale list, thereby allowing large undertakings to manufacture these items and undercut smaller businesses through economies of scale. But most of the traditionally child-labour-based industries have remained unaffected by the new policies. The state continues as a mute spectator to the blatant violations of the very laws that it enacts with seeming enthusiasm (Saini 1999, 1995b; Patel and Desai 1995). In relation to CLPRA enforcement problems, government officials hide behind the alibi of the 'harsh reality' theory of the existence of child labour. This theory explains child labour as a necessary evil and a product of the high incidence of poverty in the country. But the national government has not been able to ensure effective management of the primary education system, which is one of the key factors perpetuating the child labour problem.

As noted above, there is no dearth of laws, including constitutional measures, to deal with the problem of child labour and illiteracy due to the lack of compulsory primary education, but the laws have simply not been enforced. Even if prosecution for violations of the CLPRA does take place, according to the inspectors interviewed at the National Labour Institute training sessions, the punishment imposed by the courts is merely a fine and not imprisonment, hardly a sufficient deterrent. This is true of violations of other labour laws as well.

Another important aspect of Indian child labour law is that child labourers are disqualified from becoming members of a registered trade union under the 1926 Trade Unions Act. By not banning child labour, but prohibiting these workers from unionizing, this statute increases the defencelessness of child labourers and provides a disincentive for trade union federations to advocate on behalf of children. Indeed, trade union federations in the country have almost never demanded abolition of child labour or improvement in children's working conditions with any degree of seriousness (Ramaswamy 1999). Thus, child labourers have no organization to fight for wages, working conditions or hours of work.

In summary, an analysis of these legal provisions and policy/advocacy measures reveals only half-hearted attempts towards solving the problem of child labour and illiteracy. It appears that there have been only 'subjective benevolent intentions and endeavours' reflected in state behaviour (Pankaj 1995: 2530), which cannot resolve key contradictions in the institution of child labour. The question then becomes whether Indian advocates for the abolition of child labour and compulsory education for children can look to international directives for either binding or persuasive support.

Child labour abolition, human rights and international initiatives

In a country that claims to be the largest democracy in the world (and that for more than half a century), it is intriguing to note that many or even most of the important initiatives in attaining the abolition of child labour have come from outside Indian society and polity. But for the pressure of the ILO and the UN, India might not have declared the fight against child labour as one of its principal political goals. Because most affected children belong to poor families from lower castes who have little voice in the opinion-making dynamics in the country, community participation in the fight against child labour is perhaps unthinkable. Any determination of the government to abolish child labour would involve setting out a workable social change agenda as a fundamental value pursued by an enlightened society. Since this has never been attempted, pressures from international institutions are desirable.

Some of the earliest attempts to articulate human rights for children at the global level were in the form of declarations. In 1924, the Geneva Declaration on the Rights of the Child talked of 'mankind's obligation towards children', owing to them 'the best it has to give' (Freeman 1996: 2). The United Nations Declaration of the Rights of the Child was adopted in November 1959, stressing certain principles, including 'entitlement to education, which should be free and compulsory, at least in elementary stages'. These principles envisaged a wider scope than that of the Geneva Declaration, their emphasis being on protection and welfare. But these principles, too, were mere declarations without involving any binding obligations on the member states. The ILO adopted the Minimum Age (Industry) Convention 1989 (No. 5), prohibiting children under fourteen years of age from working in industrial establishments. Later, the ILO adopted a number of sectoral conventions on the minimum age of admission to employment. These related to industry, agriculture, trimmers and stokers, maritime work, non-industrial employment, fishing and underground work. Primarily, the international initiatives on child labour abolition have come about through the Conventions and Recommendations of the ILO and the UN Convention on Child Rights in 1989.

Conventions and recommendations of the ILO Perhaps the most comprehensive ILO initiative on child labour is the Minimum Age Convention No. 138 (1973) and Recommendation No. 146. The former is based on an understanding of the close interrelationship between various stages, levels and extents of human development, including physical, biological, mental, emotional and spiritual. The Convention states that all ratifying countries should fix a minimum age for admission to employment and should undertake to pursue a national policy aimed at ensuring the effective abolition of child labour, and applies this rule to all sectors of economic activity, including factories, mines, plantations and the sea – whether children are in paid employment or otherwise. Ratifying countries should also progressively raise the minimum age for admission to employment or work to a level that is consistent with the fullest physical and mental development of young persons. Recommendation No. 146 can be seen as supporting the goals of Convention No. 138 as it provides a broad framework and essential policy measures for prevention as well as elimination of child labour.

The principles on which Convention No. 138 are based include: the minimum age for work should not be less than fifteen, or the age of completion of compulsory schooling, if later than fifteen; the minimum age should be progressively raised to a level consistent with the fullest physical and mental development of young persons (countries with insufficiently developed educational facilities can set the age initially at fourteen); a higher minimum age of eighteen should be established for hazardous work that is likely to adversely affect the health, safety or morale of young persons; and the type of employment in which children can be employed should be determined by national laws of the country concerned. The Convention allows countries to initially limit the scope of its application to specific activities. Nevertheless, it requires that seven sectors be covered, including mining and quarrying, manufacturing, construction, electricity, gas- and water-related activities, sanitary services, transport, storage and communication enterprises, and plantation and other agricultural undertakings (excluding family and small-scale holdings mainly producing for local consumption and not regularly employing hired workers).

The ILO treats Convention No. 138 as one of its seven Core Conventions and, since 1995, it has launched a vigorous campaign for its ratification by the member states. Nevertheless, India has not currently ratified this Convention. The key reason for this is that labour legislation is a matter in the Concurrent List, which means that both the central government as well as the states can enact laws in the field. As a result, several laws with different ages for entry into various employment settings, including factories, mines, plantations, motor transport undertakings, shops and establishments, have been passed by different states. The central government's policy appears to be that of gradually raising the minimum age for entry into employment to fourteen (except for the Plantations Act, which does not provide for any minimum age of entry). The regulation of shops and establishments is purely a state matter, and different states have enacted laws setting the age of entry into employment at between twelve and fourteen years.

The ILO has passed two other recent conventions to prevent child labour, both of which are also considered by it as Core Conventions. At its conference on 18 June 1998, the ILO adopted the 'ILO Declaration on Fundamental Principles and Rights at Work and its Follow-up', dealing with: 1) the right to organize and bargain collectively; 2) the elimination of all forms of forced or compulsory labour; 3) the abolition of child labour; and 4) the elimination of discrimination in employment and occupation. The declaration stipulates that all member states have the obligation to implement these Core Conventions even if they have not ratified them. The ILO is even offering support to countries that are working to ensure these fundamental rights of workers, including those working in the informal sector and free trade zones. At its eighty-seventh session in Geneva in June 1999, the ILO passed the Immediate Abolition of the Worst Forms of Child Labour Convention. This document urges ratifying members to take immediate measures to prohibit and eliminate the worst forms of child labour, including all forms of slavery, forced or compulsory labour and serfdom, use of children for prostitution and pornographic perform-ances, use of children for production and trafficking of narcotic drugs and psychotropic substances, and all other activities that jeopardize the health, safety or morals of children.

LDCs view the motives behind these core standards as not pure and simple human rights of workers, as usual with the conventions and dec-larations of the ILO. Rather they witness a changing ILO succumbing to demands by the AFL-CIO (the US trade union federation) and the Interna-tional Confederation of Free Trade Unions (ICFTU), which are interested in the ILO adopting a strong stand on enforcement of core standards. Regardless, since its inception the ILO has done precious little to eradicate many abominable labour practices. Therefore, the developed countries are demanding that these labour standards be incorporated in a social clause connected to trade agreements that are part of the WTO system.

The Child Rights Convention: the beginning of a shift in the child labour abolition agenda The adoption by the United Nations General Assembly of the 1989 Convention on Rights of the Child (hereinafter referred to as CRC) is one of the most significant developments in international human rights law related to child development and child labour abolition – indeed, a landmark in the history of child rights. Its fifty-four articles are perhaps the most comprehensive treaty on child rights, comprising a set of interna-tional standards and measures that are intended to promote the well-being of children in society. The most important guiding principle of the CRC is the 'first call for children', which provides that the essential needs of children should be of paramount importance when allocating resources. The state is expected to 'respect and ensure' that children get a fair and equitable 'deal' in society.

Articles 12, 28 and 32 of the CRC are especially relevant to child labour. Article 12 requires state parties to guarantee to a child who is capable of forming his or her own views the right to express those views freely in all matters affecting the child. Article 28 requires that primary education should be made 'compulsory and available free to all'. Article 32 requires the member countries to protect children from performing any work that is 'likely to be hazardous, or to interfere with the child's education or to be harmful to the child's health or physical, mental, spiritual, moral or social development'. The CRC provides four sets of basic rights – the right to survival, protection, development (including a reasonable standard of living, health and basic services, social security, education and leisure) and participation. Thus the Convention may be viewed as 'a means of empowering children and creating an environment in which all children are able to live securely and realize their full potential of life' (UNICEF 1994: 1).

Prior UN documents, for example the 1924 Geneva Declaration on Rights of the Child and the 1959 Universal Child Rights Declaration, while emphasizing the protection and welfare of children, positioned children as merely *objects* of concern. The CRC, on the other hand, seeks to confer 'autonomy' on the child, deviating from the 'parent (usually the father) knows best' theory. For many children, the home is a site of oppression and the CRC, recognizing this, seeks to provide state power to protect the child from such oppression. Thus, even though children frequently need the protection of their parents, the CRC enables them to claim rights on their own behalf. In addition, the CRC is considered 'a breakthrough in international human rights standard-setting' as it interlinks civil, political and economic, social and cultural rights (Toope 1996: 34).

It is interesting to note that probably 'no other international instrument has been responded to so rapidly by so many' states (Freeman 1996: 4). The CRC has been ratified by 191 member states, including significantly India (Mishra 2000: 191), arousing a greater seriousness about children's rights. But the outpouring of signatory endorsements should not be confused with implementation nor distract attention from the enormity of the problem, especially in developing countries such as India with massive poverty, a high incidence of child labour, and a not-so-high government concern about the negative social effects of child labour. For example, the Indian government, aware of these realities when it ratified the CRC on 12 November 1992, registered its qualification with the UN in the following terms:

... objectives and purposes of the Convention ... can be progressively implemented. In the developing countries, subject to the extent of available resources and with the framework of international cooperation ... being aware that it is not practical immediately to prescribe minimum ages for admission to each and every area of employment in India. The Government of India undertakes to take measures to *progressively implement the provisions of Article 23, particularly paragraph 2(a)*, in accordance with its national legislation and relevant international instruments to which it is a state party (emphasis added). (Heredia and Mathias 1995: 293)

This instrument, therefore, makes the Indian ratification of the CRC only conditional.

In response to the CRC, leaders of nine high-population developing nations that had ratified the CRC – Indonesia, China, Bangladesh, Brazil, Egypt, Mexico, Nigeria, Pakistan and India – held an 'Education for All Summit' in 1996. The summit affirmed each country's commitment to make primary education universal. It also pledged, by the year 2000 or earlier, a place for every child in a school or appropriate programme according to his or her capabilities, and further stated that no child would be deprived of education for lack of a teacher, learning material or adequate space. Funding for the costs of this educational system was promised through public and private sources (see Venkata Ratnam 1998: 1001).

The structural framework of the CRC, its ratification by most nations and the subsequent summit on its implementation reveal a sense of urgency about the connection between child labour and literacy. In addition, these factors evidence an emerging trend to conceptualize children's work as part of the broader framework of child rights.

The social clause, children's rights discourse and recent developments in the child labour reform agenda

Many progressive scholars and activists attack 'globalization' as reflective of imperialistic thinking. They charge that, by superimposing the 'rationality' of market functioning, globalization is wiping out components of the welfare state and the basic rights of working people.

Even though there might be truth in these observations, a highly charged debate over a 'social clause' connected to international trade agreements may constitute a silver lining for workers in countries that violate certain basic human rights, including employment of child labour. In this context, a social clause is a special agreement, inserted in international trade agreements, that sets forth minimum demands for ensuring labour dignity, not a comprehensive set of labour rights. These demands should be understood with reference to some of the more fundamental Conventions and Recommendations of the ILO. As noted in the earlier section, these core standards were adopted in the agenda of the ILO in its 1998 annual conference (allegedly at the behest of the developed world). They include, among others, abolition of child labour as one of the core priorities of the international community.

The social clause is being vehemently opposed by the developing countries, however. They see it disguising a revival of neo-protectionism in international trade and imperialism by the developed world – a mechanism for the developed world to undermine the comparative advantage of developing countries. They argue that the right authority to implement core labour standards is the ILO, not the WTO.

A brief history of the evolution of the social clause controversy should be sketched. The issue of a social clause came to the fore for the first time at the concluding session of negotiations in the Uruguay Round of GATT in 1993, when the industrialized countries and the International Confederation of Free Trade Unions (ICFTU) placed this issue on the agenda as a means of preserving basic labour rights. But the matter was not pursued owing to opposition from the developing countries. A ministerial round met in April 1995 in Marrakesh (Morocco), where representatives from North America and the European Union again demanded the introduction of a social clause in the newly founded WTO connecting adherence to labour standards by member countries with trade negotiations. At another WTO ministerial conference in December 1996, the issue of inclusion of a social clause in trade negotiations mandating core labour standards was rejected owing to opposition by the developing countries. The controversy was raised again in Seattle at the 1999 third ministerial meeting of the WTO, when then US President Bill Clinton threatened trade sanctions against countries violating minimum labour standards (Hensman 2000: 1247). No consensus has so far been reached on the issue, and the developed and the developing worlds remain divided on its inclusion in trade negotiations. There are charges and counter-charges from both sides about the hidden and manifest intentions of the social clause.

One may suspect the genuineness of the developed world's concern for human rights globally, given the fact that the WTO is a trade organization. And it has been appropriately said that 'to consider that trade policy measures will be based on morality is nothing but wishful thinking and frustrating innocence' (Chisti 2000: 2669). Trading partners, naturally, are guided by trade and business exigencies. Otherwise, how can one see trade unions, employers' associations and governments (the three actors in industrial relations) coming together almost totally in favour of the social clause in the US and the same three sets of actors in India and other developing countries taking a diametrically opposite view to the social clause philosophy? But the important question is: should we reject the concept of a social clause, viewing it mainly as a ploy to seek business advantage by certain nations, or should we explore its potential to assist the world in developing as an enlightened society respecting basic or core human rights?

How do we situate the debate over the 'social clause' within the emerging complex international poverty law (IPL) discourse? How do we assess which aspects of this discourse will eventually empower or disempower the poor? We have noted two aspects of IPL in relation to child labour and poverty: i) the lesser or non-controversial ones, which include the Universal Declaration of Human Rights, ILO Conventions and Recommendations and the 1979 Child Right Convention; and ii) the controversial one, charged with a sense of protectionist rejuvenation in world trade by means of the high-cost North seeking to impose the social clause on the cheap-labour South. While the first set of measures aims to confer human dignity on working children pro-actively, the latter seeks to ensure their human rights by mixing the morality of these rights with business rationality.

Against the background of these developments, it is pertinent to ask how we view the child labour issue in relation to trade negotiations, for example, in India. In an earlier section, I have analysed the incidence and causal roots of child labour in India and discussed the Indian constitutional proclamations and legal framework for abolishing child labour and ensuring universal basic education. The failure to accomplish these measures and incorporate these policies, however, reflects bureaucratic indifference, executive lawlessness (see Saini 1999 and 1995b for an analysis of poor labour enforcement in general) and a lack of political will.

The law, of course, is so structured and implemented that it legitimizes the state's underlying indifference to the plight of the poor and the powerless in a hierarchical, caste-ridden and highly unequal India. Nader (1975: 1687), a legal anthropologist, has argued that, especially in developing nations, law will play a great part in ensuring that the more powerful and wealthier members override and superimpose their views on the poorer, less powerful sections by means of the law, and 'law is fashioned to legitimate the status quo'. The history of child labour and attempts to abolish it in India amply show that the child labour problem has yet to be tackled effectively despite international efforts and multiple laws (Nath 1998). There is no doubt that law is often 'opportunistically' used by the oppressive forces to serve their narrow ends (Nonet and Selznick 1978). By and large, state mechanisms have looked the other way in the face of blatant violations of the basic rights of children, and have used the pretext of poverty to explain child labour. The government has not satisfactorily discharged its statutory duty of either bringing about compulsory primary education or enforcing the legal prescriptions for child labour abolition.

That being said, the debate over the social clause and the adoption of the CRC have helped to build tremendous pressure within the developing countries on the hitherto half-hearted treatment of issues relating to universal primary education and child labour abolition.

First and foremost, the resulting international pressure has led to a serious debate in India among academics, government functionaries, NGOs and labour rights organizations. This, by any standard, is no small achievement (see, for example, Chisti 2000). Through this discussion, people have begun to see the other (positive) side of the social clause (Nath 1998: 1005). The allocations to primary education in the central government budget configurations over the past few years bear testimony to this, although one should not expect miraculous results just from this one development.

Second, an impressive number of programmes are being undertaken by the central government to eradicate child labour, although the result of these initiatives is quite limited. One of the key programmes is the National Child Labour Project (NCLP), which has been set up in various states with the main objective of withdrawing children working in hazardous occupations and putting them into mainstream formal school systems. In addition, a major focus of this project is the establishment of special schools to provide non-formal education, vocational training, supplementary nutrition, stipends and healthcare to children withdrawn from employment. The budgetary allocation for this scheme in the Ninth Five Year Plan has gone up to Rs 248.60 crores from a mere Rs 15 crores in the Eighth Five Year Plan (Government of India 2000). The NCLP in various states covers 1.9 lakh children who have been removed from work. These children are from different socio-economic backgrounds and have different skills and experiences. Often normal schools may not cater to their specific needs. The special schools established under this programme essentially act as a bridge to facilitate these children's entry to formal school. The monitoring of this programme is not quite systematic, however, and requires a more efficacious management (ibid.: 163).

Also, the terms of the CRC, ratified by India, required the country to create appropriate institutions to enforce the CRC provisions. To this end, a National Authority on Elimination of Child Labour (NAECL) was created in 1994, with nine secretaries from the relevant central government ministries serving as ex officio members and the central labour minister serving as chair. NAECL is required to report to parliament at least once a year. In

1995 the NCAEL suggested the creation of eleven child labour cells in eleven states with a high incidence of child labour. These cells (forums) were expected to determine the incidence of child labour in different states and devise effective steps for its abolition and rehabilitation. NAECL also established district committees in each of these areas, who mandatorily report to the NAECL (Chaudhri 1997b: 61).

Third, international pressure was instrumental in the announcement of the National Agenda for Governance in 1998. The agenda states, among other things, that its aim is to ensure that no child remains illiterate, hungry or lacks medical care, and that measures will be taken to eliminate child labour. In pursuance of this agenda, the Cabinet Committee on Economic Affairs has recently approved an expanded NCLP programme.

Fourth, in 1993 the government set up a National Resource Centre on Child Labour (NRCCL) at the National Labour Institute (Noida) with financial support from the central government and UNICEF. The NRCCL conducts important research studies on child labour, and assists the central and state governments, NGOs, policy-makers and other social groups in developing capabilities for the progressive elimination of child labour.

Fifth, the ILO launched the International Programme on Elimination of Child Labour (IPEC) in December 1991; this became operational in 1993. India was the first country to join it in 1992. Until 1996, the programme focused on NGO action through a large number of small programmes, covering nearly all the Indian states. The second phase, in 1998/99, involved large and sustainable programmes covering entire areas in certain selected districts. The government's NCLPs are now being used as vehicles for ILO's outreach strategy. Nearly 100 thousand children were covered under the IPEC programme between 1992 and 2000.

Apart from direct efforts at child labour abolition, the central government is paying more attention to the development of primary education through its *Sarva shiksha Abhiyan* (Universal Education Mission), which seeks to provide eight years of 'quality elementary education' for all children up to the age of fourteen in 'a mission mode with a thrust on community ownership' (*Economic Times* 2001: 2). This scheme seeks to involve the community in ensuring that children are sent to school. In 1995, the government launched a national programme of nutritional support to primary education, called the 'Midday Meal Scheme'. It aims to improve enrolment, attendance and retention by upgrading the nutritional status of students in primary classes. Under this scheme, students studying in classes I to V in all primary schools run by state governments and local bodies are provided with cooked/processed food. The central government reimburses the cost of food grains.

Very recently, the Indian parliament passed the Constitutional (93rd Amendment) Bill, 2002, now officially referred to as the Constitution (86th Amendment) Act, 2002, making education for six-to-fourteen-year-olds a Fundamental Right within the meaning of Chapter III of the constitution. In other words, Article 21, providing for a Fundamental Right to Life and Personal Liberty, is amended to make education up to high school a Fundamental Right for all citizens of India. The amendment has not yet been implemented (the date of its enforcement will be determined and announced by the Department of Education in the Ministry of Human Resource Development), and in a country that has a sad history of laws remaining largely symbolic, it remains to be seen how many years or even decades will go by before this law actually becomes effective. But even these modest efforts reflect the sense of urgency and pressure placed on the Indian government, and presumably other developing countries' governments, as a result of the ratification of the CRC and the threat of the social clause in international trade being wielded by the developed world.

Towards conclusions

Child labour has a multiplier effect, perpetuating economic, social and cultural poverty. The concern of developed countries, as expressed through their government and trade representatives, although of course contested within their societies, about the presence of child and forced labour in various developing countries, is predominantly driven by trade exigencies rather than guided by concerns relating to humanity and morality. While the social clause may be viewed by progressives as necessary for preserving workers' rights, it is also a non-tariff barrier in favour of the developed world. In addition, there is a world of difference between states' projections and actual poverty alleviation, especially in LDCs, where the covert nexuses between the powerful vested interests against the less powerful are very strong, and where those who have assets and power are largely oblivious to the problems of child labourers. Thus, the opposition to the social clause on the part of governments, employers and the trade unions, both within LDCs and the developed world, is complex and highly problematic.

Many governments in developing countries have the political goal of ensuring the success of globalization because they have been led to believe that their economic survival depends on a global economy, which necessitates the subordination of social justice and human rights issues to the wider imperatives of globalization. This creates a still greater incentive for employers to minimize costs through the perpetration of child labour. In fact, there is evidence that in post-globalization India a greater degree of casualization of labour is taking place, largely for female and child labourers, who tend to offer their services at wages lower than market rates (Gupta and Mitra 1997). Also, because of the general decline of pluralism and the countervailing power in society, the social health in poorer countries is likely to be under greater strain. In view of these realities, it is essential to look outside the traditional viewpoints of both the developed world and the LDCs to question how best to respond to what appears to be a bleak future for child labourers and the poor in a globalized world. Despite my belief that the intentions of the developed world regarding the social clause are not fully genuine, my intuitive uneasiness repeatedly compels me to support the social clause as a means to address child labour and hence illiteracy. I am limiting my pro-social-clause conclusion to the issue of child labour, because other aspects of the social clause advocated by the developed world are more problematical and beyond the scope of this chapter. I sincerely wish to see the social clause as an important part of the emerging international poverty law, however, alongside the UN Convention on Child Rights, in order to put the requisite pressure on governments to realize their fundamental responsibility for implementing universal primary education. Historically, there are not very many instances of the use of trade sanctions to combat child labour. But it happened in the 1930s in connection with trade between states of the US. The federal government used trade sanctions that were under its jurisdiction to prohibit the use of child labour by the states (see Chaudhri 1997a: 791; Brown et al. 1992).

An acceptable social clause applicable only to the case of child and forced labour can possibly be devised through a more constructive dialogue between developed and developing countries. Since the ILO does not have an impressive record of enforcement of labour standards, greater hope can be expressed for the enforceable labour clause of the WTO. Unions and advocates for children in the LDCs must consciously engage in illuminating the neglect of basic rights of children and those who have been subjected to bonded labour. What is needed is a 'conscientization campaign' (Gupta and Voll 1999: 129); and I doubt whether that is really possible without pressure through something like the social clause. This will both contribute to the success of programmes of child labour abolition and universal primary education, thereby removing illiteracy and reducing poverty. It will also help in enhancing the stature and purposiveness of the emerging international poverty law. There is much more to the problem of child labour abolition than the mere amendment of the Indian constitution to provide for primary education as a fundamental right. This amendment should not be seen as an end to the debate on social clauses; to make this law effective pressure is needed on a state that tends to slip into entropy when confronted with issues of children's human rights.

Notes

1 I would like to thank Lucy Williams for her helpful comments on an earlier draft of this chapter, which led to alterations of many earlier positions. Of course, the usual disclaimers apply.

2 See also, Amartya Sen's views expressed on similar lines in Shaikh (2001: 8).

3 Census in India is conducted every ten years. Only the main results of the census conducted in February 2001 are available; details related to child population are expected to be available in the course of time. Therefore, a mix of data from the censuses of 2001 and 1991 has been used in this chapter.

4 The latest poverty estimates were released by the Planning Commission of India on 22 February 2001. These are based on a large sample survey of consumer expenditure completed by the National Sample Survey Organization (NSSO) between July 1999 and June 2000.

5 Operations Research Group puts the figure of child labour in India at 44 million (Ramaswamy 1999: 54). Pankaj (1995) puts the figure at 55 million and gives its distribution in various occupations. Sahoo (1990) quotes a figure of 44 million.

6 Chapter III of the constitution is entitled 'Fundamental Rights' and contains a bill of rights guaranteed to all citizens. In case of violation of any right prescribed in this chapter, a citizen has the option of directly approaching the Supreme Court of India. Chapter IV is entitled 'The Directive Principles of State Policy'. These directives guide state policy; they are technically unenforceable in a court of law, but are nevertheless considered fundamental in the governance of the country. Some legal scholars have described Chapter IV as representing a social revolution as it embraces important goals that the Indian state is supposed to pursue. Courts in India have frequently referred to various articles in Chapter IV of the constitution while justifying liberal interpretations of certain laws seeking to promote social justice.

7 *Unni Krishnan JP* v. *State of AP* (1993) 1. SCC 645.

References

Agnivesh, S. (1999) 'A critique of selective Western interventions and WTO', in Voll (1999)

Ashraf, S. (1999) 'The elimination of child labour in the carpet belt of north India: possible NGO and trade union strategies', in Voll (1999)

Bardhan, P. (2001) 'Social justice in a global economy', *Economic and Political Weekly*, 3–10 February, pp. 467–80

Baxi, U. (1994) 'The justice system: is it child friendly?', Paper presented at the International Conference on Shaping the Future by Law: Children, Environment and Human Health, Indian Law Institute, New Delhi, 21–25 March

Brown, M., J. Christiansen and P. Phillips (1992) 'The decline of child labour in the US fruit and canning industry: law or economics', *Business History Review*, 66, winter

Burra, N. (2001) 'Cultural stereotypes and household behaviour: girl child labour in India', *Economic and Political Weekly*, 3–10 February, pp. 481–8

Castle, R. et al. (1997) 'Labour clauses, the World Trade Organization and child labour in India', *Indian Journal of Labour Economics*, 40 (1)

Chaudhri, D. P. (1997a) 'A policy perspective on child labour in India with pervasive gender and urban bias in school education', *Indian Journal of Labour Economics*, 40 (4)

— (1997b) 'Labour clauses, the World Trade Organization and child labour in India', *Indian Journal of Labour Economics*, 40 (1)

Chimni, B. S. (1999) 'Marxism and international law – a contemporary analysis', *Economic and Political Weekly*, 6 February, pp. 337–49

Chisti, S. (2000) 'World trade and labour', *Economic and Political Weekly*, 22 July, p. 2669

Dreze, J. (1998) 'Elementary education as a pro-poor strategy in India: myth and reality', *CROP Newsletter*, 5 (3): 1–2

Economic Times (2001) 'Despite tall promises, little funds for education: experts', New Delhi, 5 March, p. 2

Freeman, M. (ed.) (1996) *Children's Rights – a Comparative Perspective*, Vermont: Dartmonth Publishing

Government of India (1969) *Report of the National Commission on Labour*, New Delhi: Ministry of Labour and Employment

— (1984) *Sanat Mehta Committee Report on Child Labour*, New Delhi Ministry of Labour and Employment

— (1986) *National Policy on Education,* New Delhi: Ministry of Human Resource Development (Department of Education)

— (1997) *Annual Report 1996–1997*, New Delhi: Ministry of Labour

— (2000) *Annual Report 1999–2000*, New Delhi: Ministry of Labour

Gupta, I. and A. Mitra (1997) 'Child labour: a profile of Delhi slums', *Indian Journal of Labour Economics*, 40 (4)

Gupta, M. and K. Voll (1999) 'Child labour in India: an exemplary case study', in Voll (1999)

Hensman, R. (2000) 'World trade and workers' rights': to link or not to link', *Economic and Political Weekly*, 8 April, pp. 1247–54

Heredia, R. and E. Mathias (eds) (1995) *The Family in a Changing World – Women, Children and Strategies for Intervention*, New Delhi: Indian Social Institute

Hirway, I. et al. (eds) (1991) *Towards Eradication of Child Labour*, New Delhi: Oxford and IBH Publishing Co.

Janardhan, V. (1997) 'Globalization of capital, multinational corporations and labour: towards a perspective', *Economic and Political Weekly*, 32 (35)

Kirmani, N. (1994) *International Trade Policies: The Uruguay Round and Beyond*, Washington, DC: International Monetary Fund

Kjonstad, A. and J. H. Veit Wilson (eds) (1997) 'Introduction', in *Law, Power and Poverty*, Comparative Research on Poverty (CROP), Bergen

Kothari, S. (1983) 'There is blood on those matchsticks: child labour in Sivakasi', *Economic and Political Weekly*, 2 July, pp. 1191–2002

Lee, E. (1997) 'Globalization and labour standards', *International Labour Review*, 36 (2): 173–89

Liemt, G. V. (1989) 'Minimum labour standards and international trade: would a social clause work?', *International Labour Review*, 128 (4): 438–41

Maskus, K. E. (1997) *Should Core Labour Standards be Imposed Through International Trade Policy?*, Washington, DC: World Bank (Development Research Group)

Mehta, S. S. (1991) 'Why child labour? The Indian case', in Hirway et al. (1991)

Mishra, L. (2000) *Child Labour in India*, Delhi: Oxford University Press

Nader, L. (1975) 'Forums for social justice: a cross-culture perspective', *Journal of Social Issues*, 31: 151

Nath, G. B. (1998) 'Linking international labour standards with trade: implications for India', *Indian Journal of Labour Economics*, 41 (4)

Nonet, P. and P. Selznick (1978) *Law and Society in Transition*, New York: Harper Colophon

Pankaj (1995) 'Plight of child labourers', *Economic and Political Weekly*, 25 November, p. 2980

Patel, Arjun and K. Desai (1995) 'Rural migrant labour and labour laws', in D. S. Saini (ed.), *Labour Law, Work and Development*, New Delhi: Westvill Publishing House

Patel, B. B. (1991) 'Child labour in India: dimensions, issues and policies', in Hirway et al. (1991)

Pratim Mitra, P. and A. Kausal (1998) 'International labour standards in India: some key issues', *Indian Journal of Labour Economics*, 41 (4): 1013–19

Ramachandran, V. (2000) 'Literacy, development and empowerment', in Rekha Wazir (ed.), *The Gender Gap in Basic Education – NGOs as Change Agents*, New Delhi: Sage Publications

Ramaswamy, E. A. (1999) 'Child labour in the larger context of industrial relations', in Voll (1999)

Sahoo, U. C. (1990) 'Child labour and legislation', *Economic and Political Weekly*, 17 November, pp. 2529–30

Saini, D. S. (1995a) 'Children of a lesser god, child labour law and compulsory primary education', in Heredia and Mathias (1995)

— (ed.) (1995b) *Labour Law, Work, and Development*, New Delhi: Westvill Publishing House

— (1998) 'Combating child labour in India – compulsory primary education in the contex of child rights', *Labour & Development*, 3 (1 and 2)

— (1999) 'Labour legislation and social justice: rhetoric and reality', *Economic and Political Weekly*, 25 September–2 October

— (2001) 'INDIA: Social Security Law', in R. Blanpain (ed.), *International Encyclopaedia of Laws*, The Hague: Kluwer Law International

Schildkrout, E. (1980) 'Children's work reconsidered', *International Social Science Journal*, XXXII (3): 479–89

Shaikh, J. (2001) 'Quote-unquote: men of note compare notes … ', *Delhi Times* (a supplement of *The Times of India*), New Delhi, 24 February, p. 8.

Sinha, R. (1994) 'Violation of child rights', *Economic and Political Weekly*, 8 October

Sinha, S. (1994) 'Child labour and compulsory education', Paper presented at the International Conference on Shaping the Future by Law: Children, Environment and Human Health, Indian Law Institute, New Delhi, 21–25 March

Srinivas, M. N. (1991) 'On living in a revolution', *Economic and Political Weekly*, 26 (13)

Times of India (2001) 'Only 26% of Indians are poor, claims plan body', 22 February, p. 1

Toope, S. J. (1996) 'The Convention on the Rights of the Child: implications for Canada', in Freeman (1996)

UNICEF (1994) 'The right to be a child', Unpublished background paper, New Delhi: UNICEF

Venkata Ratnam, C. S. (1998) 'International labour standards and India', *Indian Journal of Labour Economics*, 41 (4): 993–1003

Voll, K. (ed.) (1999) *Against Child Labour: Indian and International Dimensions and Strategies*, New Delhi: Mosaic Books

Weiner, M. (1991) *The Child and the State in India*, Delhi: Oxford University Press

8 | Privatizing human rights? The role of corporate codes of conduct

AURORA VOICULESCU

I call on you – individually through your firms, and collectively through your business associations – to embrace, support and enact a set of core values in the areas of human rights, labour standards, and environmental practices. *Address of UN Secretary-General Kofi Annan to the World Economic Forum in Davos, Switzerland, 31 January 1999*

[Business] would look askance at any suggestion involving external assessment of corporate performance … The Global Compact is a joint commitment to shared values, not a qualification to be met. *Maria Livianos Cattui, Secretary-General of the International Chamber of Commerce, 'Yes to Annan's "Global Compact" If It isn't a License to Meddle',* International Herald Tribune, *26 July 2000*

It is often claimed that, in the long run, a global market will benefit the poor, that economic growth will trickle down, resulting in progressive improvement in the working conditions and the living standards of the poorest of the world. Globalization, however, is a very complex process, whose equation might not always take into account our hopes, unless we choose to actively incorporate these hopes into that equation.[1] What is the process of globalization, and how could one make sure that human rights, labour standards, environmental protection and concern for the most deprived sectors of the world population will have a place in this process? Among the main features of the process of globalization are an increasing reliance on a deregulated global market, free trade, uncontrolled flow of investment, and an increasing role for the international financial market, with the Bretton Woods institutions becoming the guardians of the market-oriented world.[2] In this context, the transnational corporations (TNCs) become the most active players.[3] They generate a growing economic interdependence, an increased volume and variety of cross-border transactions in goods and services, and heightened international capital flow. These processes are accompanied by important developments in science, technology, communications and information processing, but also by employment crises and growing inequality between and within countries. Moreover, the participation of the less developed countries (LDCs) in the global economy is accompanied by imposed Structural Adjustment Programmes and considerable foreign debt.

In this very complex socio-economic context, it has become increasingly evident that the direct investment and the undeniable economic growth accompanying the presence of TNCs in the global market are not necessarily linked to a reduction in poverty.[4] Addressing poverty in the context of globalization has more than ever stopped being both an issue that concerns only nation-states and solely a matter of national policy. Given their considerable economic power, TNCs can, and should, contribute to the alleviation of poverty. The question, however, is how to facilitate this contribution: by allowing the TNCs to freely operate their businesses or by harnessing their activities more purposefully through national and international programmes targeting human development?[5] Arguments for the latter seem to have gathered pace lately, not least because of an increased awareness about the impact of globalization upon the poorest of the world.

The importance of direct investment and the activity of TNCs in the LDCs have increased considerably. Increasing capital mobility and declining transport and communications costs give TNCs enormous bargaining power in relation to territory-bound states and trade unions. In this context, industrial relations, and the way they are regulated (or deregulated) by the national states, become themselves a factor in global competition.[6] Although not totally 'footloose', TNCs are adapting investment strategies to the new paradigm via, for example, lean production, global sourcing and offshore funding.[7] Therefore, the new rules according to which the economic activities are pursued can have a great impact on national economies generally, and on the individual welfare of the most deprived sectors of the world population in particular.

This chapter addresses the capacity of the corporate voluntary codes of conduct to promote, in the present regulatory framework, a meaningful notion of corporate social responsibility and to bridge more consistently the gap between economic growth and poverty and human development. The chapter argues that this dimension of the transnational corporations' activity is positively encouraged by two important UN documents: the UNDP 'Poverty Report 2000', and, most directly, the UN Global Compact. But it also looks into regulatory, non-legally enforceable international mechanisms that seek in different ways to engage transnational corporations in more socially responsible economic activities. Three of these documents are discussed: the UN Draft Code of Conduct for Transnational Corporations, the ILO Tripartite Declaration of Principles Concerning Multinational Enterprises and Social Policy, and the OECD Guidelines for Multinational

Privatizing human rights?

Enterprises. The importance and role of the voluntary codes of conduct in the global market are also set out here. This analysis, together with the level of effectiveness of the ILO and OECD initiatives, as well as the UN Global Compact, in shaping the concept of corporate social responsibility, is then used to assess the extent to which the codes of conduct, as part of a process of privatization of human rights, can lead to effective social regulation of globalization addressing poverty and human development.

Transnational corporations in the global market

The process of globalization is, in a way, defined by the new breed of social agency represented by the TNCs.[8] It is, therefore, not surprising that many international institutions have attempted to contribute, albeit in a 'soft' way, to the regulatory framework within which the TNCs pursue their activities. Reflecting this interest, a Centre on Transnational Corporations was created at UN level. This centre tried to promote a comprehensive code of conduct for a number of years. This code, however, never went beyond the stage of a Draft Code of Conduct on Transnational Corporations, remaining as a form of authoritative wishful thinking. In this 1977 Draft Code, the TNCs were defined as ' … enterprises, independent of their country of origin and their ownership, including private, public or mixed, comprising entities in two or more countries, regardless of the legal form and fields of activity of these entities, which operate under a system of decision-making centres in which these entities are so linked, by ownership or otherwise, that one or more of them may be able to exercise a significant influence over the activities of others and in particular, to share knowledge, resources and responsibilities with the others'.[9]

The special status and importance of the TNCs in the global market lie in the fact that, as main agents of international direct investment,[10] they can make an important contribution to the promotion of economic and social welfare, to the creation of employment opportunities and, not least, to the promotion of basic human rights.[11] At the same time, and lately mentioned more often, the TNCs have the potential to undermine all these values through either actively opposing or simply ignoring them.[12]

The global markets in which TNCs operate bestow net benefits on advanced economies. Even in these economies, however, the low-skilled workers are often subject to at least some harmful effects. Moreover, the benefits are unequally distributed,[13] not least because in recent decades, through the TNCs' activities, the growth of global production systems has outpaced the growth of trade-based systems in international economic interaction. The investment flows, therefore, tend to be greater than the trade flows, which is particularly problematic for the host countries, usually

LDCs. Also, the same countries are comparatively disadvantaged by an intra-firm international division of production. One of the results of this process is the creation of an international secondary labour market that does not share in the diffusion of technical skills and wealth generated within the global networks. Within these systems, production takes place more and more 'at arms'-length', through subcontracting, licensing and franchising. One result of all these changes is a widening of the gap in income and opportunities.[14]

Given the importance and the role played by TNCs in conveying both advantages and disadvantages, both prosperity and poverty, governments often face a difficult choice in deciding how to treat TNCs. They often have to choose between mass unemployment and the presence of 'working poor', that is between a heavily regulated economy which tries to keep under control national as well as transnational companies, and the business-friendly economy, which attracts direct investment but leaves the work force largely unprotected. The fact that, in search of the absolute comparative advantage, TNCs have become increasingly 'footloose' forces governments to create an attractive regulatory framework, or to give clear signals of a favourable informal preferential regime for the TNCs. The proliferation of methods whereby firms may remove themselves from domestic jurisdiction also pushes governments gradually to eliminate capital controls in order to remain competitive. In this way, national states surrender even more of their sovereignty in exchange for short-term capital flows.[15]

Thus the TNCs are in a position of largely regulating and limiting them-selves. The pressure to do so, however, generally comes not from national governments, but rather indirectly from other national and international social agencies. Under considerable market pressures (for example, con-sumer boycotts, stakeholders' actions and non-governmental organization campaigns),[16] the TNCs 'voluntarily' put themselves under a set of rules that often express some kind of organizational social responsibility. In doing so, corporations transport themselves beyond their narrowly defined profit-oriented rationale.[17] Therefore, while initially Western companies developing their activities abroad were urged not to get involved in issues other than those strictly related to trade and economic activities, and not to interfere in the domestic affairs of their host states,[18] now they are prompted to get involved in areas that were until not long ago considered the exclusive domain of the state.[19] There is a shift in expectations towards a more active commitment and participation by the business community in fields such as environmental protection, promotion of socio-economic as well as civil and political human rights, or even engagement in seeking a dynamic democratic stability in their host countries.[20]

Traditionally, there were two public levels at which such social and political issues could be addressed: within the governments of home or host countries, and within international forums. But this is no longer the case, or at least not to the same extent as it was previously.[21] For practical and technical reasons, in a global interdependent world, labour issues, environmental concerns and socio-economic as well as civil and political rights cannot be addressed meaningfully by the national governments alone. The TNCs, some of whose economic power is greater than that of many nation-states, must actively contribute to the realization of these social dimensions. Establishing duties and responsibilities of the TNCs beyond their economic personae, however, is not an easy task.[22] The fact that TNCs are largely unregulated at the national level represents a significant democratic deficit. Through their activity, the TNCs can have a considerable impact on national policies regarding, for example, social security and environmental protection of their host countries. This is especially true for the LDCs, which can do very little to protect themselves. This impact, though, is more subtle than it was a few decades ago. While in the 1970s, for instance, the concern over TNCs focused on potential interference with national policies, today there is the more fundamental worry that economic activity is being conducted on a truly transnational plane which bypasses the 'geographical logic' of the nation-state altogether.[23]

The TNCs' home states, usually developed countries seeking comparative advantage, have a vested interest in the TNCs' freedom of action and relatively little incentive to regulate them. Therefore, all the international documents aimed at establishing socially responsible TNCs are largely not binding upon either TNCs or their home governments. The aborted UN Draft Code of Conduct mentioned above constitutes a good example of this result.

On the other hand, at the international level, there are currently no supranational institutions that directly regulate the practices of the TNCs beyond the strict economic needs of the free market.[24] International law, directed mainly at nation-states, has had little or nothing to say about the transnational social effects of corporate activities. It is states which are held responsible for the protection of human rights within their jurisdictions. TNCs, therefore, appear only as object and not as subject of public international law. The issue of voluntary codes of conduct should, therefore, be situated within this context of a vacuum of consistent and meaningful global regulation addressing TNCs directly, or at least of mechanisms that would be capable of producing a global impact on the TNCs.

UN positions on poverty and corporate social responsibility

Traditional views on human rights still distinguish between public and private actors. The state is allegedly the main entity responsible for implementing programmes to reduce poverty and promote human development.[25] This once widely accepted dichotomy between state and non-state agencies, however, was always, and increasingly has been, perceived as blurred. Private actors, whose rights are established and enforced by state action, may now be deemed liable for violations of economic, social and cultural rights, as well as often being seen as responsible in conjunction with the state for the implementation of policies that would enhance the realization of these rights.[26]

The problem with the state as the main repository of the responsibility for the elimination of poverty and for the promotion of human development is that the new market mechanisms specific to the global economy make increasingly redundant those structures through which the state was expected to retain a certain control over the domestic economy. Hence, the implementation of socio-economic rights through state policies becomes to a certain extent more difficult.[27] In this context, the voluntary codes of conduct adopted by the different transnational corporations appear as a supplement to the less than perfect governmental regulatory framework, as one of the mechanisms through which these important economic actors are harnessed to those policies that target poverty and, more generally, aim at the realization of socio-economic rights.

This need to supplement and support state policies for eradicating poverty and promoting human development has lately been acknowledged at international level through a set of documents. Two such documents significant from the point of view of this chapter are the UNDP Poverty Report 2000[28] and the UN Global Compact.[29]

The UNDP Poverty Report 2000 is relevant to the analysis of voluntary codes of conduct from two points of view. First, the 'Poverty Report' emphasizes the need to reinforce the state structures fighting poverty with non-state, civil society mechanisms and initiatives. The report, therefore, looks beyond the regulatory role of the state towards 'soft-law' alternatives that provide practical solutions to the complex problems faced by societies today in relation to the process of globalization.

Second, the Poverty Report links trade and poverty by arguing that trade rules must address and be tied more directly to anti-poverty policies in order for trade to benefit the poor. In this context, targeting becomes a key issue. The report states that one of the main problems with today's approaches to poverty is the perceived and false dichotomy between addressing economic growth and addressing poverty. According to the report, there is a two-track

Privatizing human rights?

approach to poverty reduction which stands in the way of integrated poverty programmes, with growth on one track and human development on the other.[30] The two tracks rarely intersect: economic policies are not designed to be pro-poor, while increasingly weakened social services are assigned the burden of directly addressing poverty. According to the Poverty Report, this two-track approach is a legacy of old-style Structural Adjustment Programmes, which approached poverty as a residual social issue.[31]

Although the UNDP Poverty Report 2000 addresses these issues mainly within the nation-state context, the message is unmistakable: the nation-state is no more alone in being expected and able, by itself, to address the complex issues of poverty. New non-state, national and international structures and agents are necessary to support a systematic approach to diminishing and finally eliminating poverty, especially in the LDCs. Moreover, an important point in the report is that market forces are expected to contribute more actively and directly to the eradication of poverty. In this sense, the report states that if trade expansion is to benefit the poor, the international rules of the game must be made fairer.

In a global market, however, fairness is a concept easier to discuss rhetorically than to achieve practically, as the 1999 WTO Seattle Summit underscored.[32] Therefore, while waiting for world leaders to develop suitable solutions, those who advocate pro-poor policies have targeted the TNCs. Not surprisingly, as much effort is put into making corporate social responsibility attractive to TNCs as is put into regulating their activity at international level.

A second UN document, the UN Global Compact,[33] is important in building up the attractiveness of corporate social responsibility. This document tries to develop a bridge between the discourse of human rights, as a source of entitlement to human development, and the economic discourse of growth through the market economy. According to UN Secretary-General Kofi Annan, these two arenas can be mutually supportive in building up a global compact of shared values and principles, giving a human face to the global market. From the point of view of TNCs' activities and of the voluntary codes of conduct, the Global Compact places these issues in a wider international perspective. It recognizes that the spread of markets has outpaced the ability of societies and their political systems to adjust to them and, even less, to guide the course they take. In addition, the compact recognizes the fact, also suggested by Acosta in this book's chapter on biodiversity and biotechnology, that such an imbalance between the economic, social and political realms cannot long be sustained without becoming a source of fundamental injustice.

The Global Compact is also relevant to the voluntary codes of conduct because, implicitly, this declaration made at the highest international level legitimizes voluntarism and self-regulation as major tools for harnessing TNCs' activity to the process of weaving social responsibility into the fabric of global trade. The codes of conduct, therefore, become a tool for addressing issues of poverty in those countries where the state cannot afford to protect its citizens against market failures and the worst side effects of globalization.

The shared values and principles proposed in the Global Compact are not necessarily new.[34] They cover three dimensions – human rights, labour standards and environmental protection – each with its specific impact on human development. Vis-à-vis human rights, the secretary-general asked the world business community to incorporate into their activities two principles: support of and respect for the protection of the recognized international human rights within their sphere of influence, and ensuring that their own corporations are not complicit in human rights abuses. With regard to labour standards, the secretary-general asked business leaders to uphold the 'values that lie at the heart of Decent Work': freedom of association and the effective recognition of the right to collective bargaining, the elimination of all forms of forced and compulsory labour, the effective abolition of child labour, and the elimination of discrimination in employment and occupation. In terms of the environment, the compact supports a precautionary approach to environmental challenges, undertaking initiatives to promote greater environmental responsibility and encouraging the development and diffusion of environmentally friendly technologies.

In one form or another, many of these values have been implicit in different corporate codes of conduct for some time. The novelty of the Global Compact, however, is that the UN, through its secretary-general's declaration, stepped down from its high position as guardian of international values and principles and proposed a partnership with the business world. The extent to which this partnership is going to be beneficial to the international community, and especially to the millions of dispossessed of the world, remains to be seen.[35]

In brief, the UN secretary-general invites world business to assume a socially responsible position in conducting its economic activities, in exchange for being allowed to retain a self-regulatory status.[36] The Global Compact is essentially proposing two ways of achieving this goal. First, the TNCs could lobby to empower the international multilateral institutions, i.e. the International Labour Organization, the United Nations High Commissioner for Human Rights and the United Nations Environmental Programme, to actively promote and implement the different values, principles and standards encompassed in the Global Compact. It is relatively early to evaluate the extent to which this invitation will be beneficial.[37] For the time being, one can only speculate as to why TNCs would give the UN institutions more power, authority and resources than the TNCs would like nation-states themselves to exercise towards them.

The second path towards corporate social responsibility proposed by the Global Compact is direct action by the corporations themselves in their own spheres of corporate activity. According to the Global Compact declaration, the TNCs, through their activities across the world, have the opportunity to create a widely spread culture of rights and accountability, even in countries where the nation-state is too weak or unwilling to enforce the same values and principles.[38]

By upholding human rights, decent labour conditions and environmental standards directly through their own corporate conduct, the TNCs could voluntarily commit themselves to certain social standards of economic action. The Global Compact appears, from this point of view, to be an invitation to widely use tools such as codes of conduct. Given the spread of TNCs' codes of conduct in recent decades, one should look at how they have been shaped thus far and what impact they have had on addressing human development in the LDCs. The Global Compact itself is more a declaration of intent than a well-structured policy paper that incorporates the necessary tools for realizing its goals. Therefore, an analysis of at least some of the previous experiences with the codes of conduct and self-regulation can be very useful in evaluating whether the Global Compact itself will become an anti-poverty document.

Codes of conduct and their impact upon human development

The voluntary codes of conduct, together with other types of private initiatives, such as consumer boycotts, labelling, shareholder actions and ethical investment, are actions that attempt to harness the forces of global markets to address the needs of the broader community, as well as those of the corporate entities and shareholders.[39] Such private initiatives are by-products of the simultaneous, but unfortunately separate, universalist processes of the globalization of both market economy and human rights.[40] The promotion of the codes of conduct is one of the many ways in which various stakeholders in the global game attempt to instil into markets a missing ethical dimension or to keep at bay dreaded legal accountability.[41] At the same time, the reliance on codes of conduct is an example of the privatization of human rights. In this process, private actors, such as the TNCs,[42] are encouraged to become directly involved in defining the procedural paths and mechanisms for the realization of human rights. Given the intricate connection between the procedural and the substantive dimension of rights, there is a high probability that these private actors may end up defining not only the procedure but also the substance of certain human rights. It is unlikely that private actors, such as the TNCs, with significant economic and lobbying power, will challenge the status quo on which the present approach to poverty is based.[43] Therefore, their participation in defining human rights should be consultative rather than controlling.[44] As long as there are well-thought-out democratic checks and balances in the process of defining the values and standards to be enforced and the way in which all the stakeholders have their voices heard, however, the difficulties stemming from allowing a multitude of agents to take part in generating ideas for these mechanisms and procedures should be reduced.[45]

Currently, there is an inflation of rhetoric about rights, values and standards, and relatively few signs of effective mechanisms for implementation other than the TNC voluntary, internally sanctioned codes of conduct.[46] As we shall see in the following pages, the effectiveness of these codes depends upon a multitude of factors not always easy to congregate. And, indeed, effectiveness is the keyword through which both the codes and the Global Compact should be assessed. The voluntary codes of conduct have been developed not because of a lack of other regulatory initiatives addressing the human rights issues related to the TNCs' activities, but exactly because of a lack of effectiveness of the different initiatives taken by the international bodies. Most notably, one should mention the UN's own initiative in regulating the TNCs, the ILO Tripartite Declaration of Principles Concerning Multinational Enterprises and Social Policy, and the OECD Guidelines for Multinational Enterprises. A brief presentation of these initiatives will offer an insight into the difficulties faced by the UN Global Compact in its attempt to entice the TNCs towards self-assumed social responsibility.

The UN Draft Code of Conduct on Transnational Corporations

Reflecting an increased awareness of the impact that the TNCs can have upon the economic and social environment in which they act, in 1977 the United Nations Centre on Transnational Corporations (UNCTC) initiated negotiations among the member states designed to establish a code of conduct for the TNCs. The main goal of this code was to establish a convergence between the economic activity of the TNCs and the national development goals pursued by the host countries. In order to achieve these goals, the UNCTC had the task of identifying the rights and responsibilities of both TNCs and the countries in which they operated.

The UNCTC aimed to establish a rapport between the TNCs and the host countries resulting in mutual supportiveness. Major provisions of the Draft Code included respect for national sovereignty and observance of domestic laws, regulations and administrative practices, adherence to national economic goals and development objectives, policies and priorities, and review and renegotiation of contracts or agreements between governments and TNCs. The Draft Code also included an acknowledgement that states have the right, after paying an appropriate compensation, to nationalize or expropriate the assets of a TNC operating in their territory. Particular importance was given to the protection of the environment in which the TNCs operated.[47]

If adopted and implemented, the code would have had a significant impact on the way in which the TNCs operated in their host countries. Disclosure requirements, for instance, would have forced TNCs to provide information on issues such as health and safety records of their employees, and details of any prohibitions, restrictions and other regulatory measures imposed on their products in any other country. Also, they would have had to disclose any possible hazardous effects of their products through proper labelling, and through informative and accurate advertising.

In spite of some progress, difficult disagreements brought the negotiations to a halt, and in 1992 the UNCTC abandoned the code. One of the major stumbling blocks, especially in the context of North–South tensions, was the issue regarding the code's position within the international law system and the United Nations' role in administering the code. This should be a warning sign for proponents of the new UN Global Compact approach, especially in assuming that implementation might result from TNCs lobbying their home governments to give the UN bodies the necessary power and resources to promote human rights, labour standards and environmental values. Another very contentious point in the Draft Code was the possible use of economic sanctions.[48]

On the one hand, from these failed negotiations, we inherit the first systematic definition of the TNC and a general acknowledgement that TNCs can have a lasting and not always positive impact upon the economies and politics of their host countries. On the other hand, the message sent by the negotiations on the substantive elements of the Draft Code was that consensus is difficult to achieve when dealing with a treaty that is too broad, and that obscure and imprecise language can only hamper achievement of the articulated goals.

TNCs under the ILO standards

The International Labour Organization (ILO) also has given special attention to TNCs by adopting in 1977 the Tripartite Declaration of Principles

Concerning Multinational Enterprises and Social Policy (the Declaration).[49] To a certain extent the Declaration was in response to the pressure from the LDCs during the 1960s and 1970s for a legally binding code for the TNCs. An enforceable code was strongly opposed, however, by the employers' representatives, who, not surprisingly, favoured a voluntary code.[50]

Through the process of adopting this Declaration, the ILO succeeded in avoiding some of the mistakes made during the UN Draft Code negotiations. Notably, it succeeded in reaching a consensus among all the interested parties by clearly and narrowly defining the scope of the Declaration,[51] defining the aim so as to encourage the positive contribution that multinational enterprises (MNEs)[52] can make to economic and social progress and to minimize and resolve the difficulties raised by their various operations. The Declaration states that, through international direct investment and other means, the MNEs can bring substantial benefit to both home and host countries by contributing to a more efficient utilization of capital, technology and labour.

The Declaration recognizes, however, an even deeper correlation between the activity of the MNEs and human development by anticipating MNEs' potential to make an important contribution to the promotion of economic and social welfare, to the improvement of living standards and the satisfaction of basic needs, to the creation of employment opportunities, and to the enjoyment of basic human rights throughout the world. At the same time, spelling out the underlying rationale of the Declaration, the document emphasizes that the advances made by MNEs in organizing their operations beyond the national framework may lead to abusive concentrations of economic power and to conflicts with national policy objectives and with the interests of workers. The Declaration also gives voice to a deeper social anxiety derived from the complexity of MNEs and the difficulty of clearly perceiving their diverse structures, operations and policies.[53]

The Declaration refers to several ILO Conventions and Recommendations. Supported by governments and employers' and workers' organizations, it invites all governments of member states of the ILO, the employers' and workers' organizations concerned and the MNEs operating in their territories to observe the principles embodied in the Declaration and in the referenced Conventions and Recommendations. It calls on member states to ratify ILO conventions numbers 87, 98, 111 and 122, along with Recommendations 111, 119 and 122, referring to freedom of association, the right to organize and to bargain collectively, discrimination in employment and occupation, and employment policy.[54]

When adopted in 1977, the ILO Declaration did not provide for any follow-up machinery. This weakness was addressed in 1980 by the ILO Governing Body, which established a Committee on Multinational Enterprises (the Committee). The Committee fulfils three tasks. First, it receives periodic reports on the implementation of the Declaration. These reports take the form of answers to questionnaires sent to union and business organizations through national governments. Second, the Committee conducts periodic studies on labour issues related to MNEs' activity. Third, it fulfils an interpretative function, through a dispute procedure that was revised in 1986. The procedure is not judicial in nature and serves merely to clarify the standards contained in the Declaration. Although the Committee can issue such a clarification only in the context of a concrete situation, the Committee offers no resolution of disputes over facts and laws.[55]

An important feature of this document is that, being based on consensus, the Declaration encourages dialogue between the MNEs and the home and host country governments.[56] Given the fact that all consulted parties agreed with its aims and objectives, to a certain extent the Declaration is changing the ethos in which governments and the MNEs function. Its general acceptance, by governments and employers' and workers' organizations, implies that it constitutes standards that society as a whole requires to be upheld. Although the Declaration does not provide a forum for all the social stakeholders to take part in the negotiation of these standards, its tripartite dimension gives the Declaration a certain morally binding character.

The fact that it is a selective tool, considering certain stakeholders but not others, is not the only drawback of the ILO Declaration. Since it is not legally binding, the Declaration cannot be used to redress misuse of power by the MNEs, even when such power breaches the Declaration itself. It only invites governments of member states of the ILO, the employers' and workers' organizations concerned and the MNEs operating in their territories to observe the principles embodied therein. Besides, the Declaration does not require MNEs to engage in socially responsible activities over and above what is required by law in the host countries. Given the declared powerlessness of the governments of the LDCs with respect to the MNEs, this aspect is an important limitation on the potential of the Declaration to bring about any change in the ethos of the global market for the benefit of the weakest parts of society.

Another, more recent ILO document which addresses the need for socially responsible actions on the part of MNEs is the Declaration on Fundamental Principles and Rights at Work.[57] This Declaration was adopted by the International Labour Conference in June 1998, and states that all members, even if they have not ratified the conventions in question, have an obligation, arising from the very fact of membership of the organization, to respect, promote and realize, in good faith and in accordance with the constitution, the principles concerning the fundamental rights that are the subject of those conventions, namely: (a) freedom of association and the effective recognition of the right to collective bargaining, (b) the elimination of all forms of forced or compulsory labour, (c) the effective abolition of child labour, and (d) the elimination of discrimination in respect of employment and occupation.

The advantage of placing the MNEs' social responsibility more solidly within the ILO system of conventions is that the ILO offers a supervisory mechanism. This mechanism obligates the states to periodically submit reports on their efforts to meet the principles and objectives of the ratified conventions. In addition, general complaint procedures have been established to supervise compliance with the ratified conventions. The ILO has created a Committee of Experts on the Application of Conventions and Recommendations, consisting of independent experts who give their opinion on the application of the ratified conventions and other obligations under the ILO constitution relating to international labour standards. This Committee is responsible for indicating the extent to which each state's situation appears to be in conformity with the conventions and the obligations undertaken by that state pursuant to the ILO constitution. It also provides guidance on how to apply the standards in specific circumstances.

While there has been some progress regarding supervision of compliance from the 1977 ILO Tripartite Declaration to the 1998 Declaration, the mechanisms instituted by the ILO could not be characterized as real enforcement mechanisms. Through its well-established and coherent system of negotiated conventions, however, the ILO represents a source of inspiration and substance to be incorporated in other potential documents, such as voluntary codes of conduct adopted by TNCs. In this sense, it should be noted that the secretary-general's declaration on the Global Compact refers to the ILO conventions as an authoritative source for labour standards which should be upheld by the TNCs.

TNCs under the OECD Guidelines

The OECD Declaration on International Investment and Multinational Enterprises, adopted in 1976 by all OECD member states, takes the form of a recommendation from OECD governments to MNEs[58] to abide by a set of Guidelines annexed to the Declaration.[59] The Guidelines are reviewed periodically, most recently in June 2000. The Guidelines cover a range of issues, including general policy, information disclosure, competition, financing, taxation, employment and industrial relations, the environment, and science and technology.[60]

The Declaration is a legally non-binding instrument that recommends that MNEs and member countries observe certain rules of conduct in the course of their economic activities in a host country. Thus the observance of these rules is, yet again, voluntary and not legally enforceable. The Guidelines give priority to national laws, in that the obligations that the Guidelines place on MNEs can only supplement, never contradict, obligations stemming from national laws. Also, the General Policies section of the Guidelines outlines a number of requirements that are vague and insufficiently clear and, therefore, incapable of establishing actual standards of behaviour.

The Guidelines established a complaint procedure that appears to have a tripartite format: governments, labour and business. In reality, however, labour (Trade Union Advisory Committee – TUAC)[61] and business (Business and Industry Advisory Committee – BIAC)[62] lobbies have only consultative status. There is no institutional structure for implementing and monitoring the commitments issuing from the Guidelines, apart from a network of regional offices or National Contact Points (NCPs).[63] These NCPs are not pro-active enough to be widely recognized or to have a real impact on implementation.

The Guidelines also lack teeth from another point of view. In the case of a dispute, the OECD Council has the power to adopt decisions clarifying the Guidelines, which are binding on all OECD members. The matters are raised 'hypothetically' before the Council, however, thus resulting in decisions formulated as 'clarification of the Guidelines'. The Council does not judge the conduct of individual enterprises and therefore the decisions neither accept nor reject the truth of any actual situation.

Given the euphemistic character of these clarifying decisions, the OECD system cannot be viewed as influencing actual behaviour. TNCs are reluctant to report on compliance with the Guidelines in their annual reports, suggesting that the code has not been assimilated into mainstream corporate practice. On the contrary, business's general formal support for the Guidelines reflects the fact that the Guidelines do little to constrain business in any practical way. All these elements suggest, as was stated in a paper disseminated by the Friends of the Earth organization, that the Guidelines are 'business-friendly to the point of being ineffective'.[64] Moreover, '[they] are moderate, non-specific, voluntary, poorly-implemented and fail to call for public disclosure of information regarding TNC breaches of the Guidelines. In addition, they are in many cases not well-known and in all cases poorly regarded.'[65]

Voluntary codes of conduct and the marketplace

So far, it appears that institutional attempts to give the global market and its agents a human face have not been very successful.[66] In the last few decades, it has also become obvious that national governments cannot, in isolation and without the cooperation of the business world, address global issues such as human development and poverty, environmental protection and the democratic accountability of different international financial institutions and, of course, the TNCs.[67] The ILO Tripartite Declaration and the OECD Guidelines on Multinational Corporations have some formal influence on the TNCs' attempts to regulate themselves through voluntary adherence to social standards of economic activity. In practical terms, however, the weaknesses of these documents are reflected in a rather poor record. This situation has prompted certain non-governmental organizations (NGOs), consumer movements and shareholders' associations, as well as TNCs themselves, to choose the path of private action through promoting voluntary codes of conduct that would regulate the TNCs' activities in areas where national and international norms have failed to do so, by reflecting best practices as well as internationally acknowledged standards.[68]

The codes of conduct adopted by the TNCs are non-legal regulatory arrangements that aim to shape corporate behaviour in the marketplace by establishing benchmarks for both individual and organizational behaviour. They add a new dimension to a corporation's charter, helping to consolidate into the TNCs' activities a set of values and principles which, although not economic in character, are seen as paramount in mitigating conflicting social interests. Generally speaking, such codes encourage, or are hoped to encourage, organizations to conduct business in ways that would benefit both themselves and the community in which they operate. They are usually initiated in response to NGO campaigns, consumer or competitive pressures, real or perceived threat of new legislation, regulation or trade sanctions, or a combination of these factors.[69]

The apparel and footwear industries offer several examples of codes of conduct that provide guidelines for specific activities.[70] These industries frequently rely on the use of subcontractors in developing countries, where labour is cheap and working conditions are often deplorable. Their products are sometimes made under intolerable circumstances, with use of forced, bonded or child labour. As a result, companies have been pressured to adopt ethical rules with regard to the activities of their subcontractors. The codes of conduct of C&A, Gap, Levi Strauss, Nike and Reebok are only a few examples of such rules. Although these codes are far from perfect, they do incorporate a broad range of ethical standards concerning labour relations, the environment and human rights. While these standards are often ignored in practice,[71] no TNC would openly declare its disregard for them on the basis that they are outside the corporate legal framework. While the codes of conduct cannot be enforced by a court of law, often their underlying moral value indirectly lends a normative force to the stated principles.

When carefully designed, a code of conduct is supposed to advance the interests of all parties involved. Social stakeholders, such as consumers, NGOs, labour and governments, can all benefit by bringing to the economic agenda the recognition of certain values, principles and standards that otherwise would not be viewed automatically as belonging to the liberal economic paradigm. When properly monitored, for instance, the codes serve as a sign that an organization's products or services meet certain social standards that go beyond the reliability of products or quality of service.

Another advantage of voluntary codes is the ability to further public policy objectives through non-regulatory means, complementing and expanding existing regulatory regimes, and avoiding jurisdictional and constitutional obstacles.[72] Also, voluntary codes can set and adjust standards more quickly than laws and regulations. Moreover, by going beyond what is currently the standard set by law, the codes can prepare society in general and the economic environment in particular to accept higher ethical standards as legal mandates at a later stage. The relationship between voluntary codes of conduct and the law is, therefore, a dynamic one, with the codes sometimes preceding legislative initiatives, while at other times simply filling in the legal gaps.[73]

The main question is, of course, why would a TNC find it economically viable to voluntarily adhere to such a social charter? One good reason would be that, by working collectively to reduce the negative impacts of their activities, the corporations can put themselves in a more favourable light with, for example, customers, governments, potential ethically minded shareholders and investors. Other potential advantages can be an improved market share for the corporation and a better diffusion of new technologies and best management practices within an industry, as well as proving adaptability and responsiveness by providing prompt feedback on consumer preference. By volunteering to uphold certain values or standards, TNCs also have the collective benefit of fending off pressure for new, tougher national or international regulations. Considering all these profit-oriented incentives while not excluding the possibility of genuinely assumed corporate social responsibility, one has to remain realistic about the TNCs' rationale in adopting voluntary codes of conduct.

Building an environment of corporate social responsibility outside the hard core of the legal framework, through a system of voluntary codes, is not always an easy task. Consistency, effectiveness and substance are values difficult to attain under such a system. For instance, not all the codes address the same problems, and even specific codes of conduct do not always effectively address fundamental problems such as the use of forced and bonded labour. Also, many codes fail to include the right to organize and the right to collective bargaining, two empowering tools that could make a significant difference in an anti-poverty campaign.[74] Instead, the codes usually lay down general ethical standards that the companies intend to uphold.

The enforcement mechanism of such standards is generally weak or non-existent, with no sanctions or remedies in case of non-compliance. There is usually no proper complaint procedure and no basis for legal claims by third parties. These characteristics can limit considerably a code's usefulness as a vehicle for social policy.[75] Furthermore, the vaguely formulated standards included in most existing corporate codes of conduct fail to offer sufficiently clear guidance in specific situations, even to the well-intended companies.

Where provided, the implementation and supervisory mechanism of most codes frequently lacks a high level of transparency and accountability. Most corporate codes of conduct claim to be designed as instruments to assign or assume social responsibility by guiding a company's activities through the expression of values. Assigning responsibility should not, however, imply only identifying responsibility, but also accounting for it, and this is an aspect often left unclear in a code of conduct.[76] Not surprisingly, this ambiguity has consequences for controlling the implementation of the values and standards promoted through the codes.

Of all the weaknesses of a voluntary system, perhaps the most difficult to deal with is not establishing a consistent and useful content of the code, but rather the practical implementation, finding a way to internalize external values and standards in a corporation's organizational charter, influencing the ethos by which that corporation conducts its business.[77] One solution to this problem could be developing a system of procedures of non-financial/social auditing. Once the substantive parameters of a code have been established or, as suggested in the Global Compact, once a TNC has signed up – via the Global Compact, for instance – to a set of conventions and declarations already present in the international public domain, there is no reason why accounting firms could not be able to verify assertions regarding the corporate social performance.

Environmental auditing, for instance, has gained increasing legitimacy in the last two decades, while social and ethical auditing is in its early stage. Human rights, however, is the area where audit procedures are weakest.[78] Given the fact that accounting firms are expert in audit methodologies, but not in human rights and labour standards, new procedures need to be developed with strong input from human rights and labour experts.

These experts will have to assist the business world in developing auditable measures of performance and methods to generate data substantial enough to be worth auditing. For instance, the ILO has substantial knowledge, authority and expertise in the labour domain. Thus, this institution should have significant input in designing auditing models, as well as in norm-setting and application processes.

External accounting would require clear and public standards and an independent assurance process. Unfortunately, so far, most existing corporate codes of conduct focus on values, not on norms or rights. When they refer to human rights at all, they usually do not provide sufficiently clear guidance for specific situations. A focus on values brings about amorphous standards, resulting in vague commitments that risk leading to the obfuscation of norms. This type of imprecision renders social auditing practically impossible, a fact that spares the TNCs the embarrassment of being accused of violating their own standards. Effective public reporting and independent auditing – which would identify a company's social policy and analyse all the stakeholders' expectations – are, however, manifestly interesting not only to society but to the corporate actors as well.[79] A company that adopts human rights standards will have an obvious interest in showing that its acts are in compliance with these standards. Clearer and firmer mechanisms of implementation and control would enhance the company's credibility and serve to legitimize its operations in the eyes of the public.

Thus far, however, independent supervision and audit of implementation has contributed very little to a more appropriate marriage between the globalization of market economy and the globalization of human rights. Rather, the shaping of corporate social responsibility has distinctly followed a path of privatization of human rights, whereby TNCs endorse codes of conduct proclaiming universally recognized human rights values, while at the same time retaining a monopoly over their implementation and realization. Given the close relationship between these mechanisms of implementation and actual human rights, the substance of these rights is also likely to be affected. If the ILO, the OECD and the UN through its Global Compact are unable to offer a coherent mechanism of implementation and control, we are left cautiously following only this path of privatization of human rights, with the hope that, sooner or later, it will develop into an independent and effective road for the promotion of human rights.

Conclusion

Judging from the current evolution of the voluntary codes of conduct and from the ethos created by documents such as the UNDP Poverty Report 2000 and the UN Global Compact, it appears that 'private' initiatives such as the voluntary codes will occupy a significant place in policies addressing the social shortcomings of globalization,[80] including social exclusion, poverty, environmental pollution and democratic deficit. International institutions, such as the UN, that choose to favour a form of voluntary codes over other means of regulating the global market should be cognizant of and carefully consider a number of issues.

First, clarity is a virtue lacking in many current codes of conduct. The aims, roles and responsibilities included in a code should, therefore, be as precisely formulated as possible, in order to eliminate false expectations and avoid future controversies to the extent possible. That being said, of course, words are always subject to interpretation, and the formulation of the purpose and ground rules should recognize that the code retains flexibility, and can be interpreted to address new circumstances. Codes should also be complemented – as suggested in the UNDP Poverty Report – by some type of transnational element, such as inter-governmental co-operation and/or transnational regulatory systems.

Second, the codes should have an open and transparent implementation mechanism that involves all stakeholders in the globalization process, for example workers, suppliers, competitors, consumers, NGOs and governments. The participation of all stakeholders will increase the effectiveness of the codes and enhance their credibility. The same process should incorporate effective channels for a regular flow of information through self-reporting, public reporting, third-party monitoring and compliance verification. Last but not least, an effective and transparent dispute resolution system should be in place.

In addition, the designer of the code should not ignore the efficacy of traditional methods of inducing compliance, i.e. the carrot *and* the stick. As for carrots, the code should provide meaningful incentives to the signatories of the code, so that commitment and participation make good business sense. Examples of such inducements could be access to information, technology or marketing tools not available to others, and eligibility for public procurement contracts. The UN Global Compact, as a preamble to a voluntary system, provided two such elements: the promise of avoiding or discouraging domestic or international regulation, and the possibility for those involved in the Global Compact partnership of using the UN logo as an advertising tool. The rewards for responsible corporate behaviour should be significant enough to constitute a commercially attractive motivation and, at the same time, to appear as a loss and a 'comparative disadvantage' for the corporations that choose not to join the code. As for the corporations that adhere to, but fail to comply with, the code, the repercussions should be easier to design (at least theoretically), 'hitting where it hurts'. One such repercussion, for instance, could be making public the act of non-compliance and naming the non-compliant TNC in the hope that effective consumer pressure would be brought to bear. Alternatively, fines could be applied for failure to comply with the code. As noted earlier, however, fines are quite an uncommon component in the current world of voluntary corporate ethics.

Therefore, the UN invitation to the TNCs to form a social responsibility partnership should be approached by all parties involved with much caution. Failure to pay due attention to the elements mentioned above will frustrate the realization of human rights in general and of socio-economic rights in particular. Codes that are not backed by good mechanisms of implementation and monitoring can actually do more harm than good. If it does not function properly, the presence of a code may actually impede the emergence of a legal remedy that could address the undesired practices in a more appropriate and firmer fashion. An ineffective code, adopted only as part of a public relations exercise, could result in lack of credibility among the affected stakeholders, and a backlash against economic processes that could otherwise bring real benefits to the societies participating in those endeavours.[81]

Thus, while the TNC codes of conduct should not be rejected outright, they should not be regarded as a regulatory panacea either. The UN policy of initiating a partnership with the world business community might in the end bring results that have largely eluded other declarations, guidelines and standards set by the international community. In order to secure optimal results, however, such processes of privatization of human rights cannot remain purely private. There must be a finely tuned implementation and monitoring system applied to carefully designed policies which would account for the rights and interests of all the stakeholders. Only in this way can self-assumed corporate social responsibility begin, as suggested in the UNDP documents and the UN Global Compact, to complement effectively the international and domestic policies addressing poverty and human development.

Notes

The author would like to thank Michael Likoski, Claire Mayer and Lucy Williams for their detailed comments on an earlier draft of this paper, as well as Margarita Gabriela Prieto Acosta, Khandakar Quadrat-I Elahi, Marius Olivier, Linda Jansen van Rensburg and Asuncion Lera St Clair for their helpful comments during the Law and Poverty IV workshop, where an earlier version of this paper was first presented. The author would also like to acknowledge the support received from the British Academy, Lincoln College, Oxford University, and the Centre for Socio-legal Studies, Oxford University.

1 For an analysis of the demands of the process of globalization on social
and economic structures, see Greider (1997).

2 Trying to encapsulate the main characteristic of the process of globalization, Robé (1997: 45) writes that '[the] really new phenomena brought about
by the so-called globalization of the economy do not rely merely on the
increase in international commerce. What is new, in its relative importance,
is that the control of fragmented production processes, spread all over the
world, is now exercised by *organizations* which have themselves spread
beyond state frontiers. This development throws into confusion such classical
legal notions as the sovereignty and impermeability of the various state legal
orders.'

3 The reference to transnational corporations (TNCs) follows the terminology used in United Nations documents and publications such as UNCTC,
'Transnational Corporations in World Development' (1986), and 'United
Nations Code of Conduct on Transnational Corporations' (1986). The doctri-
nal differences between this term and others, such as multinational corporation, multinational enterprise or international company, are not engaged in
this chapter. The choice of terminology is deliberate, however, trying to convey
the key tensions between the TNC as an economic entity and the national
normative environment. When referring to regulatory instruments, or quoting
from authors using another terminology, this chapter will adopt that specific
terminology. For instance, in accordance with the ILO and OECD practice,
where appropriate 'multinational enterprise (MNE)' will be used instead of
'TNC'. No distinction is intended in this chapter, however, between these
terms. For a description of the nature and activities of transnational corporations, issues that are not approached here, see Muchlinski (1999); Barnet and
Muller (1974); Vernon (1971, 1977); Modelski (1979). For an analysis of the
legal aspects, see Blumberg (1993), and for the economic perspective, Lall
(1980). The intersection between transnational corporations' activity and the
human rights implications is exhaustively addressed in Addo (1999).

4 For a systematic analysis of this problematic relationship between economic growth and poverty, see Øyen (2000).

5 According to some authors, the relevant question in economic policy
is not whether we need a neo-liberal or a socially sensitive economic policy
model but how to make a market-oriented economic system more 'socially
sensitive' (Kirton et al. 2001: 15).

6 Breitenfellner (1997: 531–55).

7 For a socio-legal perspective on the economic aspects of globalization
and their importance for the emergence of a global legal pluralism, see Snyder
(in press).

8 Ostry (1997: 5); Gilpin (1987: 234).

9 UNCTC (1986) 'The United Nations Code of Conduct on Transnational
Corporations', UNCTC Current Studies Series A, no. 4, UN Doc. ST/CTC/SER.
A/4, September.

10 According to Richard E. Caves, foreign direct investment is an integral
part of the global corporate strategy for firms operating in oligopolistic
markets (Caves 1982). Referring to foreign direct investment, Gilpin writes

that '[whereas] traditional portfolio investment is driven by differential rates of return among national economies, foreign direct investment is determined by the growth and competitive strategies of the oligopolistic corporations. Although the former has most frequently been concentrated in government loans and infrastructure types of investment, direct investment tends to be sector-specific and is usually based on the existence of some competitive advantage over local firms, advantages that the corporation wishes to exploit or preserve. As this type of investment creates economic relations of an integrative nature and involves the corporation in the internal economic affairs of a country, it has become extremely controversial' (Gilpin 1987: 233; see also Julius 1990).

11 Using quantitative analysis, William H. Meyer seeks to establish a certain positive correlation between the level of direct foreign investment and the practice of civil and political rights in developing countries. In his study, Meyer also correlates positively direct foreign investment with the Physical Quality of Life Index, measuring longevity, nutrition and education. Meyer concludes that in the modern world TNCs are engines of progressive development, associated with improved civil and political, as well as socio-economic, rights (Meyer 1996: 368–97). For a debate and his methods and conclusions see also Meyer (1998).

12 Gilpin (1987: 247f, 262).

13 Krugman and Venables (1995).

14 Vaitsos (1974).

15 Altvater writes that '[the] idea of sovereignty having a territorial character is rendered ridiculous in times of globalization' (1999: 289).

16 OECD (1996: 199).

17 For an elaborate way of defining corporate social responsibility, see Ethos (2000).

18 Compa, L. and T. Hinchliffe Darricarrere (1995: 663–89); Wilkins (1974); Gilpin (1987: 238–41).

19 Of course, the state has contributed decisively to the definition of this public–private dichotomy, through the 'identification' of apparently neutral concepts that are in fact meant to perpetuate specific power structures. See, for instance, Williams on the definition of the concept of 'right' and 'entitlement' in the US welfare regulations (Williams 1998: 569–90). At the same time, an important aspect of the global dynamics is exactly the fact that, although the state has been giving the first kick to the ball of globalization and has established the rules of the game, rules that are still favouring the elites, the state is no more the only, or the main, player in the game. Moreover, now the state has often to run a lot harder after the ball in order to remain in the game. At this point in the globalization process, the only way in which the state can regain the monopoly it used to have over the running of socio-economic affairs would be unrealistic: simply to take the ball and 'go home'. This would practically stop the game completely, with consequences that would be hard to predict.

20 For this last aspect, see McCrudden (1999: 167–201). Regarding the

social standards that apply to business agents, according to the United
Nations High Commissioner for Human Rights it appears that there is a wide
variety of human rights standards which apply, in varying degrees, to the private sector: 'Principles that directly affect a business's employees; Principles
that involve a company's business partners, and their employees, both in the
public and private sector; Principles that affect the community and general
human rights environment in which a company operates; "Hybrid issues" that
may implicate a company and public institutions to various degrees, or may
involve concern for individual human rights, the environment, and community concerns' (UNHCHR 2000).

21 See, again, Snyder (in press).

22 This is fully proven by the development at the domestic level of the
concept of corporate collective agency and responsibility. Establishing
meaningful corporate social responsibility appears for some to be impossible,
owing to the final reduction of a corporation from a collectivity to its individual members, or to specific dimensions of a corporation's charter. See, respectively, Velasquez (1991: 111–31); and Donaldson (1982). Other authors argue,
however, that with the right mechanism the corporate organizations can be
induced to internalize a much-desired dimension of social responsibility. In
this sense, see Stone (1991); Selznick (1994: 396–402). Building on the domain
of organizational structure, Peter French offers a theory of corporate collective responsibility in which he moves from the causal attribution of liability,
with its requirement of intention and action in the same body, to a collective
attribution that requires a coincidence of action and 'reasons for action' in
the same structure. See French (1991: 133–51). For the responsibility of more
ambiguous organizational structures, see Held (1991: 89–100); Voiculescu
(2000, especially chs 4 and 5, pp. 165–259).

23 '[Globalization]', writes Snyder, 'has tended to weaken, fragment, and
sometimes even restructure the state, but has not by any means destroyed or
replaced it. Globalization has also altered radically the relationship to which
we have become accustomed in recent history between governance and territory. It thus has blurred and splintered the boundaries between the domestic
and external spheres of nation-state and of regional integration organizations;
fostered the articulation of systems of multi-level governance, interlocking
politics and policy networks; and helped to render universal the discourse of
and claims for human rights' Snyder (in press: 2). See also Ohmae (1990).

24 Analysing the emergence of a global legal pluralism, of which domestic
law is only one element, Teubner writes that '[the] fragmentation of world
society creates a very peculiar form of global law which should not be measured against the standards of unified national legal systems [...]. Its peculiar
characteristics can be explained by the relative absence of political and
institutional support on the global level and by its close dependency on other
globalized social processes' Teubner (1997b: xiv).

25 '[The] sovereign state', writes Falk, 'is changing course due primarily to
the widespread adoption of neoliberal approaches to governmental function
... The role of the state is changing in response to a transformed global setting, but not uniformly. States are very differently situated and endowed, and

Privatizing human rights?

have at their disposal a wide range of adjustment strategies and capabilities. Nevertheless, there exists a broad cumulative trend toward the social disempowerment of the state. This trend encourages private sector "solutions" to such social issues as poverty, unemployment, and alienation, including the emergence of the billionaire philanthropy as practiced by such exemplary figures as Ted Turner, George Soros, and Bill Gates' Falk (2000: 1).

26 Referring to a complementarity of responsibilities for the protection of human rights, Dias writes: '*Limburg* and *Maastricht* focus solely on State obligations. However, given the increasing significance of non-state actors, it may well be argued that the *obligation to respect* applies to all actors, state and non-state alike. So, too, the *obligation to protect*, at least against the consequences of one's own acts, could apply to all actors, state and non-state alike' Dias (2000).

27 See Schachter (1998: 31–44).

28 UNDP (2000).

29 UN (1999).

30 For a critique of this approach, see De Waart (1998: 109–31).

31 On this aspect, see also Williams (1998).

32 '[The] capacity of the "local" to disintegrate the "global" should not be underestimated,' writes Muchlinski. 'Forced globalization will marginalize communities that do not possess the economic, social and political structures that are conducive to the effective pursuit of MNE activities. These may be entire countries or regions or districts within countries. Such areas will be forced to redefine their way of life in the absence of significant MNE presence. Such counter-cultures may be informed by the same capitalist ideology as the globalizing culture, or they may not. They may be stigmatized as criminal, as in the case of black markets or illegal drugs cartels. They may be seen as "other-worldly," as in the case of ecological or spiritual movements. However, the extent to which such counter-cultures gather pace will be a significant variable to determining the growth and future history of the "global Bukowina" and its legal projects' Muchlinski (1997: 103).

33 UN (1999).

34 These values and principles are defined, however, in relation to the WTO/GATT trade regime and its need of social updating as 'the new trade agenda'. See Gilpin (2001: 225–31); Destler and Balint (1999); Esty (1994).

35 According to some, the Global Compact is a sign that the UN has engaged on the 'slippery slope toward privatization and commercialization of the UN system itself' Bruno and Karliner (2000). Highlighting the danger that the UN could become a tool that would 'create benefits for a small privileged minority at the expense of an increasingly disenfranchised majority', citizen organizations and movements have proposed a compact between the UN and civil society, regarding the UN's relationship with the private sector, with the scope of safeguarding the image, mission and credibility of the United Nations as it deals with the private sector. See TRAC (2000a). Related to the same aspects, there is presently a new UN initiative which focuses on capturing, in a document of a yet undefined normative weight, the responsibilities of

TNCs. The most recent draft text of this document is referred to as the 'Draft Norms of Responsibilities of Transnational Corporations and Other Business Enterprises with Regard to Human Rights' and was produced by the UN Sub-Commission on Human Rights (UN Doc. E/CN.4/Sub.2/2002/13, 15 August 2002). For details on this document see <www1.umn.edu/humanrts/links/tncreport-2002.html> or <www.business-humanrights.org>.

36 In his address to the World Economic Forum, UN Secretary-General Kofi Annan stated that '[there] is enormous pressure from various interest groups to load the trade regime and the investment agreements with restrictions aimed at preserving standards in the three areas [human rights, labour standards and environment]. These are legitimate concerns. But restrictions on trade and investment are not the right means to use when tackling them. Instead, we should find a way to achieve our proclaimed standards by other means. And that is precisely what the compact I am proposing to you is meant to do' (UN 1999).

37 A precedent, for instance, would seem to confirm this worry. The Global Sustainable Development Facility, a partnership for poverty alleviation between the United Nations Development Programme (UNDP) and a group of transnational corporations, had to be abandoned in June 2000 since 'it did little to advance the UNDP's mission of serving the world's poor'. For details, see TRAC (2000b).

38 According to a report prepared by the Office of the High Commissioner for Human Rights, by being a UN initiative the Global Compact might be seen as giving employers a greater voice with governments and in international policy matters (OHCHR 2000).

39 See OECD (1996: 199–204).

40 Compa and Hinchliffe Darricarrere (1996: 181f).

41 Diller (1999).

42 NGOs also play an important and increasing role in this process of privatization of human rights. See Forsythe (2000: 163–89).

43 See, for instance, in this book, Bas de Gaay Fortman's chapter on 'Poverty as a failure of entitlement'. 'Poverty', writes Fortman, 'is to be seen as "a brutal denial of human rights" ... Hence, rights-based strategies [of tackling poverty] confront the status quo. As such they differ from development approaches based on a harmonious striving for progress ... the basic orientation is not national resources, but the constraints in poor people's daily struggle for sustainable livelihoods .' For an example of how the concept of 'right' can be defined in a fashion that would preserve the status quo, see Williams (1998).

44 Forsythe (2000: 12–13). For a wider perspective on the detrimental impacts of economic globalization and the creative initiatives that are emerging in many settings in response to these impacts, see Falk (1999: 137–52).

45 In this sense, Teubner writes that 'when the frame of rule hierarchy, with constitutionally legitimated political legislation at its top, breaks under the pressures of globalization, then the new frame which replaces it can only be heterarchical' (Teubner 1997b: xiv).

46 Forsythe (2000: 201).

47 UNCTC (1986) 'The United Nations Code of Conduct on Transnational Corporations'.

48 On this aspect, see Rodman (1998: 19–42).

49 ILO (1978).

50 Robinson (1983: 171).

51 For a discussion of cases arising under the ILO Declaration, see Glade and Potter (1989).

52 See above, note 3.

53 ILO Tripartite Declaration, Introduction, para. 1. In relation to this concern expressed in the Declaration, and for a well-informed analysis of the evolution and the legal forms of TNCs, see Muchlisnki (1999: 19–89).

54 ILO Tripartite Declaration, General Policies, para. 9.

55 ILO Doc. GB. 232/12/15 February/March 1985, cited in Muchlinski (1999: 459).

56 Diller (2000: 67–88). Referring to the need for a wider participation of all social stakeholders in the process of globalization, Mark Halle states that '[it] is time to recognise that there is an emerging global standard for transparency, participation and access to judicial processes, which cannot be ignored. It is the basis of the new global governance' Halle (2000: 13–14).

57 ILO (1998). See also Kellerson (1998: 223–8).

58 See above, note 3.

59 OECD (1976).

60 Ibid. See also Campbell and Rowan (1983).

61 The Trade Union Advisory Committee to the OECD is an interface for labour unions with the OECD. It is an international trade union organization which has consultative status with the OECD and its various committees (<www.tuac.org>).

62 The Business and Industry Advisory Committee to the OECD (BIAC) was constituted in March 1962 as an independent organization officially recognized by the OECD as being representative of business and industry. BIAC's role is to provide the OECD and its member governments with comments based on the interests and the practical experience of the business community.

63 The Council provides that '[adhering] countries shall set up National Contact Points for undertaking promotional activities, handling inquiries and for discussions with the parties concerned on all matters covered by the Guidelines so that they can contribute to the solution of problems which may arise in this connection [...]. The business community, employee organisations, and other interested parties shall be informed of the availability of such facilities' (OECD 2000).

64 FoE (1998).

65 Ibid.

66 Secretary-General Kofi Annan spoke about 'globalisation with a human face' as the goal of the Global Compact. See UN (1999).

67 See Blanpain and Hanami (2000: ix–xi). In this sense, the OECD governments have acknowledged in the Guidelines for Multinational Enterprises that '[the] common aim of the governments adhering to the Guidelines is to encourage the positive contributions that multinational enterprises can make to economic, environmental and social progress and to minimise the difficulties to which their various operations may give rise. In working towards this goal, governments find themselves in partnership with the many businesses, trade unions and other non-governmental organisations that are working in their own ways toward the same end.' See OECD (2000).

68 For a survey of company initiatives, see Makower (1994).

69 Murray (1998: 45–115). See also Snyder (in press).

70 For an overview of labour issues addressed in codes of conduct in the garment, sportswear and toy industries, see, for instance, the Clean Clothes Campaign (1998).

71 Ibid.

72 See Snyder (in press).

73 Analysing the Sullivan and MacBride Principles, two private initiatives addressing mainly equality of employment opportunities in, respectively, South Africa and Northern Ireland, McCrudden writes that '[both] codes acted as a stimulus to the development of law in their areas of concern, operating like water that seeps into rock and, by continually freezing and unfreezing, creates fissures and cracks that contribute to collapse and its subsequent replacement by something different'. Exemplifying even more the teasing relationship between the voluntary codes and the law, McCrudden adds that ' ... [the] challenging role of the MacBride Principles remained even after significant changes in the area. They continue, unlike the Sullivan Principles, to act like a putty that fills in the cracks of existing hard law, in this case the cracks in enforcement, making the hard law more effective and longer lasting. In this sense, the MacBride Principles now operate by shadowing hard law, ready to jump in when (or if) the enforcement of the hard law stumbles or falls' (McCrudden 1999: 198, 200). For an analysis of corporate self-regulation as possible evidence of intracorporate 'global proto-law', see Muchlinski (1997: 80–85); Teubner (1997: 3–28).

74 See Snyder's account of the Code of Business Practices of the International Council of Toy Industries (ICTI), established in 1974 and revised in 1998 (Snyder in press: 20–22).

75 None of the existing codes provides mechanisms for redressing loss caused by failure of the corporation to enforce the provisions of its code. The International Chamber of Commerce (ICC) 'Bribery Code' is the only one which makes bribing an act of 'unfair competition' for which damages may be applied. International Chamber of Commerce (ICC) 'Rules of Conduct on Extortion and Bribery in International Business Transactions', Paris: ICC, 1996.

76 Forcese (1997).

77 According to Stone, society can redesign the map of responsibilities of a corporation not by preventing the organizational structure from evaluating the environment and pursuing its own corporate goals, but by inducing in

that structure new evaluative mechanisms (Stone 1991: 123–5, 145–9). See also French (1984); May (1992).

78 Concerning labour practices, for instance, systematic use of confidential interviews with workers, independent workers' organizations and other local sources will be of vital importance to the quality of the auditing process. A Global Compact without such tools will find it difficult to command credibility. Nike offers a good example in this sense. Nike has been among the first TNCs to adhere in 1999 to the core values of the Compact. In a mission statement, Nike pledged to lead in corporate citizenship through pro-active programmes 'that reflect caring for the world family of Nike, [its] teammates, [its] consumers and those who provide services to Nike'. In the same statement, Nike sets out policies and programmes 'affecting the lives and well-being of people making Nike products around the world'. See ICC (2001). In spite of this pledge, in February 2001 an independent compliance audit performed by Verité, a non-profit labour and trade monitoring organization, established through confidential worker and management personnel interviews, analysis of factory documents, factory walk-throughs by the auditors, daily reports from observers and consultation with independent and impartial legal experts that the Kukdong International Mexico factory, a Nike subcontractor, needed to take decisive corrective actions in a number of areas. Those areas included harassment and abuse, health and safety, and freedom of association and collective bargaining. See Verité (2001). Also regarding Nike, in October 2000 a BBC *Panorama* programme made public the fact that the company was allegedly violating its own code of conduct and pledge to the Global Compact by using child labour in one of it subcontracting factories in Cambodia. Regarding this incident, as well as those reported by Verité, Nike promised to take immediate remedial action. See <www.nikebiz.com/labor/bb.-state.shtml>.

79 Breton (2000).

80 Referring to labour practices in the processes of toy production in China, Snyder writes for instance that '[the] codes of conduct elaborated under the aegis of multinational companies and sector-specific trade associations may be much more important in practice than formal national or local legislation' (Snyder in press: 20).

81 Pierre Sane, head of Amnesty International, warned in this sense that only independent monitoring, with public reporting of the companies' performance, along with strong enforcement mechanisms such as sanctions, would give the Global Compact credibility (CorpWatch 2001).

References

Addo, M. K. (ed.) (1999) *Human Rights Standards and the Responsibility of Transnational Corporations*, The Hague: Kluwer Law International

Altvater, E. (1999) 'Restructuring the space of democracy: the effects of capitalist globalization and the ecological crisis on the form and substance of democracy', in N. Law (ed.), *Global Ethics and Environment*, London: Routledge

Barnet, R. J. and R. E. Muller (1974) *Global Reach: The Power of the Multinational Corporation*, New York: Simon and Schuster

Blanpain, R. (ed.) (2000) 'Multinational enterprises and the social challenges of the XXIst century: the ILO declaration on fundamental principles at work. Public and private corporate codes of conduct', *Bulletin of Comparative Labour Relations*, The Hague: Kluwer Law International

Blanpain, R. and T. Hanami (2000) 'Introduction: the global challenges,' in Blanpain (2000), pp. ix–xi.

Blumberg, P. (1993) *The Multinational Challenge to Corporation Law*, Oxford: Oxford University Press

Breitenfellner, A. (1997) 'Global unionism: a potential player', *International Law Review*, 136 (4): 531–55

Breton, J. R. (2000) 'World affairs social audit', <world-affairs.com/audit.htm>

Bruno, K. and J. Karliner (2000) 'Tangled up in blue: corporate partnerships at the United Nations', TRAC – Transnational Resources & Action Center: CorpWatch, <www.corpwatch.org/trac/globalization/un/tangled.html>

Campbell, D. C. and R. L. Rowan (1983) *Multinational Enterprises and the OECD Industrial Relations Guidelines*, Philadelphia: The Wharton School, University of Pennsylvania

Caves, R. E. (1982) *Multinational Enterprise and Economic Analysis*, New York: Cambridge University Press

Clean Clothes Campaign (1998) 'Codes of conduct for transnational corporations: an overview', <www.cleanclothes.org/codes/overview.htm>

Compa, L. and T. Hinchliffe Darricarrere (1995) 'Enforcing international labour rights through corporate codes of conduct', *Columbia Journal of Transnational Law*, 33: 663–89

— (1996) 'Private labor rights enforcement through corporate codes of conduct', in L. A. Compa and S. F. Diamond (eds), *Human Rights, Labor Rights, and International Trade*, Philadelphia: University of Pennsylvania Press, pp. 181–98

CorpWatch (2001) 'Corporatization of the United Nations', <www.corpwatch.org/trac/globalization/un/gccc.html>

Destler, I. M. and P. J. Balint (1999) *The New Politics of American Trade: Trade, Labor, and the Environment*, Washington DC: Institute for International Economics

De Waart, P. (1998) 'Quality of life at the mercy of WTO Panels: GATT's Article XX an empty shell?', in F. Weiss, E. Denters and P. De Waart (eds), *International Economic Law with a Human Face*, The Hague: Kluwer Law International, pp. 109–31

Dias, C. J. (2000) 'Towards effective monitoring of compliance with obligations and progressive realisation of ESCR', UNDP, Second Global Forum on Human Development, 9–10 October, Rio de Janeiro, <www.undp.org/hdro/Rioforum.html#summary>

Diller, J. M. (1999) 'A social conscience in the global market? Labour dimensions of codes of conduct, social labelling and investor initiatives', *International Labour Review*, 138 (2)

Privatizing human rights?

— (2000) 'Social conduct in transnational enterprise operations: the role of the international labour organisation', in Blanpain (2000), pp. 67–88

Donaldson, T. (1982) *Corporations and Morality*, Englewood Cliffs, NJ: Prentice Hall

Esty, D. C. (1994) *Greening the GATT: Trade, Environment and the Future*, Washington, DC: Institute for International Economics

Ethos (2000) 'Ethos indicators: on corporate social responsibility. Introduction to version 2000', Instituto Ethos de Empresas e Responsabilidade Social, <www.ethos.org.br/>

Falk, R. A. (1999) *Predatory Globlization: A Critique*, Cambridge: Polity Press

— (2000) *Human Rights Horizons: The Pursuit of Justice in a Globalizing World*, New York: Routledge

FoE (Friends of the Earth) (1998) 'A history of attempts to control the activities of transnational corporations: what lessons can be learned?', International Forum on Globalization: Toward a Progressive International Economy, Washington, DC, December, <www.foe.org/progressive-economy/history.html>

Forcese, C. (1997) *Commerce with Conscience? Human Rights and Corporate Codes of Conduct*, Montreal: International Centre for Human Rights and Democratic Development

Forsythe, D. P. (2000) *Human Rights in International Relations*, Cambridge: Cambridge University Press

French, P. A. (1984) *Collective and Corporate Responsibility*, New York: Columbia University Press

— (1991) 'The corporation as a moral person', in L. May and S. Hoffmann (eds), *Collective Responsibility: Five Decades of Debate in Theoretical and Applied Ethics*, Savage, MD: Rowman & Littlefield, pp. 133–51

Gilpin, R. (1987) *The Political Economy of International Relations*, Princeton, NJ: Princeton University Press

— (2001) *Global Political Economy: Understanding the International Economic Order*, Princeton, NJ: Princeton University Press

Glade, B. and E. Potter (1989) 'Targeting the labor practices of multinational companies', in *US Council for International Business; Focus on Issues*, New York: US Council for International Business, <www.uscib.org/ilodecl.html>

Greider, W. (1997) *One World, Ready or Not: The Manic Logic of Global Capitalism*, New York: Simon and Schuster

Halle, M. (2000) 'Seattle and sustainable development', in *Bridges: Between Trade and Sustainable Development*, International Centre on Trade and Sustainable Development, year 4, no. 1, pp. 13–14

Held, V. (1991) 'Can a random collection of individuals be morally responsible?', in L. May and S. Hoffmann (eds), *Collective Responsibility: Five Decades of Debate in Theoretical and Applied Ethics*, Savage MD: Rowman & Littlefield, pp. 89–100

ICC (International Chamber of Commerce) (1996) 'Rules of conduct on extortion and bribery in international business transactions', Paris: ICC

— (2001) 'The UN–business Global Compact: working with the UN', <www.
iccwbo.org/home/menu-global-compact.asp>

ILO (1978) 'Tripartite Declaration of Principles Concerning MNEs and Social
Policy', 17 ILM 422, International Labour Organization

— (1998) 'Declaration on fundamental principles and rights at work', Geneva:
International Labour Organisation, <www.ilo.org/punlic/english/stand-
ards/decl/declaration/tindex.htm>

Julius, D. (1990) *Global Companies and Public Policy: The Growing Challenge of
Foreign Direct Investment*, London: Pinter

Kaldor, M. (2000) 'Transnational civil society', in T. Dunne and N. J. Wheeler
(eds), *Human Rights in Global Politics*, Cambridge: Cambridge University
Press, pp. 195–213

Kellerson, H. (1998) 'The ILO Declaration of 1998 on Fundamental Principles
and Rights: a challenge for the future', *International Labour Review*, 137 (2):
223–8

Kirton, J. J., J. P. Daniels and A. Freytag (2001) 'Introduction', in J. J. Kirton,
J. P. Daniels and A. Freytag (eds), *Guiding Global Order: G8 Governance in
the Twenty-first Century*, Aldershot: Ashgate

Krugman, P. and A. J. Venables (1995) 'Globalization and the inequality of
nations', *Quarterly Journal of Economics*, 110 (4), November

Lall, S. (1980) *The Multinational Corporation*, London: Macmillan

McCrudden, C. (1999) 'Human rights codes for transnational corporations:
what can Sullivan and MacBride principles tell us?', *Oxford Journal of Legal
Studies*, 19: 167–201

Makower, J. (1994) *Beyond the Bottom Line*, New York: Simon and Schuster

May, L. (1992) *Sharing Responsibility*, Chicago, IL: Chicago University Press

Meyer, W. H. (1996) 'Human rights and multi-national corporations: theory v.
quantitative analysis', *Human Rights Quarterly*, 18 (2): 368–97

— (1998) *Human Rights and International Political Economy in Third World
Nations: Multinational Corprations, Foreign Aid, and Repression*, Westport,
CT: Praeger

Modelski, G. (ed.) (1979) *Transnational Corporations and World Order*, San
Francisco, CA: W. H. Freeman

Muchlinski, P. T. (1997) '"Global Bukowina" examined: viewing the multinational enterprise as a transnational law-making community', in G. Teubner
(ed.), *Global Law without a State*, Aldershot: Dartmouth, pp. 79–108

— (1999) *Multinational Enterprises and the Law*, updated edn, Oxford: Blackwell

Murray, J. (1998) 'Corporate codes of conduct and labour standards', in
R. Kyloh (ed.), *Mastering the Challenge of Globalization: Towards a Trade
Union Agenda*, ILO, pp. 45–115

OECD (Organization for Economic Cooperation and Development) (1976)
'OECD Guidelines for Multinational Enterprises', 15 ILM 967–79

— (1996) 'Private-party mechanisms', in OECD, *Trade, Employment and
Labour Standard: A Study of Core Workers*, pp. 199–204

Privatizing human rights?

— (2000) 'Guidelines for Multinational Enterprises: Decision of the Council', OECD, June, at <www.oecd.org/daf/investment/guidelines/decision.htm>

OHCHR (Office of the High Commissioner for Human Rights) (2000) 'Business and human rights: an update', prepared by the OHCHR for the Global Compact meeting, 26 July, New York, <www.unhchr.ch/businesupdate.htm>

Ohmae, K. (1990) *The Borderless World: Power and Strategy in the Interlinked Economy*, New York: Harperbusiness

Ostry, S. (1997) *A New Regime for Foreign Direct Investment*, Washington, DC: Group of Thirty

Øyen, E. (2000) 'Six questions to the World Bank on the World Development Report 2000/2001: "Attacking Poverty"', <www.crop.org/wdroyen1.htm>

Robé, J.-P. (1997) 'Multinational enterprises: the constitution of a pluralistic legal order', in G. Teubner (ed.), *Global Law without a State*, Aldershot: Dartmouth, pp. 45–77

Robinson, J. (1983) *Multinationals and Political Control*, Aldershot: Gower

Rodman, K. A. (1998) 'Think globally, punish locally: non-state actors, multinational corporations, and human rights sanctions', *Ethics and International Affairs*, 12: 19–42

Schachter, O. (1998) 'The erosion of state authority and its implications for equitable development', in F. Weiss, E. Denters and P. De Waart (eds), *International Economic Law with a Human Face*, The Hague: Kluwer Law International, pp. 31–44

Selznick, P. (1994) 'Self-regulation and the theory of institutions', in G. Teubner, L. Farmer and D. Murphy (eds), *Environmental Law and Ecological Responsibility: The Concept and Practice of Self-organization*, Chichester: Wiley, pp. 396–402

Snyder, F. G. (in press) 'Governing globalisation', in M. B. Likosky (ed.), *Transnational Legal Processes*, Butterworths

Stone, C. (1991) *Where the Law Ends: The Social Control of Corporate Behaviour*, Illinois: Waveland Press

Teubner, G. (1997a) '"Global Bukowina" : legal pluralism in the world society', in G. Teubner (ed.), *Global Law without a State*, Aldershot: Dartmouth, pp. 3–28

— (1997b), 'Foreword: Legal regimes of global non-state actors', in G. Teubner (ed.), *Global Law without a State*, Aldershot: Dartmouth, pp. xiii–xvii

TRAC (Transnational Resource & Action Center) (2000a) 'Citizens compact on the United Nations and corporations', <www.corpwatch.org/trac/globalization/un/citizenscompact.html>

— (2000b) 'UNDP abandons perilous partnership', CorpWatch, <www.corpwatch.org/trac/undp/>

UN (United Nations) (1999) 'A Compact for the New Century', <www.unglobalcompact.org/gc/unweb.nsf/webprintview/thenine.htm>

— (1999) 'Secretary-General proposes Global Compact on Human Rights,

Labour, Environment, in address to World Economic Forum in Davos',
1 February (SG/SM/6881), <www.unglobalcompact.org/>

UNDP (United Nations Development Programme) (2000) 'UNDP Poverty
Report 2000: Overcoming Human Poverty', <www.undp.org/povertyreport/
exec/english.html>

UNHCHR (United Nations High Commissioner for Human Rights) (2000)
'Business and human rights: a progress report', UNHCHR, <www.unhchr.
ch/business.htm>

Vaitsos, C. (1974) *Intercountry Income Distribution and Transnational Enterprises*, Oxford: Clarendon Press

Velasquez, M. G. (1991) 'Why corporations are not morally responsible for
anything they do?,' in L. May and S. Hoffmann (eds), *Collective Responsibility: Five Decades of Debate in Theoretical and Applied Ethics*, Savage,
MD: Rowman & Littlefield, pp. 111–31

Verité (2001) 'Comprehensive factory evaluation report on Kukdong International Mexico, SA de CV', at <www.nikebiz.com/labor/index.shtml>

Vernon, R. (1971) *Sovereignty at Bay: The Multinational Spread of US Enterprises*, London: Longman

— (1977) *Storm over the Multinationals: The Real Issues*, London: Macmillan

Voiculescu, A. (2000) *Human Rights and Political Justice in Post-communist
Eastern Europe: Prosecuting History*, Lewiston, NY: Edwin Mellen Press

Wilkins, M. (1974) *The Maturing of Multinational Enterprise: American Business
Abroad from 1914 to 1970*, Cambridge, MA: Harvard University Press

Williams, L. A. (1998) 'Welfare and legal entitlements: the social roots of
poverty', in D. Kairys (ed.), *The Politics of Law and Progressive Critique*, New
York: Basic Books, pp. 569–90

9 | Developing universal anti-poverty regimes: the role of the United Nations in the establishment of international poverty law

GABRIEL AMITSIS

The evaluation of anti-poverty regimes developed by international organizations active in the field of social welfare challenges the thinking of scientists and experts on poverty issues. Analysis of international actions to eradicate poverty became a hot issue in light of globalization. Globalization theories focus on economic factors, however, paying little or marginal attention to institutional and judicial activities. Initially, this chapter identifies advantages and disadvantages created during the implementation of legal norms and techniques applied by the United Nations (UN) to combat poverty and social exclusion. The chapter then addresses, from a methodological point of view, the traditional normative distinction between 'International Declarations' and 'Binding Conventions', assessing, within the UN framework, both categories' impact on member states as well as on citizens and persons. Particular attention is paid to the analysis of the Universal Declaration of Human Rights (UDHR), the International Covenant on Economic, Social and Cultural Rights (ICESCR) and UN Action Programmes in the field of human rights. The resulting analysis is based on an investigation of certain aspects of anti-poverty regimes (i.e. rights to social assistance, rights to an adequate standard of living, and social equality clauses) and their monitoring systems (i.e. reporting procedures and relevant supervisory committees). In this context, the chapter examines issues of normative effects (direct applicability), particularly where the guarantee of enforceable rights for interested persons is concerned.

The chapter concludes that human rights instruments designed by UN organs form the cornerstone of international poverty law (IPL). Despite political and ideological conflicts that emerged during the implementation by member states of UN human rights instruments, the development of IPL mechanisms could benefit from further actions promoted by the international social rights monitoring bodies. Such action is the first step in highlighting the political and judicial principles of IPL.

The role of international organizations in the development of anti-poverty law

The scientific and political debate about poverty has been rapidly changing during the last few decades. Poverty has become one of the controversial issues in national social policy regimes, while its transnational variations have led to the internationalization of relevant enquiries.[1] International agencies and organizations promote activities to combat poverty through global social policy interventions.

But the concept of poverty has attracted intellectual and political interest for hundreds of years. Emphasis was placed on the scientific definitions of poverty, as distinct from social explanations for income inequality. During the twentieth century, three alternative conceptions of poverty evolved as a basis for international and comparative work, based principally on the formulation of subsistence, basic needs and relative deprivation.[2]

The idea of subsistence, which includes food, shelter and clothing as relevant needs, as a tool to define poverty has both advantages and disadvantages in terms of its contribution to the development of anti-poverty policies. The main criticism put forward by social rights promoters regarding this approach is that human needs are interpreted as being predominantly physical needs rather than social needs. The idea of basic needs includes two primary elements:

- certain minimum conditions necessary for private consumption (adequate food, shelter, clothing, housing, furniture and equipment); and
- essential services related to public goods (water, sanitation, public transport, health, education, training and cultural facilities).

While the concept of basic needs is regarded as an enlargement of the subsistence concept, it has nevertheless been described as inappropriate to deal with the complexity of poverty. Noted shortcomings include the fact that people's needs cannot be defined simply by reference to their physical needs.

The concept of relative deprivation places poverty in relationship to social and institutional structures, not viewing poverty as simply an issue of relatively low disposable income. According to this approach, poverty may best be understood as affecting not just those who are victims of a maldistribution of resources but, more precisely, those whose resources do not allow them to fulfil the elaborate social demands and customs that have been placed upon citizens of a given society: they are materially and socially deprived in a variety of ways that can be observed, described and measured.[3]

These three concepts influence legal actions in the global social policy field,[4] particularly with reference to the establishment of basic social rights. A comparative overview of international legal instruments on social rights[5] in the field of welfare indicates that international policy-makers have given preference to a combination of the subsistence and the basic needs approaches:

a) Social rights within the 'jurisdiction' of the UN follow the traditional subsistence concept. UN social rights are established through the development of international conventions[6] on the legal regulation of entitlements and duties.[7] These Conventions promote measures to combat absolute poverty, placed in the global context of transnational social policy.

b) Social rights in the domain of the Council of Europe follow a more liberal, participative approach, strongly related to the basic needs concept. The Council of Europe introduced a specific framework for the guarantee of social rights through European conventions, which impose obligations on contracting member states.[8] These conventions (particularly the European Social Charter of 1961[9] and the European Code of Social Security of 1964[10]) promote measures to combat relative poverty through benefits and services based on enforceable rights, adapted to the Western tradition of human rights machineries.

c) Social policies in the European Union (EU) framework introduce restrictive elements, given that they are largely connected to the social protection of wage earners as opposed to the social coverage of poor persons. EU primary and secondary law promotes the coordination of national social security schemes for workers, while member states apply domestic policies in the field of social welfare.[11] In 1999, however, the European Commission introduced a new strategy on social exclusion[12] through an open method of coordination between national welfare schemes,[13] which strengthens the possibilities for concerted legal actions in the area.

The EU introduced innovative measures to combat poverty and social exclusion[14] that do not create enforceable rights owing to the strict application of the subsidiarity principle.[15] These measures are based on specific provisions of primary Community law[16] that situate the fight against poverty in the broader framework of the European Economic Space.

At the European Councils in Lisbon and in Feira (2000), the member states of the EU took a major initiative by incorporating the fight against poverty and social exclusion as one of the central elements in the modernization of the European social model. Policy-makers agreed that the Council should set suitable objectives having a decisive impact on the eradication of poverty before the end of 2000. They also concluded that policies for combating social exclusion should combine national actions and EU support measures.

According to the new EU approach,[17] national anti-poverty schemes should follow the coordination technique, which will combine national action plans with a Community Support Programme. The European Council agreed at the Nice Summit in December 2000 that member states should be requested to implement two-year National Action Plans on Social Inclusion (referred to as NAPincl to distinguish them from National Action Plans on Employment) for combating poverty and social exclusion, setting targets, taking into account national, regional and local differences, and listing the indicators used to assess progress. Member states submitted the national plans to the Commission for the first time in June 2001. The Commission has examined these national plans, applying specific social indicators developed by the Social Protection Committee, a body charged with the task of monitoring the progress of the European strategy to combat poverty and social exclusion. The monitoring of the plans, as the first instrument for the Open Method of Coordination on Social Inclusion, was documented in the Joint Report on Social Inclusion published by the European Commission in 2002. These action plans set forth a set of principles and measures to combat poverty and social exclusion at the national level. They should fulfil four broad objectives:

- to facilitate participation in employment and access by all to resources, rights, goods and services;
- to prevent the risks of exclusion;
- to help the most vulnerable; and
- to mobilize all relevant bodies (social partners, NGOs, public and private social service providers).

Objectives 2 and 3 establish a soft, non-binding EU anti-poverty framework. According to this framework, member states should take the following measures:

- to exploit fully the potential of the knowledge-based society and of new information and communication technologies and ensure that no one is excluded, taking particular account of the needs of people with disabilities;
- to put in place policies that seek to prevent life crises that can lead to situations of social exclusion, such as indebtedness, withdrawal from school and homelessness;
- to implement action to preserve family solidarity in all its forms;
- to promote the social integration of people who are at risk of persistent

poverty because, for example, they have a disability or belong to a group experiencing particular integration problems;

- to move towards the elimination of social exclusion among children and give them every opportunity for social integration;
- to develop comprehensive actions to assist areas and regions significantly affected by exclusion;
- to promote, according to national practice, the participation and self-expression of people suffering exclusion, particularly with regard to their situation and the policies and measures affecting them; and
- to mainstream the fight against exclusion into overall policy.

Mechanisms to promote mainstreaming of anti-poverty policies include:

- the mobilization of public authorities at the national, regional and local level, according to their respective areas of competence;
- the development of appropriate coordination procedures and structures between EU authorities, national administrators and social partners;
- the adaptation of administrative and social services to the needs of people suffering exclusion and ensuring that front-line staff are sensitive to these needs; and
- the development of dialogue and partnership between all relevant bodies.

In Lisbon, the Council also called on the Commission to report annually on the structural indicators of the progress of member states, and at Feira two years later the Council requested the Commission to ensure the necessary coherence and standard presentation of indicators. At the Nice Summit in December 2000, the Council endorsed the Commission's proposals for moving forward the European Social Agenda. The Council also gave an important role to the Social Protection Committee (formerly the High Level Group on Social Protection), which has established a Sub-group on Social Indicators that started meeting in February 2001. At the Stockholm European Council in March 2001, the Heads of Governments asked the Council to agree on indicators for monitoring progress in combating social exclusion by the end of 2001.[18] Relevant indicators were adopted in the Laeken European Council of December 2001 on the basis of a report compiled by the Social Protection Committee.

The impact of the United Nations on the establishment of international anti-poverty law

The United Nations and its agencies are regarded as the global policy-makers for the establishment of international anti-poverty law for two principal reasons:

- the UN applies specific legal competencies[19] in the field of human rights, strongly related to poverty issues;[20] and
- the UN international agencies provide financial means for the eradication of poverty through social development programmes.[21]

From a legal point of view, the UN has introduced binding and non-binding legal instruments as a means to combat poverty. Binding instruments include international covenants and treaties that prevail over domestic law after their incorporation in the national legal order; non-binding instruments include international declarations that introduce policy guidelines or recommendations.[22]

This chapter identifies the legal status of UN instruments and clarifies their applicability as the main mechanisms or foundations of international anti-poverty law. This is an intellectual process of great importance given that it highlights the legal aspects of international anti-poverty policies.

The Universal Declaration of Human Rights The non-binding Universal Declaration of Human Rights, adopted in 1948, forms the cornerstone of international anti-poverty law.[23] It codifies adequate living standards and protection against income insecurity as fundamental human rights.[24] Relevant provisions are found in Article 25:

> 1. Everyone has the right to a standard of living adequate for the health and well-being of himself and of his family, including food, clothing, housing and medical care and necessary social services, and the right to security in the event of unemployment, sickness, disability, widowhood, old age or other lack of livelihood in circumstances beyond his control.

> 2. Motherhood and childhood are entitled to special care and assistance. All children, whether born in or out of wedlock, shall enjoy the same social protection.

Article 25 constitutes the legal basis for the promotion of anti-poverty policies through the machinery of international human rights.[25] It introduces two specific social rights: the right to an adequate standard of living (mainly applied through a social assistance model) and the right to social security (mainly applied through a social insurance model).[26]

In strict legal terms, the Declaration contains neither enforceable rights for citizens nor binding obligations on member states. It simply acknowledges the international dimension of human rights and the goal of progressive realization in their entirety: civil, political, economic, social and cultural. On the other hand, it codifies general principles of international customary law that can be used as a normative instrument in its own right.[27]

The Declaration was followed by two executing instruments which provide specific norms for the implementation of recognized human rights: the International Covenant on Civil and Political Rights (ICCPR) and the International Covenant on Economic, Social and Cultural Rights (ICESCR), both adopted in 1966. A systematic analysis of these texts[28] as well as an evaluation of their practical effects[29] lead to the conclusion that the ICCPR does not form part of the international anti-poverty law machinery in that it covers only traditional civil and political rights.[30] Its provisions could be used, however, through extensive interpretive techniques – as a means to strengthen the social role of civil rights.[31]

The ICESCR constitutes, therefore, the single executing instrument for the legal formation of international anti-poverty policies that guarantee social rights. In order to assess its impact, attention should be paid to legal effects on contracting states and individuals bound by relevant norms.

The International Covenant on Economic, Social and Cultural Rights The ICESCR introduced a detailed codification of economic, social and cultural rights at a global level.[32] It guarantees, *inter alia*, specific social rights that may be used as significant legal instruments for the development of anti-poverty policies. These rights are found in Articles 9 and 11.

a) Article 9 constitutes the legal foundation of the right to social security, which is implemented through the social insurance model.[33] It is a traditional social right, recognized at the international level through ILO Convention No. 102 on social security minimum standards.[34]

b) Article 11 is the legal foundation of four interrelated social rights:

- the right to an adequate standard of living;
- the right to adequate food;
- the right to housing; and
- the right to clothing.

These rights are deduced through a substantive interpretation of the original text, which states that:

> 1. The States Parties to the present Covenant recognize the right of everyone to an adequate standard of living for himself and his family, including adequate food, clothing and housing, and to the continuous improvement of living conditions. The States Parties will take appropriate steps to ensure the realization of this right, recognizing to this effect the essential importance of international co-operation based on free consent.

2. The States Parties to the present Covenant, recognizing the fundamental right of everyone to be free from hunger, shall take, individually and through international co-operation, the measures, including specific pro-grammes, which are needed ...

Article 11 is one of the broadest and most general of the articles in the Covenant, including a host of concerns that are usually addressed in the context of state development.[35]

The impact of both Articles 9 and 11 on poverty requires a legal under-standing of the enforceability and definition of the rights contained therein, which can be viewed from two perspectives:

- The first argument is that the ICESCR establishes concrete rights that give entitlements to individuals to receive social welfare benefits. This approach strengthens the legal status of poor persons since they are entitled to coverage in case of need.
- The second argument is that the ICESCR does not create enforceable rights that individuals can invoke before national or international courts. This approach marginalizes the legal status of poor persons, particularly under the assumption that national governments are not bound by social norms to promote anti-poverty measures.

Both arguments should be evaluated according to the 'direct applica-bility' principle.[36] 'Direct applicability' means that international rules are applied directly to a domestic legal order without specification by national legislators, administrators or policy-makers. Any individual, claiming that state organs violate his or her rights, as deduced by these rules, could therefore invoke them before national courts.

All rights enshrined in Article 11 are constructed in a vague and abstract manner that diminishes their direct applicability effect. This is particularly the case for the right to adequate living standards, given the broad defini-tion of that concept, as noted below.

A relevant theoretical approach is reaffirmed by the implementation of the Covenant by states parties[37] as well as by the 'case law' of the monitoring bodies of the Covenant. According to the system in force since 1985, the Covenant is reviewed by the Committee on Economic, Social and Cultural Rights,[38] a working group with eighteen members elected by the Economic and Social Council.

The Committee on Economic, Social and Cultural Rights makes general comments on the Covenant and the issues it raises. These comments draw on the reports submitted by states from different parts of the world with various socio-economic, cultural, political and legal systems. The intention is to help the states parties in their task of implementing the Covenant, as well as to bring to their attention deficiencies in the reports they submit and to suggest improvements in the reporting procedure. The committee's comments are also designed to accelerate action by the states parties, various international organizations and United Nations specialized agencies, which will lead to the full enjoyment of economic, social and cultural rights. An analysis of these committee inquiries into Article 11 indicates that no direct applicability effect is intended.

In addition, problems arise in trying to define relevant rights, given that applicable provisions include vague and abstract terms. As far as the right to adequate living standards is concerned, emphasis should be paid to its primary scope. If the right is understood as a synthesis of other economic, social and cultural rights, it will have little utility as an independent human right; if, on the other hand, it is read to include concerns that are not already addressed by other rights, it might usefully extend the scope of the Covenant.[39]

Thus far, the committee has not assigned a meaning to the right to an adequate standard of living that substantially extends the protection offered by other rights. In discussing Article 11, the committee has made little mention of an adequate standard of living per se. The committee has instead concentrated on the rights to adequate housing and food. Moreover, when dealing specifically with the right to an adequate standard of living, committee members have generally concentrated upon questions relating to social security, unemployment and income levels. In doing so, they have appeared to duplicate much of the work undertaken in relation to other articles of the ICESCR.[40]

A further problem concerns the measurement of living standards, given that the original text refers to adequate standards without indicators or criteria. The committee does not stipulate how these standards are measured, but rather allows the states concerned to adopt their own criteria for evaluation. The reporting guidelines of the committee suggest, however, two specific indicators that could be applied here: the Physical Quality of Life Index (PQLI) or the per capita GNP of the poorest 40 per cent of the population.

Despite their methodological value, these indicators do not give a great deal of insight into the content of the fundamental right to adequate living standards. First, the PQLI is a composite indicator intended to 'measure the performance of the world's poorest countries in meeting the most basic needs of people'.[41] It uses infant mortality, life expectancy and literacy as measurements: these indicators all have serious technical limitations[42] which created shortcomings in terms of the utility of the PQLI to the committee. Moreover, the components, which largely focus on the degree of enjoyment of health and education, were chosen primarily for their utility as indicators rather than the degree to which they encompassed the range of concerns that fall within the notion of 'quality of life'.

Second, the per capita GNP of the poorest 40 per cent of the population as a standard poverty line corresponds to a broad measure of poverty. Its strict use necessitates the introduction of a legal poverty line, a determination that many national governments hesitate to create.

Taking these considerations into account, the committee leaves the precise definition of an adequate standard of living to the state concerned. While it is entirely appropriate for states to establish their own quantitative benchmarks of 'adequacy' according to their current level of economic and social development, the committee itself should specify the qualitative aspects of a 'standard of living'.

Likewise, as far as the right to food is concerned, a more detailed consideration of the issues is needed which emphasizes the precise obligations to which states are bound. The committee should pay particular attention to the legal regulation of this right, a vital condition for its implementation in practice.[43]

In spite of enforceability and definitional limitations, however, the committee has spent a considerable amount of its time addressing issues within Article 11 as opposed to other articles of the Covenant. This is attributable to three factors:

a) First, Article 11 includes rights that are closely associated with the 'basic needs' of the individual. The enjoyment of a minimum level of the right to food, housing and clothing is a necessary condition for survival, and therefore warrants detailed consideration. These rights are legal instruments to eradicate poverty, particularly in its absolute approach.
b) Second, Article 11 includes rights that are peculiar to the ICESCR. No other international instrument has dealt with matters such as food and housing on an individual level; on the other hand, only the committee investigates – through the application of detailed legal standards – the legal commitment on relevant rights.
c) Finally, Article 11 is the legal foundation for the implementation of the other economic, social and cultural rights. Without the right to subsistence, no serious application of other rights is possible.

The effective use of Article 11 as a means to combat poverty is also linked to the introduction of legally binding obligations on states. Many view Article 11 as providing that party states have only moral obligations to realize fundamental social rights. This argument undermines the value of Article 2 of the Covenant, which reads as follows:

1. Each State Party to the present Covenant undertakes to take steps, individually and through international assistance and co-operation, especially economic and technical, to the maximum of its available resources, with a view to achieving progressively the full realization of the rights recognized in the present Covenant by all appropriate means, including particularly the adoption of legislative measures.

2. The States Parties to the present Covenant undertake to guarantee that the rights enunciated in the present Covenant will be exercised without discrimination of any kind as to race, colour, sex, language, religion, political or other opinion, national or social origin, property, birth or other status.

3. Developing countries, with due regard to human rights and their national economy, may determine to what extent they would guarantee the economic rights recognized in the present Covenant to non-nationals.

The first paragraph of this article authorizes UN organs to specify the legal obligations imposed on party states. Relevant organs have not taken advantage of this technicality, however, given that binding circulars have not been issued, nor indicators to fulfil obligations adopted. The Committee on Economic, Social and Cultural Rights is the single body that has developed interpretive techniques through its General Comments, which established minimum core obligations for member states.[44]

The committee's lack of detailed investigation into the actions or inactions of party states is partly addressed by the development of personal and material limitations placed on the scope of the Covenant by the non-binding 'Limburg Principles'.[45] These principles form a set of guidelines for states' obligations, but they do not lead to the establishment of legal norms.[46] Nevertheless, they contribute to the development of 'technical clauses', given that they identify the issue of violations of rights.

Significant legal developments in the field of economic, social and cultural rights since the adoption of the Limburg Principles led to the clarification of these principles by a group of international experts who met in Maastricht in January 1997. The participants agreed on a set of specific guidelines regarding the nature and scope of violations of economic, social and cultural rights and appropriate responses and remedies.[47] The Maastricht Guidelines adopted a violations approach for monitoring the implementation of social rights.[48] According to this approach, state obligations in the field of international social rights follow the distinction between obligations to respect, protect and fulfil and obligations of contact and result.[49] Relevant obligations clarify the nature of state parties' obligations, as deduced through the General Comments of the Committee on Economic, Social and Cultural Rights.[50]

The Vienna Declaration of Human Rights The UN General Assembly adopted the Vienna Declaration of Human Rights during the Vienna World Conference on Human Rights in June 1993. It is not a binding legal text, given that it took the form of a resolution, which includes specific guidelines to member states as well as to the UN organs. Its importance should not be underestimated, however, since it reaffirms the principles that have evolved in the development of international poverty law and strengthens the foundation for additional progress in the area of human rights.

With regard to the development of anti-poverty policies, the Declaration introduces new elements in the relationship between human and social rights.[51] Poverty and social exclusion are not regarded as simple violations of social rights, but as violations of fundamental rights, such as the rights to human dignity and the right to participation.

Relevant observations can be found in Section 25 of the Declaration:

The World Conference on Human Rights affirms that extreme poverty and social exclusion constitute a violation of human dignity and that urgent steps are necessary to achieve better knowledge of extreme poverty and its causes, including those related to the problem of development, in order to promote the human rights of the poorest, and to put an end to extreme poverty and social exclusion and to promote the enjoyment of the fruits of social progress. It is essential for states to foster participation by the poorest people in the decision-making process by the community in which they live, the promotion of human rights and efforts to combat extreme poverty.

The Vienna Declaration was followed by an Action Programme,[52] which includes specific recommendations and guidelines. Unfortunately, reflecting the traditional emphasis on civil and political rights and the marginal attention paid to the development of social rights, there is no explicit reference to poverty alleviation.

The Copenhagen Declaration on Social Development The UN General Assembly adopted the Copenhagen Declaration on Social Development during the Copenhagen World Summit for Social Development in March 1995. Since it is written in the form of a resolution, it is also a non-binding legal text, which includes specific guidelines to member states as well as to the UN organs. Its importance should not be discounted, however, because, for the very first time in a UN document, this Declaration recognizes the significance of human well-being for all.

The Copenhagen Declaration introduces certain socio-political, as opposed to legal, commitments of member states, similar to principles or objectives that were included in the previous UN declarations. These commitments establish neither enforceable rights for citizens nor legal obligations on national governments and administrations. But various sections of the text of the Declaration include specific references to anti-poverty policies. Sections 23 and 26 contain relevant provisions.

Section 23 introduces new priorities in the social protection field: 'We can continue to hold the trust of the people of the world only if we make their needs our priority. *We know that poverty, lack of productive employment and social disintegration are an offence to human dignity.* We also know that they are negatively reinforcing and represent a waste of human resources and a manifestation of ineffectiveness in the functioning of markets and economic and social institutions and processes' (emphasis added).

Section 26 codifies the twenty-one goals that should be fulfilled by national governments, including three specific goals related to international poverty policies.

Goal no. 9 reads: 'Ensure that disadvantaged and vulnerable persons and groups are included in social development, and that society acknowledges and responds to the consequences of disability by securing the legal rights of the individual and by making the physical and social environment accessible.' Importantly, the scope of this goal is broad, covering both economically needy persons and persons with special needs.

Goal no. 10 reads: 'Promote universal respect for, and observance and protection of, all human rights and fundamental freedoms for all, including the right to development; promote the effective exercise of rights and the discharge of responsibilities at all levels of society; promote equality and equity between women and men; protect the rights of children and youth; and promote the strengthening of social integration and civil society.'

Goal no. 12 pays particular attention to anti-poverty measures. It reads: 'Support progress and security for people and communities whereby every member of society is enabled to satisfy his or her basic human needs and to realize his or her personal dignity, safety and creativity.' Although this goal might be interpreted as following the basic needs approach to defining and combating poverty, its application may be extended to social development, which also takes into account relative deprivation issues.

Actions to eradicate poverty fall among the commitments described in Sector III of the Declaration. There are ten commitments, which, *inter alia*, concern social policies at national and international levels.

Commitment no. 1 highlights the need to promote a positive implementation of UN social law instruments in view of the needs of poor persons, stressing 'the realization of the rights set out in relevant international instruments and declarations, such as the Universal Declaration of Human Rights, the Covenant on Economic, Social and Cultural Rights and the Declaration on the Right to Development, including those relating to education, food, shelter, employment, health and information, particularly in order to assist people living in poverty'.

Commitment no. 2 is devoted to the eradication of poverty through the adoption of national and international measures. National actions include:

- the formulation of national policies and strategies geared to substantially reducing overall poverty in the shortest possible time, reducing inequalities and eradicating absolute poverty by a target date to be specified by each country in its national context;
- the guarantee of basic goods to persons living in poverty;
- the social coverage of persons in case of social insurance risks; and
- the coverage of basic needs – through reducing inequalities and targeting poverty – as a strategic objective of national budgets and policies.

International actions include:

- the cooperation between multilateral financial institutions and countries with the aim of eradicating poverty and ensuring basic social protection; and
- the participation of poor persons in anti-poverty programmes promoted by international organizations.

Commitment no. 8 concerns the integration of social development goals into Structural Adjustment Programmes. The focus here is on 'the promotion of basic social programmes and expenditures, in particular those affecting the poor and the vulnerable segments of society, and their protection from budget reductions, while increasing the quality and effectiveness of social expenditures'.

An Action Programme that outlines policies, actions and measures to implement the principles and fulfil the commitments adopted by national governments follows the Declaration. The special importance of this programme lies in its integrated approach and its attempt to combine many different actions for poverty eradication, employment creation and social integration in coherent national and international strategies for social development. The implementation of the recommendations contained in the programme is the sovereign right of each country, consistent with national laws and development priorities, with full respect for the various religious and ethical values and cultural backgrounds of its people, and in conformity with all human rights and fundamental freedoms.

Despite its abstract substance,[53] it should be stressed that the adoption of this programme forms a major source of international poverty law. This is due to the fact that it establishes for the very first time general principles of a complex minimum standards scheme for poor persons.

Briefly, the basic dimensions of a minimum standards scheme are:

1 A social safety net for every person without adequate resources, according to paras 72f and 38c: 'Establishing a universal and flexible social safety net that takes into account available economic resources and encourages rehabilitation and active participation in society' (para. 72f). 'Ensuring that social safety nets associated with economic restructuring are considered as complementary strategies to overall poverty reduction and an increase in productive employment. Short term by nature, safety nets must protect people living in poverty and enable them to find productive employment' (para. 38c).

2 Regulation by law, according to para. 38, which states that 'social protection systems should be based on legislation and, as appropriate, strengthened and expanded, as necessary, in order to protect from poverty people who cannot find work'.

3 A basic objective of human dignity, as para. 28c underlines that 'ensuring that policies and programmes affecting people living in poverty *respect their dignity* and culture and make full use of their knowledge, skills and resource fullness' (emphasis added).

4 Provision of traditional cash benefits with social services that promote the economic and social integration of the persons concerned, according to para. 35f: 'providing appropriate social services to enable vulnerable people and people living in poverty to improve their lives, to exercise their rights and to participate fully in all social, economic and political activities and to contribute to social and economic development'.

5 Integration of mechanisms for the legal and extra-legal protection of claimants and beneficiaries. Para. 35i is important in strengthening the integration of poor persons into the formal legal and administrative system: 'Ensuring that people living in poverty have full and equal access to justice, including knowledge of their rights and, as appropriate, through the provision of free legal assistance. The legal system should be made more sensitive and responsive to the needs and special circumstances of vulnerable and disadvantaged groups in order to ensure a strong and independent administration of justice.'

6 Prevention of social isolation and stigmatization of needy persons, according to para. 38d: 'Designing social protection and support programmes to help people become self-sufficient as fully and quickly as possible, to assist and protect families, to reintegrate people excluded from economic activity and to prevent the social isolation or stigmatisation of those who need protection.'

7 Access to social services for people living in poverty (education, vocational training and healthcare).

8 Special programmes for the integration or the reintegration of poor persons into the labour market. This task is stressed in para. 59: 'Programmes for entry or re-entry into the labour market aimed at vulnerable and disadvantaged groups can effectively combat the causes of exclusions on the labour market by:

'(a) Complementing literacy actions, general education or vocational training by work experience that may include support and instruction on business management and training so as to give better knowledge of the value of entrepreneurship and other private-sector contributions to society;

'(b) Increasing the level of skills, and also improving the ability to get a job through improvements in housing, health, and family life.'

9 A guarantee of participation by persons concerned with its operation. Para. 28a provides that: 'Involving them fully in the setting of targets and in the design, implementation, monitoring and assessment of national strategies and programmes for poverty eradication and community-based development, and ensuring that such programmes reflect their priorities.'

The minimum standards scheme is the basic measure to combat poverty. Its effectiveness depends, however, on the adoption of other actions by national governments and social administrations in the social policy and economic field, including measures to combat inequality, to guarantee the proper distribution of public goods and to cover extraordinary events.[54]

National governments should design and apply integrated policies in order to satisfy the objectives of the programme. They should pay particular attention to the following strategies:[55]

• Formulation and implementation of national poverty eradication plans to address the structural causes of poverty, encompassing action on the local, national, sub-regional, regional and international levels. These plans should establish, within each national context, strategies and affordable time-bound goals and targets for the substantial reduction of overall poverty and the reduction of absolute poverty.[56]

- Development of a precise definition and assessment of absolute poverty.[57] This recommendation also includes reference to the preparation of measurements, criteria and indicators for determining the extent and distribution of absolute poverty.

The United Nations Millennium Declaration The UN General Assembly adopted the United Nations Millennium Declaration during the Millennium Summit Treaty Event that took place in September 2000 in New York. The Millennium Summit was convened as an integral part of the Millennium Assembly of the United Nations through Resolution 53/202.[58]

The Declaration is not a binding legal text; it corresponds to a resolution that includes specific guidelines to member states as well as to the UN organs. Its importance should not be underestimated, however, given that it raises major issues about the values and principles upholding human dignity, equality and equity at the global level.

To influence the development of social welfare, the Declaration introduces a unique framework based on fundamental values and implementation techniques. A systematic analysis of this framework demonstrates that it may be used as the substantive foundation of international poverty policy.

Section 6 of the Declaration identifies general principles of international anti-poverty policies including freedom ('Men and women have the right to live their lives and raise their children in dignity, free from hunger and from the fear of violence, oppression or injustice. Democratic and participatory governance based on the will of the people best assures these rights') and solidarity ('Global challenges must be managed in a way that distributes the costs and burdens fairly in accordance with basic principles of equity and social justice. Those who suffer or who benefit least deserve help from those who benefit most').

Part III of the Declaration identifies implementation techniques related to social development and poverty eradication that should be taken seriously into account by international policy-makers. This sector includes specific non-binding norms on poverty reduction, described as follows:

> We will spare no effort to free our fellow men, women and children from the abject and dehumanizing conditions of extreme poverty, to which more than a billion of them are currently subjected. We are committed to making the right to development a reality for everyone and to freeing the entire human race from want.[59]

> We resolve therefore to create an environment – at the national and global levels alike – which is conducive to development and to the elimination of poverty.[60]

Success in meeting these objectives depends, inter alia, on good govern-ance within each country. It also depends on good governance at the inter-national level and on transparency in the financial, monetary and trading systems. We are committed to an open, equitable, rule-based, predictable and non-discriminatory multilateral trading and financial system.[61]

According to these objectives, international poverty policies should fol-low different techniques in order to achieve certain tasks:

- Extreme poverty requires a guarantee of physical subsistence means; relevant measures follow the traditional subsistence concept.
- Freedom from want concerns the coverage of basic needs; relevant meas-ures follow the basic needs concept.
- Social development addresses the participation of every human being in a stable economic and social environment; relevant measures follow the relative deprivation concept.

The Declaration makes no reference to the establishment of legal anti-poverty rights at national and international levels. This is a serious shortcoming, not covered by other provisions of the Declaration dealing with the protection of human rights.[62] Article 25, however, *inter alia*, urges member states:

- to respect fully and uphold the Universal Declaration of Human Rights;
- to strive for the full protection and promotion in all countries of civil, political, economic, social and cultural rights for all; and
- to strengthen the capacity of all countries to implement the principles and practices of democracy and respect for human rights, including minority rights.

Article 25 should be read in conjunction with Article 19 of the Declara-tion, which sets out specific tasks and indicators for anti-poverty policies. Relevant tasks concern qualitative intervention in fields such as schooling, education, housing and healthcare:

- Schooling and education policies should ensure 'that, by the year 2015, children everywhere, boys and girls alike, will be able to complete a full course of primary schooling and that girls and boys will have equal access to all levels of education'.
- Housing policies should achieve 'by 2020 a significant improvement in the lives of at least 100 million slum dwellers as proposed in the "Cities without Slums" initiative'.
- Healthcare policies should 'provide special assistance to children orphaned by HIV/AIDS'.

On the other hand, indicators to measure the effectiveness of anti-poverty policies involve quantitative interventions in different sectors, such as physical subsistence, maternal and child mortality and health:

- Subsistence objectives are to be promoted through structural policies, with the aim 'to halve, by the year 2015, the proportion of the world's people whose income is less than one dollar a day and the proportion of people who suffer from hunger and, by the same date, to halve the proportion of people who are unable to reach or to afford safe drinking water'. Further measures should be adopted, with the aim 'to reduce, by the same date, maternal mortality by three quarters, and under-five child mortality by two thirds, of their current rates'.
- Particular health objectives are identified for specific diseases. Here the aim is 'to have, by then, halted, and begun to reverse, the spread of HIV/AIDS, the scourge of malaria, and other major diseases that afflict humanity'.

Towards international poverty law

The establishment of international poverty law is inspired by the need to use specific legal norms as a means to strengthen social welfare objectives. Given the abstract nature of existing rules on social rights at the international level, a normative process reaches beyond perceived categories of human rights, applying a more purposeful analysis that poses two legal objectives:

- to codify the sources of international poverty law (based on the distinction between international customary law and 'material' law);[63] and
- to guarantee indivisibility and direct applicability of international norms.

At the global level, the UN provides a unique framework for the development of relevant sources of law through both binding and non-binding instruments:

a) Binding instruments that 'may' create obligations related to the implementation of anti-poverty rights, after their ratification by member states. The sole provision in all UN machineries that could be classified in this category is Article 11 of the International Covenant on Economic, Social and Cultural Rights. Its impact in practice is rather limited, however, particularly given the nature of its judicially enforceable effects on governments and individuals. Governments are not obliged to implement anti-poverty rights while individuals cannot invoke enforceable rights before national or international courts.

The main task here is to strengthen the impact of internationally recognized rights on governments and individuals. This is a policy problem that should be taken into account jointly by UN organs, national governments, social partners and NGOs.

b) Non-binding instruments that provide guidelines and general principles for the realization of anti-poverty policies. These instruments are to be found in Article 25 of the Universal Declaration of Human Rights, Section 25 of the Vienna Declaration of Human Rights, commitment No. 2 of the Copenhagen Declaration on Social Development, and Article 19 of the United Nations Millennium Declaration.

UN organs have focused on raising awareness, at the international level, of the significance of anti-poverty measures, thereby also increasing national awareness. During the last decade, social policy debates were promoted through: i) the World Conference on Education for All in 1990, ii) the Second United Nations Conference on the Least Developed Countries in 1990, iii) the World Summit for Children in 1990, iv) the United Nations Conference on Environment and Development in 1992, v) the World Conference on Human Rights in 1993, vi) the International Conference on Population and Development in 1994, vii) the World Summit for Social Development in Copenhagen in March 1995, and viii) the Fourth World Conference on Women in Beijing in September 1995.

The UN General Assembly also has called for a series of awareness-raising efforts on related concerns. These include: i) the International Year for the World's Indigenous People, 1993, ii) the International Year of the Family, 1994, iii) the United Nations Year for Tolerance, 1995, iv) the International Year for the Eradication of Poverty, 1996, and v) the Decade on the Elimination of Poverty, 1997–2006.[64]

The objectives of international poverty law The discourse of international poverty law (IPL) creates a new discipline[65] that may provide a fresh impetus for legal and social policy-making in the field of poverty.

The broader framework of IPL strengthens the adaptation of existing legal instruments to social and economic changes, while highlighting the need to expand new mechanisms and relevant policies. According to this approach, IPL tries to fulfil the following basic objectives:

- establishment of formal links between poverty alleviation and human rights;[66]
- clarification of the rights against poverty and social exclusion;[67]
- identification of internationally recognized social rights;

- codification of guiding welfare principles for the formulation of national anti-poverty policies;
- achievement of poverty[68] and deprivation[69] indicators that could lead to the elaboration of enforceable legal rights through the adoption of direct applicability clauses;[70]
- coordination of international agencies that develop anti-poverty policies;[71]
- mobilization of attention and commitment by social partners and NGOs through the validation of social welfare policy indicators;[72] and
- development of legal and academic doctrine in the field of anti-poverty rights.[73]

The instruments of international poverty law International anti-poverty objectives, which are judicially enforceable, may be fulfilled through two different strategies: the improvement of existing legally binding instruments and the introduction of new binding instruments addressing anti-poverty policies.

Given the *de lege ferenda* status of the second proposal, it seems that the improvement of existing binding instruments provides a more realistic goal for further action. UN organs are responsible for implementing policy tasks and should take advantage of the following techniques:

THE NORMATIVE CONSOLIDATION OF ARTICLE 11 OF THE INTER-NATIONAL COVENANT ON ECONOMIC, SOCIAL AND CULTURAL RIGHTS This regulation may be promoted through the work of the committee charged with the implementation of the Covenant.

The main task here is to design and adopt specific indicators that will support the direct applicability effects of the provisions in question. Following the committee's discussion on statistical indicators, it may be assumed that the committee will at some stage in the future specify particular rights-oriented indicators for use by states that will, to some degree, outline what the committee perceives to be the content of the rights enshrined in Article 11. The committee should particularly focus on the legal construction of the right to adequate living standards.

Further work is necessary in three main areas:

a) First, the committee needs to determine a means by which those persons without adequate resources may be identified. This process will require the establishment of qualitative criteria as well as the design of quantitative indicators, closely related to the introduction of governmental minimum income standards.[74]

b) Second, the committee should define a basic typology of anti-poverty measures that takes into account both subsistence[75] and inclusion aspects.[76]

c) Third, more consideration should be given to the general question of international cooperation regarding both the role of international agencies and bilateral assistance programmes.[77]

THE ADOPTION OF AN OPTIONAL PROTOCOL TO THE INTERNATIONAL COVENANT ON ECONOMIC, SOCIAL AND CULTURAL RIGHTS International scholars have already discussed this subject despite prevailing negative responses of national governments.[78]

The UN Committee on Economic, Social and Cultural Rights adopted a draft Optional Protocol in 1996. The draft protocol introduces the right to individual or collective complaints by persons or groups who claim to be victims of a violation by a state party of any of the rights recognized within the Covenant. It remains in preliminary form,[79] given that it has not been approved either by the UN Commission on Human Rights or other monitoring bodies.

The adoption of the Optional Protocol would provide interested persons and groups with a rather significant legal framework to address rights violations. Its effects on anti-poverty policies depend, however, on the legal regulation of the rights within Article 11.

In creating the substance of this Protocol, UN organs should take into account the provisions of the First Optional Protocol to the UN Covenant on Civil and Political Rights[80] as well as the Additional Protocol to the European Social Charter providing for a system of collective complaints.[81] Both instruments strengthen the legal status of individuals or groups that are willing to promote the respect of fundamental social rights by national governments.

Conclusion

The theoretical foundations of international poverty law lie in the inadequacy of existing international law in terms of addressing disputes between states and poor persons, as well as in the inability of existing human rights instruments to legitimize claims of individuals against other member states or international organizations. Shortcomings highlight the need to clarify the scope of international poverty law. This is a normative process which may take advantage of the rights-based approach,[82] broadening the traditional scope of the development of anti-poverty theories. These theories correlate UN law to a set of guidelines and principles that developed countries should take into account during the creation of

Structural Adjustment Programmes for poor countries. This is neither a standards-setting process nor a strategy to coordinate national anti-poverty regimes. A limitation is that it does not guarantee that poor persons have entitlements protected through the legal machinery of rights.

One of the major problems for the legal establishment of IPL is the identification of its sources. Many social policy experts argue that existing UN legal instruments should not be recognized or applied as legal sources, given that they are not substantive norms. I contend that this argument is not valid. The UN Bill of Rights and relevant non-binding instruments are legal norms that could be treated as customary sources of law. On the other hand, conventions and treaties include binding norms that develop rights and obligations. The problem lies in the absence of direct applicability to member states and not in their legal status.

To implement IPL, legal experts should discuss two theoretical scenarios based on *de jure* and *de lege ferenda* approaches:

- the legal construction of the right to be free from poverty, as deduced through Article 11 of the International Covenant on Economic, Social and Cultural Rights;
- the inclusion of anti-poverty clauses in all binding UN instruments in the field of human rights.

Given the broader scope of international social rights and the lack of effective adjudication instruments, the development of IPL can still formulate both abstract general values and detailed generalizable rules on welfare rights at national and international levels. Socially excluded persons and groups, faced with poverty risks, may then take advantage of an evolving legal doctrine, which gives them priority in the allocation of scarce state resources during fiscally hard times. This is a social policy scenario that questions the dominance of traditional international law objectives over the rights of disadvantaged human beings.[83]

Discussions about the introduction of IPL within the UN framework should highlight different approaches and options between member states. For instance, the right to food may be more attractive in comparison to the right to social welfare for developed countries within the debate on IPL, given that it concerns absolute poverty and marginalization. Persons are also faced with the consequences of relative poverty and social exclusion, however. This is the reason why we need a broader notion of international poverty law, guaranteed through 'participatory minimum standards schemes', which will cover adequate living standards.

Notes

1 See Townsend (1993: 27).

2 See Spicker (1993).

3 Relevant techniques are discussed by Midgley (1997).

4 See Townsend (1995: 5).

5 This overview takes advantage of comparative social policy methods as discussed by Clasen (1999).

6 See Higgins (1969).

7 See Eide et al. (1995: 3).

8 See Collins et al. (1992: 125).

9 See Council of Europe (1997: 15).

10 The Code covers only social security benefits, excluding social welfare cash benefits and services.

11 See Ditch and Oldfield (1999: 65–76).

12 European Commission, *A Concerted Strategy for Modernizing Social Protection*, COM (1999) 347, 1999.

13 This process is designed to help member states to develop their own policies, reflecting their individual national situations, to share their experience, and to review their outcomes in a transparent and comparable environment. It involves fixing guidelines for the Union, establishing indicators and carrying out periodic monitoring.

14 For the concept of social exclusion, see in particular Room (1997).

15 For the application of the subsidiarity principle in the social welfare field, see Spicker (1991: 10).

16 Article 2 of the Amsterdam Treaty of 1996.

17 See Official Journal of the European Communities, 'Objectives in the Fight against Poverty and Social Exclusion' (2001/C 82/02) – C 82/4/13.3.2001.

18 In the field of social inclusion, the European Commission has proposed an initial set of seven indicators for assessing national performance: 1) the distribution of income (ratio of share of top 20 per cent to share of bottom 20 per cent), 2) the share of the population below the poverty line before and after social transfers, 3) the persistence of poverty, 4) the proportion of jobless households, 5) regional disparities, 6) low education, and 7) long-term unemployment. See European Commission (2001).

19 These competencies are found in Article 1 and regulated in Articles 55–56 of the UN Charter.

20 This is discussed by Van Genugten (1997: 118).

21 These agencies include the World Bank, the International Labour Office (ILO), the International Monetary Fund (IMF), the United Nations Children's Fund (UNICEF), the United Nations Research Institute for Social Development (UNRISD), the United Nations Development Programme (UNDR) and the World Health Organization (WHO).

22 See Asamoah (1966).

23 See Eide et al. (1992).

24 See Veit Wilson (1998: 103).

25 See Eide (1997).

26 On the distinction between social insurance and social assistance, see Spicker (1988).

27 For the different theories that explain the normative status of the Universal Declaration, see Simma and Alston (1992: 82).

28 See Schwelb (1976).

29 Legal scholars may take into account the comparative work of Harland (2000: 187).

30 Van Genugten (1997) argues that 'in sum, however, the CCPR may be an important treaty, but is ineffective in dealing with poverty'.

31 Particular attention should be paid to the 'welfare construction' of the right to life. According to this approach, the right to life covers socially acceptable living standards which are to be promoted through positive state intervention.

32 For an excellent overview of this Convention, see Alston (1991).

33 Article 9 provides that 'the States Parties to the present Covenant recognize the right of everyone to social security, including social insurance'.

34 This Convention, adopted in 1951, covers the traditional social insurance risks.

35 As discussed by Craven (1998: 287).

36 For the definition of 'direct applicability', see Hohnerlein (1988: 111).

37 See Craven (1993: 367).

38 See Center for Human Rights (1991: 4).

39 See Craven (1998: 302).

40 These are the Article 6 (the right to work) and Article 9 (the right to social security).

41 As discussed by Morris (1979: 34).

42 See Turk (1990: 27).

43 See Craven (1998: 313).

44 General Comments on Article 11 reaffirm that resource scarcity does not relieve states of certain minimum obligations with respect to the implementation of economic, social and cultural rights.

45 The Limburg Principles were compiled by a group of distinguished experts in international law during a meeting at the University of Limburg in 1986. At the initiative of the Netherlands government they have been issued as an official UN document, *The Limburg Principles on the Implementation of the International Covenant on Economic, Social and Cultural Rights*, adopted by the UN Commission on Human Rights on 8 January 1987. The full text of the Limburg Principles is reprinted in *Human Rights Quarterly*, 9: 122–35.

46 See Eide (1997: 126).

47 The full text of the Maastricht Guidelines is published in *Human Rights Quarterly*, 20: 691–705.

48 For this approach, see Chapman (1996: 23).

49 See Dankwa et al. (1998: 713).

50 See the relevant General Comment no. 3, 'The Nature of States Parties Obligations', adopted by the committee on 13 December 1990.

51 Dominant legal theory highlights the significance of the normative interdependence of the two grand categories of human rights: civil and political rights and economic, social and cultural rights.

52 See United Nations, *World Conference on Human Rights*, 1993, p. 44.

53 See Townsend and Donkor (1996: 14).

54 According to para. 23, '*the eradication of poverty cannot be accomplished through anti-poverty programmes alone* but will require democratic participation and changes in economic structures in order to ensure access for all to resources, opportunities and public services, to undertake policies geared to more equitable distribution of wealth and income, to *provide social protection for those who cannot support themselves*, and to assist people confronted by unforeseen catastrophe, whether individual or collective, natural, social or technological' (emphasis added).

55 On this point, see Townsend and Donkor (1996: 14–15).

56 According to para. 26b of the programme.

57 According to para. 26d of the programme.

58 This resolution was adopted by the General Assembly on 17 December 1998.

59 Article 11 of the Declaration.

60 Article 12 of the Declaration.

61 Article 13 of the Declaration.

62 These norms have been identified in Sector V of the Declaration which concerns Human Rights, Democracy and Good Governance.

63 International customary law provisions are included in any UN treaty or declaration without binding effect.

64 The first United Nations Decade for the Eradication of Poverty was adopted by the General Assembly on 16 December 1996.

65 Rather useful concepts are elaborated by Von Maydell (1973: 348).

66 Relevant links should take advantage of the 'organic' and 'related' interdependence between human freedoms and social rights, strengthening the beneficial impact of traditional human rights on the enjoyment of social rights. For a relevant analysis, see Scott (1989: 778).

67 Both rights are concerned not only with living standards but also with the disposal of a minimum level of resources that guarantee participation in the social and economic environment. This approach may be illustrated by international poverty law mechanisms.

68 Poverty indicators may identify the proportion of people below the poverty line before and after social transfers.

69 Deprivation indicators supplement the income standards in the measurement of social exclusion, seeking to identify those experiencing exclusion at a point in time and to assess changes over time. See Nolan and Whelan (1996).

70 Legal clauses were briefly discussed during a UN Seminar on Appropriate Indicators to Measure Achievements in the Progressive Realization of Economic, Social and Cultural Rights, which was held during the World Conference on Human Rights in 1993.

71 Therefore, judicial strategies could be coordinated in light of new social protection instruments. See, for example, the new World Bank approach to social welfare, as discussed by Holzmann and Jorgensen (1999: 1005), and the International Monetary Fund Initiative on Debt Relief and Poverty Reduction.

72 Relevant indicators are advocated by MacRae (1985).

73 An example of this point is the International Commission of Jurists, which in 1995 adopted the Bangalore Declaration and Plan of Action, which is fully devoted to economic, social and cultural rights and the protective role of lawyers, both at the national and international level.

74 For the distinction between poverty measures and minimum income standards, see Veit Wilson (1998: 7).

75 See Berghman (1997a: 3).

76 See Silver (1994: 532).

77 Craven (1998: 351) states, for example, 'whereas developed States will not generally accept an obligation to provide a specific form of assistance to specific States, there may be room for strengthening obligations in the case of families or other "natural" disasters'.

78 See Van Genugten (1997: 105).

79 See UN Commission on Human Rights, Status of the International Covenants on Human Rights – Draft Optional Protocol to the International Covenant on Economic, Social and Cultural Rights, 1997.

80 Craven (1998: xi) provides a rather useful assessment of the draft protocol in view of clauses included within this text.

81 This protocol was adopted in 1995. See Council of Europe (1997: 57).

82 For a detailed summary of this approach, see Buergenthal (1997: 703).

83 This argument highlights the results of the debate on the reform of international public law towards humanitarian or security objectives, not related to social protection issues. For a general overview, see Delbrück (1993: 708).

References

Alston, P. (1991) 'The International Covenant on Economic, Social and Cultural Rights', in United Nations Center for Human Rights, *Manual on Human Rights Reporting*, New York: United Nations, pp. 39–77

Asamoah, O. (1966) *The Legal Significance of the Declarations of the General Assembly of the United Nations*, The Hague: M. Nijhoff

Badelt, C. (1999) *Social Risk Management and Social Inclusion*, Washington, DC: World Bank

Berghman, J. (1997a) 'The resurgence of poverty and the struggle against exclusion: a new challenge for social security in Europe?', *International Social Security Review*, 1: 3–21

— (1997b) 'The new social risks – a synthetic view', in J. Van Langendonck (ed.), *The New Social Risks*, The Hague: Kluwer Law International, pp. 251–61

Buergenthal, T. (1997) 'The normative and institutional evolution of international human rights', *Human Rights Quarterly*, 19: 703–23

Castaneda, J. (1969) *Legal Effects of United Nations Resolutions*, New York

Centre for Human Rights (1989) *Right to Adequate Food as a Human Right*, Human Rights Study Series no. 1, Geneva

— (1991) *The Committee on Economic, Social and Cultural Rights*, Fact Sheet no. 16, Geneva

Chapman, A. (1996) 'A violations approach for monitoring the International Covenant on Economic, Social and Cultural Rights', *Human Rights Quarterly*, 18: 23

Clasen, J. (ed.) (1999) *Comparative Social Policy*, Oxford: Blackwell

Collins, D., A. Gillet, P. Hennessy and P. Watson (1992) 'International organizations and European social policy', *Journal of European Social Policy*, 2: 125–34

Council of Europe (1997) *European Social Charter – Collected Texts*, Strasbourg

Craven, M. (1993) 'The domestic application of the International Covenant on Economic, Social and Cultural Rights', *Netherlands International Law Review*, 40: 367

— (1998) *The International Covenant on Economic, Social and Cultural Rights*, Oxford: Clarendon Press

Dankwa, V., C. Flinterman and S. Leckie (1998) 'Commentary to the Maastricht Guidelines on Violations of Economic, Social and Cultural Rights', *Human Rights Quarterly*, 20: 705–30

Dean, H. (1996) *Welfare, Law and Citizenship*, London: Harvester Wheatsheaf

— (1997) 'The juridification of welfare – strategies of discipline and resistance', in A. Kjonstad and J. H. Veit Wilson (eds), *Law, Power and Poverty*, Bergen: CROP, pp. 3–27

Delbrück, J. (1993) 'A more effective international law or a new world law? – some aspects of the development of international law in a changing international system', *Indiana Law Journal*, 68: 708

Ditch, J. and N. Oldfield (1999) 'Social assistance – recent trends and themes', *Journal of European Social Policy*, 9 (1): 65–76

Eide, A. (1997) 'Human rights and the elimination of poverty', in A. Kjonstad and J. Veit Wilson (eds), *Law, Power and Poverty*, Bergen: CROP, pp. 117–36

Eide, A. et al. (1992) *The Universal Declaration of Human Rights – a Commentary*, Oslo: Scandinavian University Press

Eide, A., K. Krause and A. Rosas (eds) (1995) *Economic, Social and Cultural Rights*, Dordrecht: M. Nijhoff

European Commission (2001), *Structural Indicators*, Annex II to the Stockholm Report, Communication from the Commission, COM (2001) 79 Final/2

Gill, I., F. Fluitman and A. Dar (eds) (2000) *Vocational Education and Training*

Reform: Matching Skills to Markets and Budgets, Joint study of the World Bank and the International Labour Office, New York: Oxford University Press

Harland, C. (2000) 'The status of the International Covenant on Civil and Political Rights in the domestic law of state parties: an initial global survey through UN Human Rights Committee Documents', *Human Rights Quarterly*, 22 (1): 187–260

Higgins, R. (1969) *The Development of International Law through the Political Organs of the United Nations*, London: Oxford University Press

Hohnerlein, E. M. (1988) 'The implementation of the European Social Charter in the Federal Republic of Germany', in A. Jaspers and L. Betten (eds), *25 Years of the European Social Charter*, Deventer: Kluwer Law and Taxation Publishers

Holzmann, R. and S. Jorgensen (1999) 'Social protection as social risk management: conceptual underpinnings for the social protection sector strategy paper', *Journal of International Development*, 11: 1005–27

International Monetary Fund and International Development Association (1999) *HIPC Initiative – Strengthening the Link between Debt Relief and Poverty Reduction*, Washington, DC

Köhler, P. (1987) *Sozialpolitische und sozialrechtiliche Aktivitäten in den Vereinten Nationen*, Berlin: Duncker und Humblot

MacRae, D. (1985) *Policy Indicators: Links between Social Science and Public Debate*, Chapel Hill: University of North Carolina Press

McDonald, R., D. Johnston and G. Morris (eds) (1978) *The International Law and Policy of Human Welfare*, Alphen an den Rijn

Midgley, J. (1997) *Social Welfare in a Global Context*, London: Sage

Morris, M. (1979) *Measuring the Conditions of the World's Poor*, New York: Pergamon Press

Nolan, B. and C. Whelan (1996) *Resources, Deprivation and Poverty*, Oxford: Clarendon Press

Ravallion, M. (1992) *Poverty Comparison – a Guide to Concepts and Methods*, Washington, DC: World Bank

Room, G. (1997) 'Poverty and social exclusion: the new European agenda for policy and research', in G. Room (ed.), in *Beyond the Threshold – the Measurement and Analysis of Social Exclusion*, Bristol: Policy Press, pp. 1–9

Schwelb, E. (1976) 'Some aspects of the International Covenants on Human Rights of December 1966', in A. Asbjorn and A. Schou (eds), *International Protection of Human Rights*, Stockholm, pp. 203–20

Scott, C. (1989) 'The interdependence and permeability of human rights norms: towards a partial fusion of the international covenants on human rights', *Osgoode Hall Law Journal*, 27: 778

— (1999) 'Reaching beyond (without abandoning) the category of economic, social and cultural rights', *Human Rights Quarterly*, 21: 633–60

Scott, J. (1994) *Poverty and Wealth – Citizenship, Deprivation and Privilege*, London: Longman

Silver, H. (1994) 'Social exclusion and solidarity: three paradigms', *International Labour Review*, 133: 531–78

Simma, B. and P. Alston (1992) 'The sources of human rights law: custom, jus cogens and general principles', *Australian Yearbook of International Law*, 12: 82.

Spicker, P. (1988) *Principles of Social Welfare*, London: Routledge

— (1991) 'The principle of subsidiarity and the social policy of the European Community', *Journal of European Social Policy*, 1 (1): 3–14

— (1993) *Poverty and Social Security: Concepts and Principles*, London: Routledge

Subbarao, K. et al. (1997) *Safety Net Programs and Poverty Reduction: Lessons from Cross-country Experience*, Washington, DC: World Bank

Townsend, P. (1993) *The International Analysis of Poverty*, London: Harvester Wheatsheaf

— (1995) *The Rise of International Social Policy*, Bristol: Policy Press

Townsend, P. and K. Donkor (1996) *Global Restructuring and Social Policy*, Bristol: Policy Press

Turk, D. (1990) *The New International Economic Order and the Promotion of Human Rights*, New York

Van Genugten, W. (1997) 'The use of human rights instruments in the struggle against (extreme) poverty', in A. Kjonstad and J. Veit Wilson (eds), *Law, Power and Poverty*, Bergen: CROP, pp. 99–115

Veit Wilson, J. H. (1998) *Setting Adequacy Standards – How Governments Define Minimum Incomes*, Bristol: Policy Press

Vierdag, E. (1978) 'The legal nature of the rights granted by the International Covenant on Economic, Social and Cultural Rights', *Netherlands Yearbook of International Law*, 9: 69–103

Von Maydell, B. (1973) 'Die dogmatischen Grundlagen des inter-und supra-nationalen Sozialrechts', *Vierteljahresschrift für Sozialrecht*, 1

Wolfrum, R. (ed.) (1991) *Handbuch Vereinte Nationen*, Munich: C. H. Beck Verlagsbuchhandlung

World Bank (2000) *World Development Report 2000/1: Attacking Poverty*, Washington, DC

About the contributors

Gabriel Amitsis, PhD in Social Security Law, is a legal consultant in social insurance and welfare policy issues. He has undertaken research and teaching at the Athens National School of Social Administration, the Greek Open University and the Technological Institute of Athens in areas relating to legal frameworks of social security, poverty and exclusion. His recent publications include *The Greek Social Insurance System* (Ministry of Labour and Social Insurance, Athens, 2003), 'The effect of legal mechanisms on selective welfare strategies for needy persons – the Greek experience', in L. Williams, A. Kjonstad and P. Robson (eds), *Law and Poverty – Poverty Reduction and the Role of the Legal System* (Zed Books, London, 2003), *Dependency of Welfare Clients on Benefits and Services – The Case of Cyprus* (Ministry of Labour and Social Insurance, Lefkosia, Cyprus, 2003) and 'Principles and instruments of social inclusion policies in Europe', in T. Sakellaropoulos and J. Berghman (eds), *Connecting Welfare Diversity within the European Social Model* (Intersentia, Antwerp, 2004).

Ahmed Aoued is a former university researcher in human rights at the University of Oran, Algeria. He taught international development law and held the UNESCO Chair for Human Rights at the same university. He has been legal consultant for several NGOs in Geneva and is now serving as legal adviser at the Permanent Mission of the State of Qatar to the United Nations Office in Geneva. He has published extensively in the area of human rights promotion and protection. He graduated from Glasgow University in 1980 (LL M) and 1992 (PhD).

Bas de Gaay Fortman has been Professor of Political Economy of Human Rights at Utrecht University, the Netherlands, since 2000, and was Msgr Willy Onclin Professor of Comparative Canon Law at the Catholic University of Louvain (2003/04). He has a Master of Laws degree (*Magister Iuris*) as well as a PhD in economics. He has taught at the Free University, Amsterdam, the University of Zambia in Lusaka, and the Institute of Social Studies in The Hague. From 1971 to 1991 he was also a member of the Netherlands parliament. Among his many publications are *God and the Goods. Global Economy in a Civilizational Perspective* (1998) and *Where Needs Meet Rights. Economic, Social and Cultural Rights in a New Perspective* (1999), both co-authored with Berma Klein Goldewijk and published by World Council of Churches Publications in Geneva. His last (co-edited) book was *From

Warfare to Welfare. Human Security in a Southern African Context (Royal Van Gorcum, Assen, 2004).

Marius Olivier teaches Labour Law and Advanced Labour Law, the tutored LL M (Labour Law) and the MPhil (Labour Law and Labour Relations) at the University of Johannesburg (formerly Rand Afrikaans University), South Africa. He is also the main presenter of the LL M (Labour Law) programmes at Vista University, the University of Zululand and the University of the Northwest. He is director of the Centre for International and Comparative Labour and Social Security Law (CICLASS), in which capacity he oversees a number of interdisciplinary projects on social security law and on development law. Professor Olivier publishes on the topics of labour law, social security law and constitutional law.

Margarita Prieto-Acosta has for the last six years taught International Biodiversity Regulation for the Durrell Institute of Conservation and Ecology and Spanish Law at Kent Law School, both part of the University of Kent. She was previously Secretary General of the Comptroller's Office for the National Treasury of Colombia and later became Acting Head of Elections Financial Auditing Control. She graduated summa cum laude in law from the Javeriana University in Bogotá, producing a ground-breaking work, *Computers and the Law: The Great Challenge for Justice* (1984), which became a university text used across Latin America. Margarita spent her early career as a lawyer for the Central Bank of Colombia, rising to Section Head of Legal Research. While there, she obtained three higher degrees in law and produced several significant publications for the bank: *Exchange Control in Colombia* (six volumes, 1987), *Monetary Control. Basic Principles* (1988) and *A Regime for Currency Exchange* (1991). Following a move to England, she obtained an LL M in Environmental Law and Conservation (1998) and has subsequently followed her research interests in the protection of indigenous peoples' rights over their traditional knowledge, on which she has spoken at many international conferences.

Linda Jansen van Rensburg is an associate professor at the Northwest University (Potchefstroom campus), South Africa. She has published several articles in peer-reviewed journals and has contributed chapters to books in the areas of social security, socio-economic rights and poverty. Her publications include 'The protection and enforcement of the right to social security', in M. Olivier et al. (eds), *Social Security: General Principles* (Butterworths, Johannesburg 1999), 'The role of supervisory bodies in enforcing social security rights', in M. Olivier et al., *The Extension of Social Security Protection in South Africa* (Siber Ink, Claremont, 2001), and

'Constitutional issues', in M. Olivier et al., *Social Security: A Legal Analysis* (Butterworths, Durban, 2003).

Debi S. Saini, PhD (Delhi), is Professor of Human Resource Management at the Management Development Institute, Gurgaon, India, and was previously a professor at the Gandhi Labour Institute, Ahmedabad (1992–94). Apart from six books (edited or authored) and three dozen research papers he has written a volume on 'Social security law: India', which forms part of the *International Encyclopaedia of Laws* (Kluwer Law International, The Hague). His specializations include industrial relations, labour laws, HRM strategy and law and society. He was the founding editor of *Management & Change* (1997–99), and has been on the editorial board of the *Industrial Relations Journal* (1998–2002). Among others, he has undertaken assignments for the ILO and GTZ (Germany). He recently drafted the All India Authority of Vocational Training (AIAVT) Bill, which is expected to be introduced in the Indian parliament for enactment soon.

Asuncion St Clair is associate professor at the Department of Sociology, University of Bergen, Norway, and secretary of the International Development Ethics Association (IDEA). St Clair's work focuses on the ethical and value aspects of global poverty and development, the role that values have and may have in building knowledge-based pro-poor policies – in particular the knowledge and policies proposed and defended by major development agencies and the ways in which these are linked to complex global processes shaping global governance. A specific concern is the tensions arising between economic neo-liberal globalization and the globalization of human rights. Her publications include *Poverty Conceptions in the United Nations Development Programme and the World Bank: Knowledge, Poverty and Ethics* (PhD thesis) and 'The role of ideas in the United Nations Development Programme', in Bøas, Morten and McNeill (eds), *Global Institutions and Development: Framing the World*, Routledge, London, 2003.

Aurora Voiculescu is Lecturer in Law at the Open University and Associate Research Fellow at the Centre for Socio-legal Studies, Oxford University. She received her PhD in law in 1999 from the London School of Economics and Political Science and then undertook research and teaching as British Academy Post-doctoral Fellow in Law at Lincoln College, Oxford University. Her main research, taking a socio-legal approach, focuses on the nexus between human rights and organizations as social and legal agencies. Her publications include *Human Rights and Political Justice in Post-communist Eastern Europe: Prosecuting History* (Edwin Mellen, 2000).

Lucy Williams has been Professor of Law at Northeastern University School of Law, Boston since 1991, and was named the School's 1994–95 Public Interest Distinguished Professor. In 1994 she was appointed by President Clinton to the Advisory Council on Unemployment Compensation, evaluating all aspects of the unemployment compensation programme and making policy recommendations to the President and Congress. She has written and lectured widely in the area of welfare law and poverty. Selected recent publications include 'Poor Women's Work Experiences: Gaps in the "Work-Family" Discussion', in J. Conaghan and K. Rittich (eds), *(Re)Producing Work: Labour Law Work and Family* (forthcoming, Oxford University Press), *Law And Poverty: The Legal System and Poverty Reduction* (co-edited with A. Kjønstad and P. Robson) (Zed Press, London 2003), 'Beyond Labour Law's Parochialism: A Re-Envisioning of the Discourse of Redistribution', in J. Conaghan, R. Fischl and K. Klare(eds), *Labour Law in an Era of Globalization: Transformative Practices and Possibilities* (Oxford University Press 2002), *Welfare Law: The International Library of Essays in Law and Legal Theory, 2nd Series* (Dartmouth Press 2001).

Index